The Trouble with Africa

The Trouble with Africa

Stories from a Safari Camp

VIC GUHRS

PENGUIN BOOKS

VIKING

Published By the Penguin Group
80 Strand, London WC2R 0RL, England
Penguin Putnam Inc, 375 Hudson Street, New York, New York 10014, USA
Penguin Books Australia Ltd, 250 Camberwell Road, Camberwell, Victoria 3124, Australia
Penguin Books Canada Ltd, 10 Alcorn Avenue, Toronto, Ontario, Canada M4V 3B2
Penguin Books (NZ) Ltd, Cnr Rosedale and Airborne Roads, Albany, Auckland, New Zealand
Penguin Books India (Pvt) Ltd, 11 Community Centre, Panscheel Park, New Delhi – 110 017, India
Penguin Books (South Africa) (Pty) Ltd, 24 Sturdee Avenue, Rosebank, Johannesburg 2196, South Africa

Penguin Books (South Africa) (Pty) Ltd, Registered Offices:
24 Sturdee Avenue, Rosebank, Johannesburg 2196, South Africa

First published by Penguin Books (South Africa) (Pty) Ltd 2004

ISBN 0 670 04797 X

Typeset and designed by CJH Design in 11/13.75pt Galliard
Cover design: African Icons
Printed and bound by Formeset Printers, Cape Town

For my daughters
Tamara and Miranda

Contents

Acknowledgements

Norman Carr gave me my first opportunity to experience true African bush life. My thanks also to his family, particularly Pamela and Adrian. To all those residents of the Valley – permanent or transient – who have provided me with the inspiration and material to write these stories, I want to say thank you. There are many who are not mentioned by name, but I think they will know who they are.

My thanks, too, to Alefer Phiri and our camp staff who looked after us all those years, accepting our family's eccentricities with good humour. To Chris Crake, who gave me my first exhibition when there was no guarantee for his confidence in me, and to Mark Read of the Everard Read Gallery in Johannesburg. And to the collectors and present owners of the paintings reproduced in this book.

I thank, too, my writer friends David Lambkin and Bobo Fuller for advice and encouragement, and Pam Thornley and Claire Heckrath at Penguin Books. And a special thank you to Jen Cowie for all her help and for believing in this book from the beginning.

Introduction

'The trouble with Africa is that it gets into your blood.'

It's a sentiment I have heard a hundred times, echoed, I'm sure, ever since the first white adventurer set foot on Africa's coast.

Hunched over my computer in a snow-bound mountain cabin on the Idaho/Wyoming border, I think of Africa. It is cold outside, the landscape white except for a few green patches where the pines show through the snow, but my thoughts are of sun-drenched plains and tall yellow grass. When I am not writing, I paint. My canvases are of elephants and lions, and the colours are saturated and bright.

This book has been a long time coming. I started making notes and writing bits of stories – beginnings, middles, and ends, but never a whole completed story – about nine or ten years ago. I'm not sure why it took me so long. Perhaps you have to leave a place in order to write about it. All my previous efforts failed, I think, because I was too close to it all, too involved, and not able to see the wood for the trees.

The first time an elephant comes in the night and leans against your house and makes the walls shake, you wake up and tell your friends in the morning, you probably write a letter home and tell your mother. The tenth time this happens, you sleep through it. Your first encounters with lions, snakes, malaria, African thunderstorms, the first time you see the Southern Cross in the African night sky, you are moved beyond words. But these events tend to lose their significance with repetition, and it is only now, with distance, that I think these stories are worth telling.

This cabin in the Idaho snow is about as far as I can get from Africa – geographically, climatically, and emotionally – and suddenly twenty-five years in the African bush are put into perspective, and I see it all clearly again. Much has been written about Colonial Africa and its colourful characters. The heroes and villains among Kenya's white settlers have been immortalised in books and movies, but little has been recorded about the Luangwa Valley, this hidden corner of Central Africa where I have spent the past twenty-five years.

There are coyotes here in Idaho; I hear them at night and I see their tracks in the snow. Their call reminds me of hyenas whooping on a clear night along the Luangwa River.

My stories are, of course, subjective, and their occasional obliqueness is deliberate. Africa does not come in epiphanies or sudden illuminations. It presents itself in sidelong glances down hidden pathways. My paintings, too, are not attempts at re-creating or copying reality. On the contrary, they deliberately set out to condense, to distort if necessary, to put a slightly different slant on things; to look for the essence, the soul. Like the stories, I hope they speak for themselves.

This is all nothing but miserable stammering. I do not know what Africa is really saying to me, but it speaks.

– C G Jung, in a letter to his wife.
15 March 1920

1   The Trouble with Africa...

'The trouble with Africa,' says a truck driver with a Cape accent, 'is that it is so unpredictable. You can never rely on anything going as planned.'

He points down to the water and across the river to the opposite shore where the Kazungula ferry lies stranded, its wheelhouse pointing into the afternoon sky at a crazy angle. Behind him, a long line of eighteen-wheelers stretches up the track that winds through the trees up the hill to the main road. All around us, four-by-fours and trucks are parked in the large rutted clearing in front of the ferry ramp.

The truck drivers are standing around in clusters, smoking, talking and kicking their boots in the dirt; some are huddled in the cabs of their trucks. We are all waiting, resigned. The sun has crushed the fight and indignation out of us.

Down by the river herons stand in the shallows and egrets swoop low in formations that look as if they have been choreographed. Somewhere upstream hippos grunt.

The man from the Cape, curly haired with uneven teeth very white against his biscuit-coloured skin, rolls his eyes sky-wards and draws up his shoulders in an exaggerated gesture of helplessness.

'I mean, look at it. *Jissis*, man, that thing's been there since yesterday. When are they going to pull their fingers out of their bums and fix it?' He kicks a small stone, sending it scuttling down towards the water's edge. 'Ag, what's the use. Might as well try and teach a baboon to fly a jumbo jet.'

He is talking to a big white man with a dirty blue T-shirt stretched tight over his stomach and a green peaked cap with 'John Deere' labels.

'Ja, man, I feel like going back and trying the Zimbabwe route. Get across at Vic Falls. But I know the Zim guys are gonna hammer me with visa fees and insurance and stuff.' He hitches up his shorts and pulls a crumpled cigarette pack out of one pocket, a lighter out of the other. '*Jislaaik*, the last thing I need is more of these sweaty customs guys crawling all over my truck.' He lights the cigarette, inhales deeply, and watches the smoke slowly curl away.

I look around as another truck comes grinding down the track with hissing brakes to join the queue. Most of us have been here before, and we know that eventually the problem will be fixed, so we wait. One thing Africa teaches you is patience.

Someone starts handing round warm beers. The sharp sting of marijuana smoke hits me on a dusty breeze. A card game has broken out in the cast-blue shade of a truck. I find a patch of shade of my own against the wheel of my Land Cruiser and close my eyes. In my head I find myself humming an old Cat Stevens song, 'Miles from nowhere'. I brush at an insect and rub my hand against my cheek. I am sunburned and need a shave. And some sleep. When I hear footsteps approaching, I open one eye and slide my hand to my shirt pocket for my passport, an old habit. It is the Cape truck driver. He thrusts a beer at me. 'Here.'

'Thanks.'

'You live over there?' His hand waves vaguely at the Zambezi.

I nod. 'In the eastern part,' I admit. 'In the bush.'

'I pity you, man. I pity you. If that's the real Africa, then give me the "fake" Africa any time. How do you handle it, man? The laziness, the inefficiency.'

I grin up at him. Being of German origin, I know only too well the antithesis of laziness and inefficiency, and wasn't so sure that it held all the answers for me. In fact, I had run away from it.

But I nod again. 'Ja, you're right. It can drive you crazy.' I sip the warm beer.

'No way I could put up with that shit.'

'It's the things under the surface that make it interesting, though. The stuff you don't see at first.'

'The less I see of it the better,' he grunts.

'The thing is that Africa doesn't care what you or I think about it.'

He gives me a long look, then turns on his heel. As he walks away, I hear him mutter, 'Oh boy, we got a philosopher here.'

I smile to myself, take another sip of the beer and close my eyes. Philosopher? Hardly. But the effect of the beer in the dusty heat makes me drowsy and I let my thoughts wander.

The trouble with Africa starts at the Zambezi. South of here, there is a very palpable European influence, there is relative wealth, and there is the kind of law and order that makes a Westerner feel almost at home. South Africa is a highly civilised country, its towns and cities more reminiscent of America than any other place. Highways, shopping malls, quiet suburbs and small-town churches tell the story of four hundred years of European colonisation.

All that changes when you cross the Zambezi. It is as if the ghosts of the early explorers and migrating tribespeople – the ghost of David Livingstone himself – have come to greet you. And to warn you that you are now crossing the threshold into a different land. It's as if you only have to turn your face into the warm breeze that sweeps along the river smelling vaguely of fish and ozone and rotting vegetation and allow it to strip away the outer layer of your skin. The layer that has for too long been absorbing the effects of civilisation; the values and trappings of a society that has tried to turn you into something you never really wanted to be: a number, a cog in someone else's machine.

Now, as you feel that breeze on your face, you are free. Like a child again, you've left your 'European' persona behind, shed the ballast of years of comfortable and safe First-World living, and are ready, like a dry sponge, to soak up all that waits for you on the other side. Ready to step forward into a strange world where nothing is ever quite what it seems, or what you had expected it to be.

Welcome to Africa.

The ferry is fixed at last. It comes chugging across the river, listing drunkenly to one side and belching hot-smelling diesel fumes. The driver stands in his elevated wheelhouse, not looking entirely sober himself, and directs the loading with exaggerated hand gestures. We roll our cars on, one truck and one car at a time. Women with babies tied to their backs, men pushing rickety bicycles, chickens and goats crowd into all other available space. Black smoke rises from the bubbling exhausts of the two big Hydromaster diesels, and slowly the ferry lurches into the powerful pull of the river. I turn my face into the fetid breeze and feel the smile spreading on my face.

My passport is stamped. A sign propped up crookedly against the customs office reads, 'The Republic of Zambia welcomes you'. It is serving double duty as a roosting post for some scruffy, flea-bitten chickens. I am on Zambian roads; I am home.

My car rocks and jolts on the broken tarmac. There are potholes on this road that could sink a small ship. A man on a bicycle overtakes me and waves cheerfully. I wave back. Cows wander into the road and stand in my car's path, chewing and looking bored and then, over the crest of a rise, a couple of yellow and red triangles, and a policeman steps into the road with a white-gloved hand held up. Three other men stand by the roadside in front of a sagging tent. Two of them wear khaki uniforms with blue stripes down the trouser legs, the other is in blue jeans and a yellow T-shirt that says 'CHICAGO RADIO SYMPHONY ORCHESTRA – JOIN THE PARTY'.

But there is nothing festive about the AK-47 that dangles from his fist. I slow down and stop beside the men and nod through the open window. The policeman with the white gloves stands in front of the Land Cruiser and points.

'Lights!' he barks. I hit the switch. 'Indicators!' Then, 'Wipers!'

The cop, apparently satisfied with the front of the car, walks slowly around it, glances at the tyres and peers into the back, at boxes and bags and camping gear.

'What's in there?'

'Oh, just some boxes ... groceries, tent, sleeping bag.'

'I want to see. Get out!'

They go through my luggage, unzip bags and open boxes, and finally one of them points to a well-worn canvas bag behind my seat.

'What's that?'

'It's a bag,' I say through clenched teeth, trying to ignore my rising irritation. 'For carrying cameras, binoculars, and things when I walk in the bush.' And matches, a notebook, a hipflask – probably empty now – and God knows what else might have accumulated in the bottom of the bag.

He opens the flap and puts his hand inside, and when it comes out holding three shotgun cartridges, I know I'm in trouble.

'What do you intend to do with these?' The policeman's eyes are blank and his voice has gone quiet.

'Nothing. I mean, I must have forgotten they were there. I have a shotgun and sometimes go shooting guinea fowl and stuff.'

He ignores this. 'You are trying to kill people here in Zambia?'

'No, I just ... I told you.'

'You've come across our border so you can kill people?' Oh Christ.

'Let's just throw him in the cells,' shouts the man in the T-shirt and raises his Kalashnikov.

'Passport. Let me see your passport,' growls the first cop.

All four of them are now crowding around me and stare at me with dead eyes.

It takes another hour. We stand in the road, flies buzzing. Two other cars and a rattling farm tractor have rumbled up the hill and been waved past. Finally the senior policeman hands me my passport.

'OK, you can go now.'

I nod wordlessly and climb into the cab.

'Here, don't forget these.' He hands me the cartridges.

'What? I mean . . .'

'Well, they are yours, they are not mine,' says the cop. 'I can't take your belongings. Here, take them. But you should hide them a bit better, otherwise you'll have the same problem at the next road-block.' He looks thoughtful for a moment, then a wide grin cracks his face. 'In fact,' he says, 'I will hide them for you. I know better about these things, so let me help you. We are all brothers, are we not?' His laugh comes from deep in his chest.

An hour later, I pass through the sleepy town of Livingstone. In the days when Zambia was still Northern Rhodesia, Livingstone was for a while its capital. The old colonial houses are decaying now, roofs sagging, windows broken, and gardens turned into jungles of weeds. Maize patches wilt in the sun where once there were lawns, and the tree-lined streets of the once quiet suburbs are potholed and full of litter. The grand old Governor's mansion is now a backpackers' rest house, 'Grubby's', where Aussie girls, intoxicated by African sunsets and too much tequila, sometimes strip off all their clothes and Scandinavian girls take their first long thoughtful look at African men.

A short distance from the bell tower in the centre of town, the Zambezi River tumbles over cliffs more than a mile wide into a narrow gorge a hundred metres below in a thundering spectacle of noise, spray and, when the sun is at the right angle, a hundred small glittering rainbows. On the south side of the river, the town of Victoria Falls has developed into one of Zimbabwe's major tourist centres, attracting countless visitors to its hotels and lodges. But on the Zambian side it seems as if time has stood still. Backpackers and a semi-permanent tribe of river rats – rafters, kayakers, bungee jumpers and other thrill seekers – tend to feel at home in Livingstone's dusty streets where the days slide by in slow motion and the word 'hurry' is an alien concept. The big-spending tourists stay on the Zimbabwe side.

The railway bridge that spans the river within sight of the Falls was completed in 1905 and the railway line began to open up the country in the interior. Timber mills, farms and settlements grew along the line of rail and eventually, in 1935, the capital was moved to the more centrally located town of Lusaka, 500 kilometres to the northeast. Today Lusaka is a bustling metropolis of more than a million people with a brand-new South African-built shopping mall, two golf courses, embassies, restaurants, international hotels.

Two main roads lead out of Lusaka: the Great North Road connects the capital to the copper mines and towns of the Northern province and beyond them the borders of Tanzania and the Congo.

The Great East Road roughly follows the Zambezi eastwards, on the north side of its wide escarpment. It snakes through sparsely populated hill country where you see few people but miles and miles of empty road, and forests that shine green in the rainy season but take on a dull greyish brown colour during the dry months when the leaves wither and fires rage all over the country; when grey clouds rise on the high ridges and wooded slopes and smoke hangs in the air like a veil and blocks out the mountains and distant tree-lines.

As I head further east, the road surface deteriorates – and sometimes disintegrates altogether – and the country seems more barren and dusty. Gradually the villages become more frequent along the roadside, and once past the truck stop of Kacholola, I am hardly ever out of sight of people walking, people on bicycles, goats

kicking up dust and small black pigs running across the road on short stiff legs.

There is little sign of trade or industry. A few tiny roadside shops, some stalls made of bamboo and grass that sell baskets and reed mats, and the occasional farm; although farming in these parts often means nothing more than chopping down all the trees on your land, slow-burning the wood and selling charcoal to

passing traffic. There is little shade or shelter here; I feel exposed and vulnerable in this vast landscape where time appears to move more slowly, where people manage to scratch out a living among the rocky hills and on the hot plains, where they survive but have never been able to make an impression on this land. Apart from the tarmac under me, there is no permanent structure anywhere, at least none more permanent than the little mud and grass huts that huddle in tight clusters and look like they might be washed away come the next rainstorm.

After a few hours on this road my eyes hurt and feel gritty and strained as if the fine dust has blown in from the horizon and penetrated my lids and made them burn. But it is not only the dust. The air is hot and seems unnaturally bright; a white-hot sun is burning down on me and reflects off the hills and the boulders and turns everything into a blinding haze.

Signs painted on the ramshackle shops tell of the hard life, of lost chances and failed crops and a harsh climate. 'The Valley of Lost Hope Shopping Centre', and 'Hard Times Grocery'. Others offer practical advice, like the 'Knowledge Is Power Bar and Restaurant' in the small settlement of Nyimba.

I see *Mosi* beer and Coke signs outside and stop to try my luck. '*Moni, mu li bwanji.* A Coke please.'

He shakes his head. 'No Coke.'

'Oh, OK. How about lemonade?'

'No.'

'Ginger ale? Soda? Sprite? In fact any cool drink. Do you have anything like that?'

His smile is wistful. 'No, nothing.'

We look at each other. Thinking briefly of the Monty Python cheese shop, I try to make sure. 'So you don't have anything to drink at all.'

His eyebrows rise a fraction. 'Yes, we do. We have orange squash.'

'Oh. All right, in that case please let me have an orange squash.'

The eyebrows fall again. 'But no glasses.'

A couple of hundred kilometres down the disintegrating road, I pass the 'Struggle Restaurant'. I suppose the name refers to the Freedom Struggle, or perhaps the struggle for daily existence, and not to the battle with the tough goat stew served inside.

As remote as the country may seem, it still has a few surprises. Trucks that have jack-knifed and ended up in astonishing positions, the trailer back-to-front halfway down a hillside, the cab suspended two metres above the road, half hidden in the trees. An old man in a black Sunday suit pushing his bicycle with a large yellow-dirty pig tied sideways to its luggage rack. I once overtook a vehicle that was part ox-cart, part motor car; a wooden contraption with wooden wheels and a Land Rover engine mounted in front that pushed it along the road at a steady 15 kilometres an hour, the driver waving casually at me from his wooden seat behind the steering wheel.

And roadblocks. All along the way from Lusaka, I encounter roadblocks.

'The trouble with Africa is that wherever you go, there's another damn roadblock!' I shout to myself as I approach the seventh of the day and take my foot off the pedal and hastily grope for the loose end of the seat belt.

On the surface, Zambian officials usually show a seriousness, sometimes arrogance, or bored apathy. But under this thin veneer, there is an irrepressible sense of playfulness. An optimism in the face of impossible odds, a fatalism that says life is hard, we are poor, and it is a continuous struggle even to feed ourselves. But you know, we're really all in the same boat; we're all human beings, so let's not take all this stuff too seriously.'

The last three checkpoints were easy, the cops merely waving me on, but this one turns out to be another annoying one. The policeman is young and officious. He wants to open my bags, check licence and insurance papers, my passport and driver's licence. He has inspected the tread on the spare wheel, the reflective tape on the rear bumper, and when he is finally finished, he flashes a big smile.

'By the way, big man, have you got a cigarette for me?'

'Sorry. Don't smoke.'

'Aaah. But my wife needs a lift to the next town. I see you have some room in the back seat.'

I see her standing in the shade of a tree with two children and an infant strapped to her back and holding a big basket with what looks like chickens inside it. It's been a long day and I don't feel like company. I shake my head.

'OK, no problem, I wish you a pleasant journey.'

As I start the car, the cop's colleague, a burly policewoman in a crisp green uniform, leans into the open window on the passenger side. Her gaze wanders around the interior of the car and finally settles on my face.

'So ...' she says with a lazy smile and half-closed eyes, '... where is your wife?'

She shrugs when I don't respond and waves me on, looking somewhat disappointed.

As I drive on, I think of Igor, a friend from Lusaka, who once tried to talk his way out of a ticket at a roadblock near the Lusaka airport. 'I know I should wear a seat belt. But I have no money on me.'

'Sorry, you have to pay.' The cop mentioned a sum of kwacha.

'I know, I know. But believe me, I don't have it.'

The policeman looked at him knowingly. All white men had money, didn't they, and this one was obviously lying just to get out of paying the fine.

'I can pay later in town, if I must, but I do not have any money on me,' Igor insisted. Then he crinkled his eyes and added, 'Alternatively, you could have the shirt off my back ...'

The cop frowned at him. 'It is easier for both of us if you pay a spot fine here,' he said.

'... or even my trousers,' said Igor and got out of the car, undid his belt, stepped out of his jeans and handed them to the policeman. Several cars had lined up behind them, some of them probably in a hurry to get to the airport. Their drivers leaned out of their windows and saw a white man standing next to his car with no trousers and a policeman vigorously shaking his head, shouting, 'No, no, I don't want them!'

And I think of the hijacking incident when a man was forced into the back seat of his car by two armed men at a traffic light in Lusaka. Driving towards the outskirts of town, his courage slowly returned and when the hijackers pushed him out of his car on to the dirt by the side of the road, he protested.

'Hey. No, man. Not only are you stealing my car ... you're leaving me out here, ten kilometres from where I live ...'

One of the car thieves dug in his pocket and handed him a few banknotes before speeding off, saying, 'Here, taxi fare.'

When Kenneth Kaunda, the first president of Zambia, invented the philosophy of

Humanism, he meant it, I believe, as a less rigid, less regulated form of socialism. The nationalising of key industries and the price controls of the day were certainly socialist in intent but the message to his people was one of kindness: of social cooperation on a practical day-to-day level.

As a political doctrine it may have failed, but it nevertheless left its mark on the people. School children were taught to go out and collect firewood for the elderly, to help people who were sick or disabled, to look out for one another. In a society where poverty is the order of the day and people are inclined to grab every available advantage for themselves, where selfishness is a survival tool, this philosophy is not as self-evident as it may seem to our eyes.

In Zambia it seems to have fallen on fertile ground, perhaps because it echoes a sentiment that is already rooted in Zambian society: life is hard, and the very essence of it is survival. Sometimes one must cheat or even steal. But at the same time, it is not possible to succeed without humour, and a sense of common destiny. Humanism is a kind of covenant, an unspoken agreement, like a secret weapon. In the end, life will defeat us. We have one chance at victory, and that is to laugh in the face of all this hardship; because if we didn't it would surely overwhelm us.

A farmer told me how he had given mango trees to all his workers. Each family

received six seedlings of specially grafted mangoes and advice on how to plant and care for them. Not a single tree got planted and when the farmer admonished his labourers, saying that in three years' time they could all be reaping delicious big mangoes, he was told that three years was just too far into the future to contemplate. We may all be dead by then.

In Chief Chitungulu's area in the

Luangwa Valley, the people are cutting down *mchenja* and tamarind trees to get at the fruit in the top branches that cannot be reached by climbing. 'What about next year?' you may ask them, and they will shake their heads and tell you patiently that next year is too far away. 'We are hungry *now*, and anyway, there are many other trees.'

Then there is the story of the fisherman sitting on the beach under a palm tree, drinking beer and listening to his radio. A tourist asks him why he is not out on the water fishing. He replies that he did go out early in the morning, caught some fish, sold them, and now it's time to relax. The tourist says no, you got it wrong. You should go out again, make some more money. After a while you'll have saved enough to buy a second boat, maybe employ your brother to go fishing with you. Then save some more to get a third boat, employ your cousin. In the end you'll have a small fleet and your whole family will have jobs. And you, my friend, you can sit under a palm tree and drink beer. The fisherman who has patiently listened to all this advice, replies with a look of puzzlement on his face, 'But that's what I'm *already* doing.'

At last, after nearly 600 kilometres of rough road that has shaken my car to its core, that has jarred my spine and has made me curse and shout in frustration, I reach the town of Chipata on the Malawi border. Chipata, formerly known as Fort Jameson, was once the hub of the Eastern Province tobacco farms – long since disappeared – and an important border post along the trade route to Nyasaland and eastwards to the port of Beira on the Indian Ocean coast. It was also, and still is, the gateway to the Luangwa Valley.

Two more hours on a dirt road that is even worse than anything I have endured thus far, where dusty children stare at me from small villages and Bateleur eagles wheel in the sky overhead, and I finally climb Mphata Hill, one of the range of wooded hills that rise along the eastern rim of the Valley.

I stop the car and get out to stretch my legs. I am home.

Geologically, the Luangwa Valley is part of Africa's Great Rift Valley, one of its southern spurs. It is nearly 500 kilometres long and an average of 120 kilometres wide. The Luangwa River meanders down its length. Fed by many tributaries that rush out of the hills in the rainy season, it winds through flat alluvial country where it changes its course often and leaves behind a random pattern of oxbow lagoons that flank the river on both sides, until it reaches the Zambezi escarpment and flows through a series of gorges and finally empties into the Zambezi.

The Valley is fertile, and its lush riverine vegetation, its dense thickets and vast *mopane* forests, its shimmering lagoons, are home to a unique variety of wildlife.

Monkeys and baboons feed high in the trees, zebras, puku and impala crop the grasses and bushes. Shy bushbuck hide in thickets and large buffalo herds roam the plains. Thornicroft's giraffe are endemic to the Valley, and at one time not so long ago, it hosted the largest elephant population in Africa, numbering close to one hundred thousand.

But there are few people here. The Valley is all but isolated from the rest of the country; surrounded by steep hills and escarpments it has until recently been virtually inaccessible except on foot. The climate is harsh, from heat and drought in the dry season to torrential flooding during the rains. There is disease, and death from malnutrition and malaria. From elephants and crocodiles too. It all adds up to the fact that throughout the last centuries, animals have thrived here but people have not; and today the Luangwa Valley National Park is possibly the last great wilderness in Africa that has not been spoiled by mass tourism.

But wait. Besides its scenery and wildlife, there is something else here, something hard to define, impossible to meet head-on. It is as if the Valley hides a secret. As if it is trying to invite us on a journey into our own past. All the mystery of Africa seems condensed here, like the calm at the eye of a hurricane.

Perhaps the Valley is offering us a glimpse into a world that our distant ancestors knew but on which we have turned our backs – that still exists in another dimension but to which we have no access for good reason.

For the trouble with Africa is also the trouble with us: as long as we insist on judging it from our Western perspective, we will be the outsiders – we will be forever baffled by it. We are so thoroughly confounded by the complexities of African attitudes that we perhaps don't see that they really are not so complex after all; that it is their very simplicity that we fail to understand. Perhaps, on the road to our civilised enlightenment, we have lost the ability to see life in its most fundamental essence.

In Africa, the magic is everywhere. It is in the wind that rattles in the *hyphene* palms and blows dust devils across the plains in August. It is in the fragrance of the *trichelia* blossoms, in the bustling marketplaces; in the bones of dead animals hidden in the tall grass and in the way a fisherman in his dugout glides silently down the river at sunset. It is in the moonlight call of the hyena, and in the stealthy footstep of the elephant who visits your camp at night and silently disappears in the cool hour before dawn when the other-worldly call of the ground hornbill echoes through the trees.

And it is in the things it makes people do. Grown men and women – people like you and me – frequently act in the most irrational ways and do things that they can never explain to themselves.

But it is not only people that howl at the moon and search for answers among the thousands of stars in the night sky; I have seen animals, too, behave in ways that won't be found in any zoology textbook. I have seen wild honey badgers play with a domestic dog, seen a wild civet wait for me at my door. I once encountered a sick kudu, normally one of the shyest of the antelope, who allowed me to walk up to him to almost touching distance, all the while regarding me with deep brown eyes as if to say, well I don't know any more, maybe *you* can help me. I've heard of elephants trekking to a graveyard in the middle of the night to 'pay their respects' to an elephant hunter who had been buried there that day.

In Africa, there is a fine line between reality and fantasy, and there is space here for both the scientist and the dreamer who will, I am convinced, ultimately come to the same conclusions.

And in the Luangwa Valley, the magic is at its most obvious. Here it is not hidden under the surface of things, you don't have to look for it – it comes looking for you. The Valley is where people of the most disparate backgrounds and from different corners of the earth come together and experience nature in its almost primeval state. Here the wild animals are not a sideshow. They are the main event and, as such, they add yet another dimension to the already strange mix.

I stretch again, raise my arms to the sky, trying to ease the stiffness out of my back and shoulders, and climb back into the car. The road has not improved in the twenty-five years I have known it. The Chipata Roads Department has several graders sitting in its yard but they are old, with peeling paint and rust patches that grow like fungus in the rain.

The trouble with Africa is that every small advance seems to be followed by an inevitable slide back into decay. In an almost predictable pattern, like a natural force. One step forward, one step back.

As the washboard corrugations rattle my bones and the car's chassis with equal ferocity, and the numb ache starts creeping up my spine with renewed vigour, I feel a wide grin starting to crack my dust-coated face. I turn to look through the open window, up at the vast domed sky. I shout: 'I love this sky! I love these trees! I love this *road*.'

2 Home

Home is where I sit on my front porch when the sun has lost its heat and watch the elephants congregating on the far side of the river, kicking up dust and biding their time until it is dark enough to cross.

If I climb the rickety steps up to our tree house and go eye-level with the baboons, I can let my eyes wander to the lazy ribbon of the Luangwa, across the tall tangled trees that line it on both banks, and into the country beyond. To the north, there are over 200 kilometres of National Park, interrupted only by the narrow corridor that separates the North and South Parks.

There are large concentrations of game in the dense vegetation along the river and around the lagoons and tributaries but inland, where water becomes scarce, so do the animals. Fifty kilometres westwards across this dry country where only warthogs and hardy zebras find enough to eat, looms the rocky wilderness of the Muchinga escarpment.

In historical terms, this is almost virgin land. It is history in the making, and the men and women who live here are busy making it. The few scattered villages have always been sparse, and it's only recently that people from other parts of the country have migrated down to the Valley.

True, several Portuguese expeditions forded this river on their way west in the late eighteenth and early nineteenth centuries. David Livingstone crossed near the Lukuzye in December 1866, and elephant hunters and ivory traders came to find their fortune over the years. But their footprints have been wiped out by the scorching October winds that still sweep across these plains and suck the breath out of us. Compared to their counterparts in other corners of Africa, almost nothing has been recorded about these men. Their campsites have long disappeared from this landscape – obliterated by sun and rain and termites until no trace was left.

When I first came here, I kept hearing stories about the men who had been here before, the first game rangers and professional hunters. Some of their adventures have become famous around the local campfires but most of the men have gone; moved on or killed by one or other of the animals that had lured them here in

the first place. Some have simply disappeared.

Where the Luangwa bridge crosses into the National Park, the river runs exactly east to west. On the day of the full moon, I can stand in the middle of the bridge and watch as the sun slips behind the western treeline at precisely the same moment as the moon rises, round and yellow, above the first bend upstream – out of the river itself, it seems.

The bridge hasn't always been here. Not so long ago, the only access to the Park was a rickety pontoon ferry that operated between the hours of sunrise and sunset but often lay moored for hours at a time for lack of business. I've been here long enough now, so that everywhere I go there are memories of my own: good and bad; humorous and not funny at all.

Chibembe Camp. This is where they brought in Geoff Wainright with his bloody kneecap hanging by a strip of tendon and the dried blood from leopard scratches all down his face, legs and chest. Somewhere here is the bend in the road where, when Arthur Taylor and Alistair Gallatly came back from a long drinking session at one of the tourist camps, Arthur fell out of the front seat of the Land Cruiser – out through the open door – and Alistair, who was driving, didn't realise this until he reached camp an hour later.

Further south, along this track here, was the spot where a hunting client was killed by an elephant.

In this stand of mopane we found the baby zebra staggering between the tree

16

trunks with a spear clean through its side. (We took it home and cleaned the wound only to watch it die a week later.)

Up the O5 road is Luwi camp, where I upset Arthur Ansell's patriotic feelings by parading outside his hut late one night with a tin washbasin on my head singing the German National anthem. It's the same spot where Huw Jones, alone in camp and without booze, felt himself slide into such acute loneliness that he crushed half a dozen malaria pills into powder and sniffed them through a straw up his nose. And then tried to feed some to Henry, the tame hyena. Downstream, along the Luwi River's dry sandy bed, a man shat his pants on a walking safari and the people walking behind him watched, fascinated, as he began to walk funny, like a stork, with his white legs sticking out from his shorts, clenching his buttocks, and finally had to let go.

Somewhere down the Nyamaluma road, Black Bob fell out of a tree he had climbed to get a look at the river. He spent the night lying unconscious in a thorn bush and when he walked into our camp the next morning, looking like he'd been through the windscreen of a car, he couldn't remember anything. Later that day, trying to show his clients a rare bird, he somehow wedged his Land Rover between two trees and was stuck for four hours before he could finally be freed with axes and saws.

This is the spot, across the Kauluzi, where the scouts tried to release a tame baboon. Someone in the Game Department had been in the mood to enforce the law that day and had sent his scouts to confiscate the animal from the guys who had adopted and raised it. 'Take that *bongwe* and release it in the Park.' But of course the baboon hadn't wanted to go. He'd become acclimatised to humans – he probably thought he *was* human – and felt far safer in people's company than in the wilds. Every time the scouts pushed him out of their Land Cruiser, he bared his teeth and screamed and loped after the moving vehicle, chasing it. Finally the men tied him to a tree and left.

The trouble with Africa is that compassion is a rare emotion. An animal is just an animal, worth nothing unless it can be eaten. The local language has only one word for both. *Nyama*, animal; *nyama*, meat.

When I first came here, this Valley was a lonely place. The men who lived and worked here were mostly alone. If they had wives or girlfriends, they had left them behind somewhere. This was no place for a white woman. Most of the men were loners anyway and preferred their own company. Their jobs were not conducive to romantic – let alone marital – bliss.

Men alone, like soldiers, sailors, cowboys, become like wolves. Self-reliant, suspicious and proud, they spend too much time by themselves and have too much time to think. And when the opportunity presents itself, they like to howl at the moon. Not that they don't dream about women, not that their stories aren't imbued with hopes, anticipations,

and wistful memories.

When they got together, they sat around campfires and, perpetuating an age-old tradition, told stories. The narrative was often helped along by a bottle of whisky or a crate of beer parked under a nearby tree. And the stories, full of bravado and self-aggrandisement and embellished with colourful detail, are nothing more than that: howling at the moon.

'Adrian, tell the guys how you bit the nun, up in Congo.'

'That wasn't me, that was Ron. We'd been hunting in the forest all season ...'

'Ja?'

'It's hard hunting up there, hands and knees stuff. I had this tracker I called Shorty. One day we're in this thick stuff where I'd seen a big buffalo, and he kept getting agitated. I said Shorty, man, keep your head down for fucksake but Shorty just smelled the *nyama*. He says, Bwana we must shoot that *nyati*, and I say no we don't, we must keep him for the client coming tomorrow; we just want to see where he goes.'

Someone interrupts. 'Hey Boetie, you're closest to the beer, I'm dying here, man.'

'Bwana, do I look like the goddamn waiter?'

'No, but you could get off your ass and hand around some frosties. We're all empty.'

Adrian takes the offered bottle and continues. 'Next thing that buff is coming flat-out. I shout to Shorty, come on bugger, let's make tracks, but he's a little *oke* and has to take two steps for every one of mine. He's falling back and the buff is catching him. So I have to shoot it. Boom! Frontal brain shot. He falls almost on top of us. And I swear that little tracker is grinning from ear to ear. He says, Bwana, now we can eat the *nyama*. I reckon he hung back just so that I would have to shoot the buffalo.'

'OK, so what about the nuns ...'

Someone gets up. 'I'm going for a piss.'

'No, listen to this.' Boetie grabs him by the leg of his shorts. 'Listen to what these buggers did.'

'Ja, anyway,' Adrian continues, 'hunting in Congo. It was a long hard season. Right at the end of it, we were invited to this mission for dinner. Only other white people for miles and miles.'

'Nuns.'

'Ja, mostly. So we made sure we all had a bath and shave, put on clean shirts. Ron even put on some aftershave. And he kept putting it in his hair, trying to make it lie flat.'

'*Oke* must have smelled like a whoopsie.'

'He did, hey? Anyway, now we're off to visit the nuns. All excited, hadn't seen a white woman in four months. Even the baboons were looking good.'

Boetie says, 'Pity there's no sheep in this part of Africa. I know you wouldn't be able resist, Adrian.'

'Fuck you. Anyway at dinner, this novice nun in her white habit, really cute Belgian girl, comes round with the soup dish and leans across Ron to serve him. Her tits are right there in front of his face.'

'I'll bet his hair was sticking up again.'

'Ja sure. By now the aftershave has dried and his hair is up and all over the show. He'd been hunting bongo that day, in that really thick forest, and his face is all scratched and red. And covered in bites. So he stares at this nun's chest and he can't help himself, he bites her left breast.'

'Embarrassed silence. The other guys are grinning behind their hands. Mother Superior's face is like a block of ice. Shit, man. So now Ron is trying to cover up and apologise, in bad French. He says, sorry, been in the bush too long ... someone says, I'll bet you'd like to be in *her* bush, and everybody's giggling. Then Ron says what's bush in French anyway, and we nearly fall off our chairs. The other guy says, don't know, why don't you try *beaver*?

'Someone is spraying soup all over the table, and the poor nuns look at each other, no idea what's happening.'

'Bet that was the last invitation you *okes* had from them.'

'Ja, for sure.'

Some evenings I sit on my porch steps with a nightcap of whisky and watch the grey shapes of the elephants as they lumber up from the river and slowly blend with the mopane trees and disappear in the forest. The moonlight makes pools of light on their backs and their footfalls are silent. If it weren't for the cracking of the branches, you'd hardly know they were there. I stub out my cigarette and look at my whisky glass. There's still an inch of whisky left, and there is too much happening in the night outside to waste it. I light another Camel because the combination of smoke and Scotch feels good in my lungs and belly.

A wood owl calls from far, far away; the sound travels through the trees and reaches my ears like a distant message. Now the Scotch is finished but my cigarette is still glowing like a red eye in the night. A new group of elephants has come up from the river like ghosts and are approaching the house. I pour another couple of fingers, a splash of soda, and go on watching as they file past the corner of the house and into the moonlit clearing where they stand as if in conference. Water is still drying on their hides from the river crossing and the lower half of their bodies is a darker shade of grey. Slowly they wander off and disappear among the mopane trees. A hyena whoops from somewhere behind me, the sound travelling along the river for miles. There is still some whisky left in the glass. Should I light another cigarette? The night is too beautiful to sleep.

But this was ten years ago when I still smoked, and when another two or three whiskies before bedtime didn't seem to matter too much. The Valley is ten years older now and, along with my nicotine habit, the elephants have disappeared from this part of the mopane forest. Where they used to drift silently up from the river, a big house now blocks their way, and there is constant noise from people and machinery.

In the last ten years or so, the Valley has become crowded. The dusty shoulders of the tar road that leads to the bridge are flanked by market stalls and dozens of tiny shops where tinny rumba music blares from radios. Mfuwe is rapidly growing into another small African town.

Among the white population in the safari camps, there are even quite a few permanent women residents: receptionists, caterers and girlfriends grace almost every camp. But even now, when people are building proper, permanent houses and plan on raising families here in the bush, they bet against long odds. Few of their plans turn out the way they envisage them. The Valley is tough on relationships, as everyone will tell you. Some couples manage to recognise the danger signs in time and move away, others wait too long and let the discontent and boredom take hold, and suddenly it's too late. And most of the men aren't really cut out for permanence. It's just not in their blood, they will say. My friend Athol Frylinck, a professional hunter, remarked recently when he heard of a couple's difficulties after a two-month affair, 'Don't ask me. I'm no expert on these long, drawn-out relationships.'

Some of the women here are every bit as tough as the men, and every bit as *different*. Eccentricity is not dependent on gender, it seems. For the people, male or female, who choose to make this their home are not the same kind of people who inhabit the insurance offices, banks and workshops of the corporate world. These are the ones who don't fit, the ones who run away and hide from the world, or maybe from themselves; who wander the globe until they find a place like this, where they feel that they can breathe, where their destinies can be fulfilled.

On the surface, they all come for different reasons (my boyfriend works

20

here … I came as a tourist and loved the place and asked for a job … my father was here twenty years ago). But deep down, in their hearts, their motives are the same; they are here because of the wild animals. They may not admit this to their friends back in the city – how would *they* understand such a strange notion? They may not even admit it, or be aware of it, themselves. But it is the mystery, the hidden secrets of this world, that draws them and keeps them here. The wonder at such natural abundance, such intricacies, such raw aggression and such sweet gentleness. How can a corporate life possibly compare with it?

One man who has felt this wonder more than any other, one of the old-timers, was still here: Norman Carr, who opened up the Valley and stayed where all the others were merely passing through, and in his lifetime became a living legend himself. His passion for this land was in every gesture he made, every word he spoke.

When the winds of the coming world war blew across Europe in the late nineteen-thirties, Norman Carr was already here, a young man hunting elephants for the Colonial administration, proud to do his bit for King and country in one of the most distant corners of darkest Africa. His official title was 'Elephant Control Officer', and his job was to deter bull elephants from raiding native village gardens – usually by shooting them. This was not as easy – nor as frivolous – as it sounds. For the villagers, saving a maize crop from

destruction – with the possible bonus of a whole elephant to eat – could be a matter of survival or starvation. For Norman Carr, it was the adventure of a lifetime.

He looks back on those days with a detached, slightly rueful nostalgia.

'I was rather younger then. Young and perhaps a little foolish.' He regards the present-day hunters with the tolerance of a parent indulging a rebel child. He well remembers the thrill of the hunt, the challenges and the dangers. But, 'how many elephants, or lions or buffalo does one have to kill to prove to yourself that you have the balls – or that you are afraid, but man enough to overcome your fear?'

Like many old hunters, Norman was now a fierce conservationist, fighting for the future of wild animals with the fervour of a heathen-turned-evangelist.

He had seen the end of the Colonial era in Africa, the passing of the glory-days when a white man with a gun was king of the savannah. He had witnessed political changes; the rising optimism and the unstoppable will to be free – as well as the dark forces of repression and bloodshed – and saw his own career cut short by the wave of the 'Zambianisation' that followed independence in his adopted country.

Turning to safaris as a livelihood and to the welfare of the animals as his life's mission, he accepted the changes with the calmness of a stoic. His pioneering spirit never left him, and apart from his role in opening up the park – building its first roads and camps, advising the game department of the day on planning strategies and policies – he always had a sympathetic ear for the plight of the local villagers, whom he has called 'my favourite people on earth'. He organised fund-raising drives for their schools, taught them the value of their wildlife and urged them to practise conservation – and on more than one occasion killed the man-eating lions that terrorised their villages.

In his time, he became Zambia's Mr Wildlife, friend to presidents and princes, and the originator, the acknowledged 'father', of the African Walking Safari.

He was also my father-in-law.

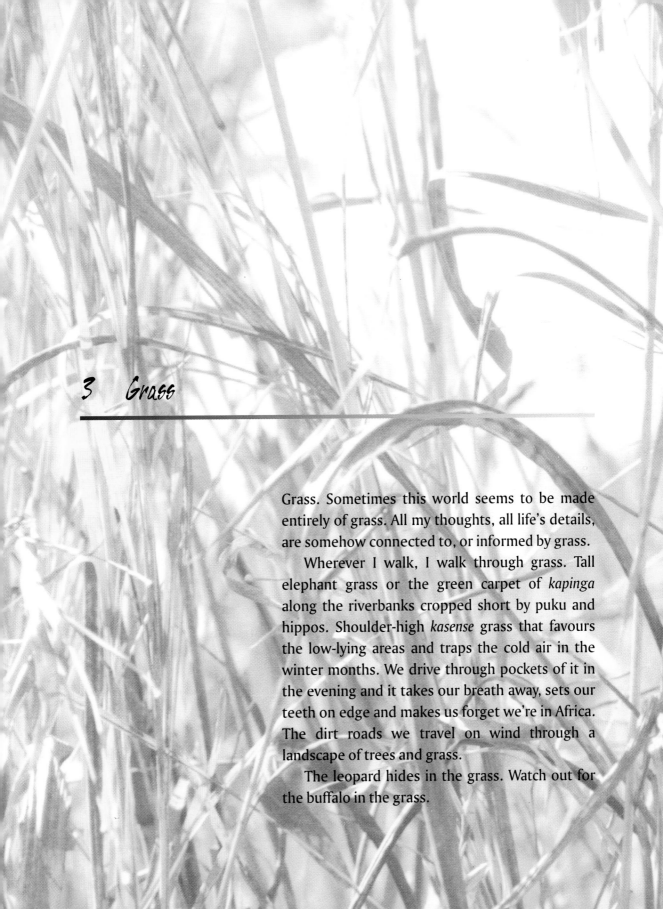

3 Grass

Grass. Sometimes this world seems to be made entirely of grass. All my thoughts, all life's details, are somehow connected to, or informed by grass.

Wherever I walk, I walk through grass. Tall elephant grass or the green carpet of *kapinga* along the riverbanks cropped short by puku and hippos. Shoulder-high *kasense* grass that favours the low-lying areas and traps the cold air in the winter months. We drive through pockets of it in the evening and it takes our breath away, sets our teeth on edge and makes us forget we're in Africa. The dirt roads we travel on wind through a landscape of trees and grass.

The leopard hides in the grass. Watch out for the buffalo in the grass.

Imagine this. You feel like going for a walk. You take your binoculars and leave camp along one of the overgrown tracks that lead you through the bush on a parallel course to the river. You try to stay on the path, and when you lose it, when it disappears among the scrub and under-growth, you try and stay in the open so that you can see any possible danger. You spot some elephants feeding a hundred yards away but they are upwind and you don't worry about them. You think it might be good to head towards the river, walk in the warm sand and watch the Egyptian geese chattering on the muddy bank. Perhaps you'll spot the Crowned Cranes with their chicks. They'll be nervous and won't let you come close but you might get a good look at the chicks through your binoculars.

There is one problem: Between the river and the point where you are standing, there is a three hundred metre wide strip of *kasense*. Grass as high as a wheat field but denser, more alive, sway-ing in the warm breeze that blows off the river. You choose a spot where the field seems at its narrowest, take a breath for courage and plunge in. Only when you are a hundred metres into the swaying dusty-yellow sea, do you suddenly think of the lion you heard calling outside camp very early this morning. Somewhere near the river. Somewhere *here.* Perhaps he is still here, lying up, sleeping off the night somewhere in this ocean of grass.

Grass mats on the floor, thatched grass on the roof. Several times a day I stop what I am doing to pick grass seeds out of my socks.

I sit under a tree in the shade, chewing a blade of grass.

The village women use grass to make their baskets.

Grass seeds lodge themselves in the radiator of my car and cause the engine to overheat. I make a screen to fit in front of the radiator to keep the seeds out.

Ticks hide in the grass. Small red pepper-ticks, smaller than a pinhead, cling to stems of grass after the rainy season, before the burning, and burrow into my skin as I walk through them, unaware. I notice them only days later, after they have crawled up my legs and dug into the skin of my groin and belly. Some even venture up into my armpits. The pink welts itch, and I smother them in Vaseline or paraffin in order to suffocate them.

Villagers burn the grass around their huts and their fields at the end of the rainy season. They stand at the edge of the flames, hoping to kill the small animals as they rush out to escape the blaze: hares, mice and rats; perhaps the odd mongoose. Tortoises are too slow, and get roasted inside their shells.

Birds gather and dive through the hot grey smoke looking for the swarming insects that rise on the hot air. Bee-eaters and Lilac-breasted Rollers feed on the wing, perilously close to the flames, it seems, swooping in and out of the crackling fire like Kamikaze pilots.

Snakes sometimes appear at the edge of the grass, sliding across a bare patch and vanishing again in the dense foliage. In the overgrown borders of our vegetable patch, I see a cobra slithering into the open. I take a step towards it, curious. The snake rears up, its head two feet in the air, and spreads its hood. I guess there must be another three or four feet of it hidden in the grass. I take a step back. The flat head sways from side to side, hood flared, round black eyes staring, tongue flicking. I step back another metre, then another. I'm no hero, it seems. Norman would laugh at me.

There are well over a hundred species of grass in the Valley, and there are over twenty species of hoofed animals that feed on them. Each of these has specialised needs; puku crop the short *kapinga* on the floodplain near the river, buffalo favour the coarser grasses. Some antelope don't eat grass at all, or very little, and prefer to browse on the new shoots and leaves of bushes. Bushbuck and kudu are predominantly browsers, so are giraffe. Warthogs root in the earth. Zebras graze.

Looking down on this world from an aeroplane, I see mostly grass. In November, with the first drops of the rainy season, tentative green

shoots start sprouting, and within days there are bright islands of green dotted everywhere in the sea of dusty brown. Impala drop their young at this time and a week from now there will be hundreds of the little fawns dotted all over the plains like spring flowers. They wobble on unsteady legs, keeping close to the flanks of their mothers and nudging their swollen udders.

'It's been a long season but I never want to leave the Valley until I've seen

the first impala fawn,' says a hunter.

The air is suddenly clear again, and the hills beyond the river seem to have edged closer. By December, the entire countryside has turned to bright emerald green. In January and February a large portion of the land is covered by floodwater. The low-lying areas have turned into lakes, their levels rising and falling with each thunderstorm and with each small stream flooding its banks. We are now at the height of the rains. Insects swarm, mosquitoes spread malaria like never before, and the grass grows so fast, we can almost watch it grow. It will be another month before the skies clear, and then another before the first fires rage through the grass and turn mile after square mile of eight-foot high elephant grass into billowing clouds of black smoke that twist and turn and choke the sky. The haze lingers for days.

Norman Carr, who has witnessed over forty of these annual cycles, says, 'If someone could only find a way to harness all this wild energy, harvest the grass before it burns, cut it, bundle it, turn it into compacted packets of fuel.'

The grass that escapes the burning provides food for an increasingly hungry population of antelope, buffalo, zebra, elephants. As the dry season progresses, the grass becomes scarce, and the previously lush stands turn into barren fields of dusty rock-hard earth, the last remaining green-grey patches trampled flat by the hooves of hundreds of antelope and buffalo. When October comes again and the grass is as dry as desert sand, we

can hear the heat ticking in the lifeless stems.

From the air, the Luangwa River resembles the lazy coils of a slow-moving yellow snake. The wide sandy river bed is the snake's belly, the brown water that bites a channel down its centre and glints when the sun finds it, is the snake's spine. Where it moves through flat sandy soils, the river bed widens, broad beaches on either side, like a fat puff adder. Where the soil is dense and full of hard clay, the river grows thin again, and moves between its steep banks like a slithering black mamba.

From the air, the river reveals its past like a storybook, a past that is not measured in geological ages or centuries but in mere human generations, decades, even in single seasons. As the floodwaters of the rainy seasons bulge its channels, the banks erode, trees are uprooted and sucked down by the current. Swollen tributaries dump their load into the main river, bringing more sand and silt and flotsam, and when the flood recedes and has spent itself in the arms of the Zambezi two hundred miles away, the river looks different. A collapsed bank here, a new sandbar there. In a sense, this river echoes our human bustle of building up and tearing down, of trying this, experimenting with that; of pushing here and retreating there, of bursting the banks, and of constantly changing.

From the air, it's easy to see where it happened. A bank has crumpled and allowed the river to cut a new channel. The old course will slowly silt up and stop flowing, allowing grasses and small shrubs to take root along its sides. Nile cabbage will arrive on a hippo's back and grow and multiply until the surface is choked with green.

The oxbow lagoons tell the river's older story; they show us where the river used to be, maybe a hundred years ago, maybe ten, maybe last year.

Here, the water is still. Birds nest in the trees and animals come to drink in the quiet of the midday heat; they come in the purple afternoons and in the cool morning mist that rises off the water to the noisy chattering of waterfowl.

If you want to build a camp on the bank of this river, you have to be aware. You must remember the river's habits, its fondness for change. Norman Carr knows this: You never build your camp on the outside of a bend where the bank will be eaten away, eroded perhaps in a matter of a few seasons. You try and position it inside a bend, or along a bank where the river runs straight. Even then, you can never be sure: the river may have other plans, long-term plans that you cannot foresee.

Chibembe Camp is built along a straight bank of the river, huddled under a grove of tall evergreens and other deep-shade trees: trichelias, sausage trees, monkey-breads, winter thorns.

Chibembe Camp: a string of twelve chalets facing the river in its first season. A second row is added the following year. A reception building, a kitchen and store-rooms are off to one side. Beyond them, downstream along the riverbank, are the grass huts where we live, with Norman, the manager and his wife, and the guides.

Birds weave their nests from grass.

We build our houses out of grass.

We live in grass houses. If we are lucky and have stands of the tall *Hyparrhenia* grass in the vicinity of camp, we will use this for our walls and roof, tied with dried strips of palm frond to a frame of bamboo and mopane poles. The more upmarket homeowners 'comb' the elephant grass. Stripping off all leaves, blades and seeds, they are left with the bare stalks, which, packed tightly, make a neat and nearly solid wall. Those of us who don't have the patience for this time-consuming and labour-intensive process, use the rougher *kasense* grass which makes the houses look dishevelled, as if they've just woken up.

Sparrow-weavers hang their nests from the branches of acacia trees, often dozens of them in a single tree. The colonies look untidy, the nests scruffy balls like the grass balls village kids make for their football games.

Our houses, if they're built with *kasense,* look a bit like that.

The floors are packed dirt. We shun cement and man-made building materials, and there are no rocks or stones to be found in the alluvial soils of the valley floor. In any case, people in grass houses shouldn't throw stones. Or play with fire.

Or mix their metaphors.

I lie on my back on my bed and stare at the grass roof through the milky gauze of the mosquito net. Something has woken me. Something is moving in the space between the top of the net and the roof, and there is a noise in that space, too. A scratching, a rustling. I am used to the walls and roof coming alive at night with the small sounds of spiders and insects in the thatch, perhaps a Spotted Bush Snake. Wood-borers are always busy in the *mopane* poles that hold up the roof, and sometimes when the night is particularly still, I fancy I can hear them as they rain their fine wood dust on to our mosquito net, like dandruff.

But this is different; louder, more aggressive somehow. As my eyes get used to the dark, I see two long whitish columns four feet above my head, like giant peeled bananas. But unlike bananas, there is a hardness to them, an inherent strength, like weapons. They move back and forth, up and down, and I suddenly realise that they are elephant tusks, and that the elephant they belong to is standing outside our hut; leaning against it, in fact. I can picture him, and I can certainly hear him now.

Our house stands under a winter-thorn tree (*Acacia albida*) and it seems that the elephant is looking for fallen seedpods on our roof, his trunk sliding on the thatch among the dead leaves and twigs that have dropped from the tree. In order to reach all of the pods, he has to stretch and lean his whole weight against the grass wall, and of course his tusks are sticking through it.

Elephants love these protein-packed winter-thorn pods. They feed on them relentlessly, all through August when the pods ripen and fall. They pick them off the ground and they pluck them off the trees, stretching to their full height, trunk extended, up on their hind-legs sometimes, to get at the high branches.

Pam is sleeping beside me, unaware of the elephant outside, oblivious to his noisy chewing. Tamara and Miranda, our two small daughters, are in the hut next to ours, a stronger one, with shuttered windows and a solid door in a tough frame. Bolted at night. Asleep in their beds with strict instructions not to go outside at night. If you need to wee-wee, call us. *Don't go outside.*

Our hut has no door. The doorframe is in place but the bamboo ran out before we could make a door and we haven't got around to cutting more. It's a long way to where the bamboo grows, and even longer to town where we could buy planks to make a *real* door. Through the open rectangle I can see the elephant lumbering off now, a large grey silhouette against the night sky. He stands by the edge of the riverbank by the low bamboo fence we have erected there to prevent the children from falling over the edge, then he slowly wanders over to Norman's house. There is another winter-thorn outside Norman's house.

But I am awake now, and it is the time of night where random thoughts and reflections come drifting obliquely across the mind.

Pam and I had finally both finished studying and were feeling the confines of the city like an acute skin rash. But being the proud owner of an Art degree doesn't necessarily make you a practising artist, let alone earn you a living. People had warned me that it would be hard but it was a shock to realise just *how* hard. The choices were few; a couple of years in a commercial design studio bridged the gap of poverty but what we craved was a bridge that would span two different worlds: from the one we had to the one that was beckoning from across South Africa's northern border.

Pam's father had been less than encouraging: 'Absolutely not. Life in the bush may seem very romantic to you now, even glamorous, but there's no career here for you.' His voice was mellow with its rich British inflections but his mouth was set in a hard line. 'There's no money in this, no security and no future. No. You stay in the city and build up a solid foundation for your lives.' I thought it odd that a man with his chosen lifestyle would lecture me on security, but it was no use arguing.

The birth of our first daughter Tamara convinced me that time was running out. It was now or never; I could make a last concerted effort at being a painter or be swallowed into the mediocrity and boredom of advertising art, live in the suburbs, drive a nice car, build a nice house.

My first exhibition at a prestigious Johannesburg art gallery was a sell-out and brought us a step closer to the dream. A year later, our second daughter Miranda was born, and the time had come for the big move out of the city. When Norman saw my determination to succeed as an artist, I began to notice a gradual thawing of his resistance, and sometimes even a grudging approval. It wasn't much longer before we packed our things – everything we needed fitted in the back of our pick-up truck – and left Johannesburg, heading north.

Sometimes our open doorway is a reminder of how vulnerable we are here, how out of place. Each night I hear elephants among the trees that surround the camp, pulling at the greenery, stripping bark off the trunks, breaking branches. Hippos come out of the river and chomp noisily along the bank. A leopard coughs and wakes a tree full of baboons that bark their alarm in the night. I feel for them, trying to imagine what it must be like, huddled together against the enemy they can hear but not see. I think I know this feeling: a few nights ago, I am suddenly, instantly awake. Nerve-tinglingly alert. I don't know how I know but I am certain without doubt that there is a lion outside the hut. Some atavistic knowledge in my brain has sounded the alarm, and I lie in bed, straining my ears to hear him.

Pam sleeps through all of this.

Three nights ago Pam and I had gone for an evening drive in the Park. We were out in the bush in one of the camp's open Land Rovers. The car had a faulty fuel gauge (a poor excuse, really) and we ran out of petrol just as the sun went down. We were too far from camp to walk back, a bad idea anyway as darkness settled quickly, and we had no torch and no water. In that short interval between day and night, when the air is still and the grass and the trees turn blue, we had a quick look around and took stock of our situation. We were at the end of a spur road that branched off the main trail perhaps three or four kilometres behind us. No problem really. We knew there was a strict camp policy to search for any vehicle that hadn't returned to camp an hour after sunset.

So we settled down to wait and watched as the blue trees faded to black. Gradually, the daytime sounds ceased. Birds and insects fell silent; we could still hear a few Egyptian geese from the direction of the river, but soon they, too, were quiet. In that short hiatus when the day has ended but the night has not properly begun, there is a hushed stillness, like the interval between acts one and two of a play. As the night sounds slowly – cautiously it seems – begin to announce their dominance, they seem unexpectedly amplified, reverberating in the gloom. A small twig breaking somewhere sounds like a gunshot, an owl's distant hoot like a sonic boom. Then the frogs start winding themselves up, their croaks rising and ebbing and rising again; and this seems to be a signal for the rest of the nocturnal orchestra to tune up.

Every so often, I switched on the headlights to see if the sounds of breaking branches, the shuffling footfalls and the grunts and rumbles were really as close as they seemed in the darkness. Once or twice we saw an elephant or a hippo crossing the path in front of us but most of the noises came from the side and from behind us, outside the reach of the headlights. This did not make them any more reassuring and when we at last heard a car horn in the distance, we smiled at each other with relief.

But our smiles were premature: we had run down the battery; it was too feeble to sound our own hooter in reply, and we heard the rescue vehicle grind its gears, the engine noise slowly fading into the distance. That's when the lions started calling. At first it seemed that they were on the other side of the river, but as they grew louder and more frequent, we could no longer be sure. Then the wind changed direction and blew towards us and suddenly the deep guttural calls sounded less than a hundred metres away, and coming closer. Elephants were feeding all around us and we could hear hippos pulling at the short grass on the riverbank.

It was almost midnight before the rescue car came back on its second run past the road junction behind us, and this time our smiles when we heard it turn off and crunch over the rutted clay towards us were rewarded.

When we had finally crawled into bed, I lay awake for a while, waiting for the adrenalin to subside and my nerves to settle down. I looked through the open doorway at the half-moon and the night wind blowing through the trees; the grass walls surrounding us seemed solid, and our hut felt as safe as a bunker.

The day before, while we were up in the main camp for dinner, two lions visited the patch of grass in front of our huts. Pam had put the children to bed; we had shuttered the windows and locked the door but there had been no time to gather up the toys left out on the grass, strewn all over a blanket and two pillows where the kids had been playing. When we returned we saw that the blanket and one of the pillows had been dragged along the ground and torn to shreds. We found the other pillow early next morning, a hundred yards away in the bush, feathers hanging in the shrubs like white blossoms in the morning dew.

Don't go outside at night!

But the elephant that must have come later in the night was peaceful: his footprints were all among the toys but he had not stepped on one of them. He had walked all around them, carefully avoiding the lego car, the rag doll with the orange hair and the book about Jemima Puddle-Duck.

Our shower stall is a grass cubicle that is open on one side with a clear view of the river. Two big oil drums are mounted on an elevated platform behind it, and it is part of our camp staff's duties to fill these drums each afternoon, one with hot water, one with cold. I stand under the shower and wash off the dust and sweat from a day in the bush. I shampoo the grass seeds out of my hair while watching the hippos snort in the river and a troop of monkeys preparing to roost in the tree above me. I feel like a hippo myself, water running down my back while the air around me is turning chilly with evening.

I dry myself and put on a long-sleeved shirt against the mosquitoes. As I walk out from behind the fence, my nose prickles with the pungent aroma of burning elephant dung. I see Norman sitting by the fire in front of his hut, facing the river. Bats are flitting along the bank catching insects that have come out with the dusk. A gust of wind blows sparks from the fire.

'Vic. Come and sit. Have a whisky.' Norman points to a sagging canvas chair with a strapped armrest beside him. 'Bit tatty, that one, I'm afraid.' Behind the chair, a bottle, a red soda siphon, and two glasses stand on an old wooden picnic box. I help myself and sit down. Norman turns towards me.

'Pam putting the girls to bed?'

I nod. 'They're still excited. We saw a mating pair on the way back from the salt-pan. The lioness was quite relaxed but the male charged us. God, that's a scary sight. They're so bloody fast.'

Norman grins at me with the indulgence of the expert. 'Well, now that you're one of us, you'll be learning a lot of new things.'

I think of the first time I met him. Pam, her brother Adrian and I sitting in an open Land Rover with him late one night watching two lions kill a buffalo. When we had finally seen enough, Norman was unable to start the car because our headlights had drained the battery. He calmly turned in his seat and said, 'Oh well, looks like you'll have to push.' The Land Rover was facing the two lions feeding not ten metres from us, and I still remember the heart-stopping relief when the engine finally fired and I vaulted back into the open car, an arm's length from the male. I remember his blank yellow eyes and the guttural growl deep in his chest. And I remember Norman grinning.

The sickly smell from the fire drifts into my face. Along with the mopane logs, Norman likes to burn dried elephant dung, which he swears keeps the mosquitoes away. He asks us to collect the brittle balls, like compacted compost, that lie in heaps around the camp perimeter.

'My eyes aren't what they used to be,' he says. 'Think I saw a bat hawk working this stretch of river.' He makes a sweeping lateral movement with his right hand, index finger extended, without spilling his whisky. 'They're jolly quick, you know. Have to be, of course, to catch a bat.'

Norman has changed, as he does every evening, from his baggy shorts into pressed khaki trousers and a short-sleeved bush jacket. His brown eyes, set in webs of deep wrinkles now, still have the dark penetrating command of the British army officer. His hair is thinning and has turned the colour of mopane ash but the hair that covers the leathery skin of his tanned fore-arms is thick and black. His nose has the self-assured hook of a Roman centurion, and watching him sitting motionless in his chair, I am reminded of the quiet authority of a bird of prey in repose.

He uses his hands when he speaks, stabbing the air with a big-knuckled index finger to make a point.

'I heard someone playing a wireless in camp today. Inconsiderate sort of chap. I'm afraid I asked him to turn it off.' He pronounced it 'orf'.

'The whole idea of being here is not having to listen to the wireless. And no newspapers. Newspapers should be banned from a safari camp. Years ago, when I started the Walking Safaris, I realised that this may be one of the few places on earth where people can escape modern life completely. Where for a few days they can pretend they're Victorian explorers. And this chap comes and plays his wireless. Rather rude, I thought.'

He takes a sip of whisky and gestures towards the river with his head. 'A couple of big bulls crossed this morning at first light and had a little scuffle with a croc.' He points downstream along the riverbank with his index finger. 'Did you hear it? Do artists get up that early?' His voice is level but I detect a trace of irony in his eyes.

Pam has come and sat down next to us.

'Kids are asleep,' she says. We sit in silence as the evening gathers around us. Hippos grunt and we watch two of them leaving the water and climbing up the bank on the other side. There are dozens of 'chutes' cut into the steep wall that enable them to shift their bulk to the top of the bank. With each footstep the earth is worn down a few centimetres more, and the chutes become easier to climb as time passes.

'Unlikely road engineers, those hippos,' says Norman. He looks at his watch.

'Oh well, I suppose it's time to go and be nice to the tourists. Much rather sit here and look at the river, but ...' He lets the sentence trail off and makes a sideways swipe with his whisky glass, a gesture of dismissal, then takes a final sip.

'Oh well, let's go and do our duty.'

The bat hawk has failed to appear.

At the bar, Norman is charming. People stand close to him, competing for his attention. He must have heard the same questions a hundred times but he answers each one patiently.

'Mr Carr, may I buy you a drink?'

'No thank you. I've had my allotted quota for the evening.'

All through dinner, he fields the questions. I see him at the next table in animated conversation, his hands always mobile, the fingers pointing or admonishing or cajoling.

Two waiters circle our table, immaculate in white tunics over starched white trousers. They carry trays with steaming soup tureens.

'Good evening,' says one. I see that his trousers are slightly too short; his scuffed shoes are showing, one sole flapping. He is new, and I know that he is struggling with his English.

'Today we have super, is tomato.'

There are polite smiles from the diners, and when they have finished their soup, he is back, offering his tray to the lady sitting next to me.

'Oh, what have we here?' she enquires, ladling a big spoonful of stew on to her plate.

'Snake and kitten pie,' comes the reply. (I remember the same waiter offering

banana filters as a dessert yesterday, and this morning, at breakfast, he announced: 'We have punched eggies, scalambala, or flying eggies. With bacon.')

The lady peers down at her plate, then at the waiter, then at me.

'It's okay,' I whisper, 'in fact, it's delicious.'

Sooner or later, most camps acquire some kind of camp animal, and in Africa this is quite often an elephant. When people site a new camp, they think about a nice view, shady trees, proximity to water, access-ibility in the rainy season, and other practical considerations. They often neglect to take into account that the beautiful shady spot they discovered might lie in the middle of an old game path, or on a stretch of river where the elephants have crossed for the last hundred years or more.

The animals were there first, and it often seems to take a bit of time for them to get used to the noise and the activity that the presence of humans brings. Most keep their distance and eventually move away from the area. But once in a while it seems as if an animal discovers that there are advantages to being around humans.

Two weeks later, and our elephant has grown bolder.

The winter-thorn pods are in full season now and lie under the trees like shed Christmas decorations. Elephants stand under the massive trees and patiently, unhurriedly, pick up the pods with sweeping circular movements of their trunks. When the pods are finished, they shake the tree until the pods rain down once more. Sometimes a bull will get up on its hindlegs, forelegs in the air and trunk raised vertically, to reach up into the high branches. Norman says he once measured the reach of a big bull, and it was close to eight metres.

The pods resemble dried apple rings.

They are a faded yellow and burnt orange in colour, and become crisp when they dry. The seeds are hard and loose inside their shells; they rattle when you shake them, a rhythmic sound like a castanet. We have started using them in our little camp band.

Our elephant comes every night now. He seems to have lost all fear of people. It's not only the pods he's after; he feeds on all the trees and bushes in camp, stripping leaves off branches with a sweep of his curled trunk, pulling up shrubs, breaking limbs off trees. It's impossible to sleep through the noise of his chewing and the rumbling of his belly.

Several times each night, I hear Norman clapping his hands and shouting, and see the thin beam of his torch through the gaps in our grass wall. 'Go on! Bugger off!'

He doesn't *have* to feed right here, I am thinking. There are other trees. Thousands of them. Why does he choose to stand here between our huts each night and rob us of our sleep. It's as if he takes a perverse pleasure in this. The Germans have a word for it: *Schadenfreude*. I fancy that I see a glint of secret satisfaction in his small eye when I shine my torch on him.

Maybe not. When I shine my torch, it is with the express wish to irritate him, to make him feel uncomfortable, to blind him. Shining the torch is the last resort, when the shouting and hand-clapping have failed and I'm forced to get out of bed and stand outside my hut with my torch.

'Go away. Bugger off. Let me sleep!'

Sometimes this works, and sometimes it has the opposite effect and he comes charging at me and I have to retreat hastily into the hut, heart pumping. Now I *really* can't sleep.

Cindy Buxton from Anglia Television is with us for the season, filming a documentary for the Anglia Survival series. She has her own camp – two grass huts inside a grass fence – adjoining ours, a mere twenty metres downstream. She, too, is showing signs of sleep deprivation: she has strung a long wire, running the length of her fence, from which she has hung empty bottles and tin cans and bits of metal she found in the scrap heap behind the workshop. Her Elephant Warning System is just as likely to wake us all up as the elephant itself.

One night, half-woken by Norman's clapping and shouting, I wait for my eyes to adapt to the darkness and slide out from under the mosquito net to peek through a gap in the grass wall of our hut. At first I cannot see anything but when I follow the direction of the shouts, I catch a glimpse of Norman, briefly, before he vanishes again. A second later I see the lumbering form of the elephant, then Norman again, and I understand what is happening.

About fifteen metres outside Norman's hut there is a round green bush, its branches trimmed by browsing animals, giving it an almost ornamental, cultivated appearance. Norman must have got out of bed and run after the elephant, clapping and shouting. When the elephant drew level with the bush, it must have changed direction and decided to go round the bush, instead of past it. Norman keeps up his pursuit, still shouting abuse.

Round and round the bush they go. Norman is naked except for his underpants – baggy Y-fronts – and the weak beam of his small flashlight does nothing to enhance his authority. I can no longer be sure who is chasing whom. I don't know the exact moment of recognition but at one point Norman must also have realised that he might no longer be the pursuer but the pursued, that the elephant was now chasing him. From my vantage point it is impossible to make a judgement on this, and I'm still pondering the problem when the elephant finally realises the futility of the situation and veers off and races out of camp with trunk and tail high in the air, trumpeting as it runs.

The whole performance is made even more bizarre by the fact that it happened in almost total darkness, as if in secrecy, in front of an audience of one.

Norman is beginning to look tired. He is always the first to rise – up at dawn, no matter how much or how little sleep he's had. 'We have to do something about this bloody elephant,' I hear him mutter.

But the day's activities have to go on, regardless of sleepless nights. Five-thirty, wake-up call, and tea and toast by the fire. Six o'clock, the drives leave camp. Seven o'clock radio schedule. Our half-hour communication slot with Lusaka head-quarters. They tell us of bookings, how many pax to expect and when. Flight details, delays, changes in itineraries. We tell them what we need. Fuel. Soap. Cook-ing oil is running out. Please. When is the truck leaving Lusaka?

The radio is our lifeline.

The camp workers call it the Roger-Roger.

Our call sign is 218. Lusaka is 210. The hunting camps are 211 to 217. Some of them are in the Kafue hunting areas on the other side of the country.

We have another slice of real life at seven in the evening. When the clients are boring and the bar is quiet, some of us drift over to the office, beer mug in hand, for thirty minutes of outside world. We listen to what the hunting camps have to say. Someone needs ammunition. Urgently. So-and-so has shot a record-book buffalo. Luawata camp is fast running out of diesel. When *is* the truck leaving Lusaka? Sometimes reception from one of the distant camps is bad and we have to relay. Lusaka, do you read? So-and-so has shot a world-class buffalo. Send some champagne. Who is in pain? No, negative pain. *Cham*-pain. Charlie Hotel Alpha Mike . . .

One night, I hear this conversation:

'217 from 210, do you read?' Call sign 217 is the Hunting Safaris field head-quarters at Chanjuzi, sixty kilometres north of here. The manager there is Anderson Mwale, who speaks only rudimentary English, and has picked up an extracurricular vocabulary from the professional hunters and their clients which often contravenes radio etiquette.

'210, reading you, go ahead. Over.'

'Anderson, good evening. Can you give me news of the grader. It needs to go to Kamira Camp urgently. Over.'

'Good evening Gerry. There is a problem. Over.'

'Anderson, what is the problem? The grader has to leave first thing in the morning. Over.'

There is a long silence; we can hear the static in the ether, the air humming in the distant spaces between the transmitters. Then the click of the microphone call button sixty kilometres away, and Anderson's voice:

'Grader hit mopane tree. Gerry . . . ?'

'Anderson. What is the damage. Please confirm, is there any damage, over.'

'Affirmative, there is great, great, great damage. Over.'

'Roger. Can you be specific, please, over.'

'Grader is fucked.'

Another pause, then: 'Anderson, you must not use that word on radio . . .'

A longer pause this time, then Anderson's voice again. 'Gerry? What word? Over.'

At this point a hunter from a distant camp cuts in.

'Anderson, this is 214. I'll be over at your camp tomorrow. Need to pick up supplies. I'll explain. Over and out.'

I have written a new song for our band. It goes,

Two-one-zero, two-one-eight. Chibembe standing by.
Half the camp is drunk again and the other half is high . . .

I see that Norman is up to something. Two of the workshop guys have come and positioned an empty oil drum, a big forty-four gallon one, outside the door of his hut. A big wooden axe handle, carved from local hardwood, hangs in the open drum, suspended by a string that runs up into the roof and disappears among the rafters.

I can see Norman himself busy inside; moving behind the grass wall, his arms lifted high. Through the gap between wall and roof I see his raised hand, the string held between his fingers.

'Norman, what are you doing?'

'Bugger!' He mutters as the string escapes his grasp. He turns and sees me standing in his doorway, 'Oh, hello, Vic. I've had enough of this bloody elephant. Just a minute, let me secure this – need a knot here, I think.' He appears at the door and points to the heavy axe handle.

'You see, the other end of the string hangs down beside my bed. Now when the elephant comes, I don't have to get out of bed any more. I simply grab the string and pull . . .' His grin crinkles his eyes as he gives the handle a push and sends it swinging against the sides of the oil drum.

'Very nice.' I nod, grinning too. 'Hope it works.'

'We'll have to see,' Norman shrugs.

At midnight the elephant approaches from downstream. I hear him crashing in the bushes, then setting off Cindy's alarm system. Bottles and cans clang in the dark as he feeds there, his back rubbing against her fence. I close my eyes and pull the blanket up to cover my ears, but five minutes later, our own house starts shaking from the attentions of six tons of bull elephant. Oh Jesus Christ.

'Go away,' I shout. 'Just … piss off. Leave us alone.' I turn my head. Pam is fast asleep. I lie rigid, with clenched teeth, debating whether to get out of bed, wondering how fresh my torch batteries are. But slowly the shaking and rubbing stops, and the rhythmic chewing fades. I drift back to sleep, only to be wide awake again a minute later. Sitting up in bed, eyes wide open, shaking my head at the banging outside: wood on metal, clamorous in the clear night. A minute later I see the grey heap lumbering unhurriedly across the dark rectangle of our open door, and no sooner have the shuffling footsteps died than the clinking of bottles on metal starts to chime again from Cindy's fence. Pam mumbles, 'Jees, whassat noise. Sounds like war.'

'It is,' I answer. 'It is.'

At breakfast, we stare numbly at each other. A tourist says, 'What was all that noise last night, that banging?' We stare at each other. No one says a word.

The days pass, and the elephant shows no sign of being intimidated by our forward defences. If anything, he's getting more aggressive himself. We do our best to ignore him. Life goes on.

Two or three nights a week Norman shows the old BBC movie about his two adopted lions, 'Return to the Wild'. Moths dance through the beam of light between the old movie projector and the screen where images of a younger Norman Carr flicker, and the soundtrack of birds and elephants competes with the noises of the real elephants outside camp.

'Welcome to the Valley of the Luangwa River where the rarest animal is man,' the commentator's voice announces in the clipped newscaster tones of the late fifties, and soon we hear Noman's voice calling his lions, 'Come, come, caaaahm!'

Afterwards, we sit around the fire and listen to his brief talk about the Valley, and his knowledgeable answers to the clients' questions. But tonight something is different. After the usual questions about the gestation period of lions or the amount of leaves and grass an elephant consumes every day, a man puts up his hand and asks: 'Why is there never enough food in camp?'

I remember the man from the day he arrived – an English ex-pat, a mechanic or technician of some kind who said that he had just finished a two-year contract on one of Zambia's copper mines. Before going home to England – Yoo-kay as they all seem to call it – he was going to spend the kwacha he wasn't allowed to take with him (due to the strict currency regulations at the time) on a trip to the Game Park. I don't recall his name but I remember that Patrick Ansell, who drove him to camp from the airport, nicknamed him the Diesel Fitter.

Things went wrong for him from the start. A fuel drum in the back of the Land Rover started leaking and dripped diesel on to the man's bag, and on to a pair of shoes in the bag. When they arrived in camp and he made this discovery, the man glared at his shoes, then looked at Patrick accusingly. Patrick apologised, but the man took his shoes to the office, demanding to see the manager.

'Very sorry, sir, unavoidable accident. Would you like us to try and clean them?'

'No. You'll spoil them even more.'

The grumbling continued all week. He didn't see a leopard. The seats in the back of the Land Rover were uncomfortable. There was not enough ice at the bar. And his shoes. What were we going to do about his shoes?

I suddenly recall that earlier today the meat loaf at the lunch buffet was finished before he got to it. There was plenty of ham, salami, and other cold meats along with the salads and the cheeses but the meat loaf was finished.

'Why is there never enough food in camp?' Norman repeats the question, staring at the man. There is a short silence with only the crackling of the flames, then everyone seems to be shouting at once.

'What? The food is marvellous … lots of everything … great variety.' I hear someone mutter, 'Low-class trash,' under his breath. 'I'm embarrassed by my countrymen sometimes.'

When the voices have died down, Norman remains resolutely polite. He stares across the flickering fire at the man.

'I think we all know how difficult things can be in this country.' He keeps his eyes on him.

'I believe you have worked in Zambia for a number of years. So you must know that there are shortages. That we sometimes struggle to get butter. Or flour. Or sugar. This camp is rather a long way from anywhere. A day's drive from Lusaka. Three hours from the nearest shop or market. Fresh vegetables are particularly difficult to come by. We try and grow them here but the elephants and baboons eat them. We have no electricity for our fridges. In spite of these difficulties, I think we do rather well.' His finger is raised like a lecturer's. There is applause from the circle.

'If anyone has any more questions, I will do my best to answer them. As long as they pertain to wildlife …' he fixes the man with a long stare, then nods almost imperceptibly, '… and after this person has left our circle.'

The next morning, three Land Rovers are lined up outside reception, ready to depart for the airport. The man has just paid his bill, reluctantly it seems. His stained shoes sit on the counter, accusingly. I see him turn to the receptionist and glare at her.

'So what are you going to do about my shoes?' Several people in the office reach for their wallets simultaneously.

'We'll replace them. How much?'

Patrick, impatient to get on the road, says, 'What size are you, anyway? Looks like about a ten.'

He bends down and slips off his own shoes. He steps forward in his socks and holds his shoes out to the man.

'Here,' he says. 'Diesel fit you.'

The elephant has got worse. He seems to have lost all his natural inhibition and walks through camp arrogantly and without fear. He has become dangerous.

Tonight, one of the guides arrives at the bar breathless, barefoot and naked except for a towel around his waist, with the elephant close behind him. Only when he dives under the safety of the thatch roof and stands panting among the drinkers at the bar counter, does the elephant retreat, his small eyes gleaming. I shudder at the malice I see there.

'Bloody thing was waiting for me outside the shower. Hiding in the bushes.' The words come out in short gasps. 'I didn't want to run to my hut, it's so dark around there, so I started running in this direction. Thought he would stop under the lights of the main camp area. Bloody thing.' He looks down at the slipping towel, then back into the night. But the elephant has disappeared.

Patrick Ansell says, 'Well, we could have a drinking competition, you and I. Have a drink out of each and every bottle at the bar.'

'Oh, shut up, Patrick.' We start discussing measures of deterrence.

'Electric fence around the camp perimeter ...'

'Naw, that'll look terrible, change the whole nature of the camp.'

'Too expensive anyway.'

'Won't work. He'll just break through it.'

'I think it's time we drill him,' says one of the guides. 'Before he flattens someone.' The manager looks doubtful.

'You can't kill an elephant just because he's a nuisance. I mean, he hasn't *done* anything.' He looks at the small knot of safari guides standing next to him at the

end of the bar, one of them nearly naked, and grins.

'Lester, I think you'd better go and put some clothes on. You look a little under-dressed.'

'No way! That thing is still out there. I'm going to have another beer and wait until I'm sure he's gone.'

Most of the guests are still in their huts, getting ready for dinner, but others are standing with drinks in their hands or sitting at the small tables. There is concern on their faces.

The manager rests his elbows on the bar counter in front him. 'We'll watch him for a few more days and see how it goes. Then we can ...'

He is interrupted by a sudden high-pitched scream from the direction of one of the guest chalets. Then the chilling rage of an elephant's trumpet, and the scream again. And again. There is genuine fear – no, *terror* – in the voice. We grab our flash-lights off the bar counter and run outside. The moon has not yet risen and the sky is dark. A few naked lights are strung between the huts and along the paths, and in the gloom of their half-light we see a woman standing on the veranda of her chalet under a bare light bulb, hands to her face, half hidden behind the menacing grey bulk of the camp elephant.

Our hand-clapping and shouting drive him off, head held high, ears flapping, each step deliberate and unhurried. Some-one throws an empty beer bottle at the retreating hulk. It bounces off his thick skin and it doesn't seem that he has even noticed. For the first time, I feel a genuine

apprehension. I feel there is something bad about this elephant, something beyond wickedness and aggression; something for which I don't have appropriate words.

Early next morning, at the first light of dawn, a gunshot wakes up the camp. We all know instinctively what it is aimed at.

'I heard him just before it got light,' says the manager. 'I went to the gun safe in the office and got the .458, followed him to the outskirts of camp. I tried to shoot over his head to scare him off but I fear I may just have nicked him.' He looks serious, acknowledging that you can't just casually wound an elephant, no matter how justfiable this may be.

'When he ran off, I followed his tracks into the bush but didn't find any blood. I think I just gave him a bad headache. Maybe this will keep him away.'

A month later, the elephant hasn't come back. But he's out there somewhere, wandering along the river, crossing it now and then at night and in the early morning, walking tall in the tall grass.

4 Leopard Blind

During the early days of Adrian Carr's hunting career, I once spent an hour sitting in a leopard blind with him. His last safari of the season was over, and the clients had left that day without a leopard trophy.

'We had three baits out,' Adrian whispered. 'The other two failed completely, it's so bloody difficult to attract a leopard at this time of year. So much natural prey around.' He shifted on the single wooden plank that served as a bench. 'But on this one, a leopard started feeding. He must have come after dark, we never saw him.' He grimaced. 'A really big tom, too, by the looks of it.' He shaped his hand in a semicircle, like a horseshoe, to indicate the size of the leopard's pugmarks.

I peered through the narrow eye-level slit in the grass fence in front of me. Thirty metres away, silhouetted against the soft blue of the late afternoon sky, stood a sausage tree. Most of its old leaves had fallen to the ground, and from a horizontal branch like a gallows, six metres above the ground, hung the bait, an impala carcass. It was secured to the sturdy branch by a heavy chain and looked unnatural – even vaguely obscene – hanging there, suspended in the air and swaying slightly in the hot breeze.

'If he comes, are you going to shoot him?' I whispered.

Adrian nodded. 'Sure. I've got a licence in my name. I'd like to give the skin to Giovanna as a present. He must be a magnificent trophy.'

Giovanna was Adrian's new girlfriend, the daughter of the recently departed Italian family who had spent the past three weeks in Adrian's camp, and shot everything they had hoped for except a leopard.

Adrian touched the .416 Rigby that leaned beside him against the grass fence.

I brushed at a fly.

We didn't speak for what seemed like an endless time. The rough plank on which we sat began to feel uncomfortable but I dared not shift my weight in case I made a noise – even the slightest sound had to be avoided.

Tiny black *mopane* flies buzzed in my ears and tried to crawl into my eyes. The man-high grass enclosure that surrounded us felt as if it was pressing in, and the feeling of claustrophobia was enhanced by the late afternoon heat that rose from the packed earth floor. I felt sweat trickling down my face and into my eyes where it burned and itched and mingled with the little black flies (minute insects that are in fact not flies at all but members of the bee family).

I did not move.

The blind was open to the sky and I could see trees swaying in the slight wind and the sun growing big and orange and slowly sliding down behind the tree tops. The silence seemed absolute.

I have no idea where he came from – I hadn't seen a single blade of grass move – but suddenly a big male leopard was in the tree in front of us. He climbed the trunk in two or three easy powerful movements to where it forked into the horizontal branch. There he paused, his claws gripping the bark of the tree trunk. He looked for a moment like he was part of the tree, a dappled shape almost indistinguishable from the surrounding vegetation. I knew I could half close my eyes and he would disappear from my gaze, vanish into the jumble of light and dark background patterns; but there he was, without doubt the biggest leopard I had seen, clinging to the tree in the slanting afternoon light, with his back to the dead impala hanging twelve feet behind him.

I could hear my heartbeat, my breath stuck in my throat. Any minute now, he would climb on to the horizontal branch, walk along the top of it to where the carcass hung, crouch down and start feeding. We waited. Seconds felt like minutes, minutes like hours. But leopards are nothing if not unpredictable.

Suddenly he was airborne.

He sailed through the air seemingly in slow motion for I thought I could see every detail of his tensing muscles: he had launched himself off the tree trunk, backwards. He twisted his body a hundred and eighty degrees in mid-air and landed on the impala carcass, sideways on, with enough force to send it swinging wildly on the heavy chain. His claws dug deep into the dead animal's flesh, his shoulder muscles bunched under the rippling skin, and they both hung there, leopard and impala in a strange embrace, slowly turning on the iron chain.

Then, unhurriedly, he began to feed.

I shot a quick glance at Adrian who was staring through the slit in the fence with wide eyes like a small boy at a puppet show. I must have smiled involuntarily, and he smiled back at me and slowly moved his head from side to side in a gesture that needed no words.

For the next ten minutes, we sat mesmerised, watching the leopard cling to the dead impala, saw his jaws and throat working, listened to the tearing of flesh as the sun sank lower, a pale yellow fire behind the trees.

Then, in a heartbeat, as suddenly and silently as he had appeared, the leopard was gone again and we were staring at an empty tree.

Adrian and I looked at each other. I saw his eyes still had an other-worldly shine.

I said, 'You didn't shoot him.'

He looked at the empty tree. 'I must have forgotten,' he said.

45

5   Cliff at the Intersection

Cliff Bishop is sitting at the bar staring into his beer. It is still early; the light is only just fading from the sky, and the river is dancing with the last highlights of the setting sun. He lifts the beer mug slowly, stares at the froth at the top of it, then sets it down again on the bar counter without drinking.

'I know a guy on the Copper Belt who does this every evening,' he says. 'Pours himself a beer but doesn't drink it, just looks at it for, I don't know, sometimes five minutes. He says, "I like to tease myself first." ' Cliff laughs and lifts the mug again and this time drinks deeply, his moustache dipping into the foam.

The manageress is in her house but when she comes out in time to welcome the clients back from their game drive, she will see Cliff already at the bar. She will sidle up to him and make a remark, like: 'Cliff, I do believe that an afternoon drive should take at least two and a half hours, if not three. And I'm sure the guests know it too.'

Cliff will shrug and say, 'Nothing much out there today – no point in boring the people.' And he'll finish his beer, slide off the bar stool and hobble back to the staff compound to shower and change. The manageress will glare after him and mutter something under her breath.

Cliff has always been his own man. He came to Chibembe Camp to work as a safari guide at the beginning of the season but almost from the outset he was bored with driving tourists around the park, and found even the five-day Walking Safaris unchallenging.

He grew up on the Copper Belt, spending weekends and holidays camping, hunting and fishing on the Kafue River. He knows how to fix engines, catch a tiger fish, skin an impala, and considers himself tougher than the rest, a man's man. His voice is gritty, reminiscent of heavy machinery rusting in the rain. Like the frontiersmen in black and white photographs of the old American West, he wears a bristly moustache. Although still only in his late twenties, the creases that are beginning to show in his face tell of too much wind and sun, and together with the moustache, they bestow on his face a

certain rugged cowboy authority.

In Cliff's opinion, the Trail Leaders are a bunch of pussycats.

'I'm just doing this to fill in some time. Soon as I get my licence, I'm out of here to join the hunting camps.'

None of the other guides has his swagger. Charlie is English, born and bred, and in Cliff's book you can't be taken seriously unless you grew up here. Charlie definitely doesn't have the swagger. Ishmail is crazy but he doesn't have it either. Patrick has it, no doubt about it, but Patrick and Robin are too young, still too eager, in Cliff's mind, to please the clients.

And shy with girls. Which Cliff isn't.

Robin had taken a high-spirited group of Italians on game drives twice a day, two days running. Among the group was a gorgeous dark-eyed girl in her early twenties, and at the swimming pool (where it was plain to see just how gorgeous), she had her eyes on him all afternoon. When Robin went to the shower room to change for the afternoon game drive, she waited just a second before she got up to follow him, adjusting her bikini top as she disappeared into the dark doorway. From behind the thin grass walls, we could hear her voice, her Italian accent like a melody, 'ooh, I'm so sorry I was looking for . . .' and we could imagine the wicked smile of invitation on her lips. But we could also imagine Robin blushing to the roots of his hair and explaining politely that this was the men's shower block – the ladies' was next door. I saw Cliff shaking his head and muttering, 'I don't believe this,' as Robin came walking back to the pool, still blushing.

Patrick's last brush with the opposite sex wasn't any more rewarding.

He told me: 'Jesus, Vic. She was sitting in the middle seat, between me and an older guy on the passenger side, who I think was her father. She had one leg on either side of the gear stick. She was wearing shorts. Quite *short* shorts. Whenever I tried to shift gears, I … well in the end I had to shift from first straight into third each time, avoiding second and fourth gears because, well you can imagine, can't you? I don't know if anyone else noticed but it was quite a bumpy sort of a drive, the way I jumped the gears.'

I shook my head. 'Patrick, I think maybe I need to explain something to you.'

'No, no, Vic, you don't understand, her crotch was right there where I would have … I mean I would have touched it with the gear lever.' Patrick stared at me belligerently.

'Ja? You don't think she was aware of that? There's a word for it, Patrick …'

'No, wait. It gets worse. And *then* …' Patrick frowned in recollection. 'Then she says, all innocence, "Do you mind if I take my top off?"'

'And?'

'Well, she did! And she had nothing on underneath!'

I could tell that his outrage was feigned, that underneath it, there lurked a secret pride. 'And all the way back I tried to stay off the main road and drive along the smallest bush tracks in case we passed another drive. Maybe even the manager.'

'Patrick, how old are you?'
When Cliff hears this story, he shakes his head again and again in frustration.

'You guys! Don't you understand, they come here to have fun. Jesus Christ, it's rare enough that we see a good-looking girl in this camp, and when one finally arrives, once in a blue moon … you guys

screw it up. You're still wet behind the ears. For Christsake they're *looking* for it. They're waiting for you to make a move. Christ, you don't see me wasting an opportunity like this.'

And we didn't. Never. Even with his bad leg, he scored. Or maybe because of it.

Halfway into the season, Cliff's dream of becoming a hunter had looked like it was coming true. He was about to assist on his first proper hunting safari, up at Luawata camp.

'See you guys around,' he said as he got into his Land Rover and drove off to meet the client at the bush airstrip, several hours to the north. His instructions were simple. Meet the client. Take him to camp, let him unpack, get comfortable, have lunch. The Number One hunter, the senior professional who ran this camp, had been hunting lechwe in the Bangweulu swamps and was delayed. 'So just explain things to the client. If he wants to, you can go out in the afternoon, maybe shoot an impala, or a guinea fowl. Keep him busy. Don't go after dangerous game, obviously. You're not licensed for that, anyway.'

The client *did* want to go out after lunch, and Cliff took him for a drive to show him around the vicinity of camp. On the way, they came across a lion in the mopane woodland not far from camp. The client got excited. 'I can shoot this, yes?'

'Sure,' said Cliff. They grabbed their rifles, got out of the car and, keeping low, slowly walked towards the lion – Cliff in front, testing the wind with the smoke from his cigarette, the client shadowing his every step. Slowly they moved into a firing position, thirty metres from the animal, and Cliff silently motioned the client to aim. The lion had been lying in an open patch of ground between the trees, and was sitting up, alert now. The first shot seemed to miss him completely. The client reloaded and in an instant fired again but the lion was already up and charging towards them.

It is the professional hunter's first priority to protect his client, no matter what the circumstances. Without hesitation, Cliff stepped out in front of the man and, standing his ground, raised his rifle and fired. The lion was now only a few metres away, and the shot hit him high in the shoulder. Anyone who has ever stood in the path of a charging lion knows the blinding speed of the charge. The impact of the bullet barely broke the cat's stride and as it leapt at him, all Cliff could do was fall backwards and raise his right boot to kick the lion in the face. His foot connected but in the next split-second he felt the lion's teeth close on his ankle, felt a sudden unspeakable pain, and through a mist of agony and shock, he heard the client's rifle go off one more time.

As he lay on the ground a few paces from the crumpled hulk of the dead lion, his femoral artery pumping blood that quickly sank into the dusty soil, Cliff's prospects did not look good.

We got the radio call at Chibembe: 'Mayday! Please try and get Lusaka on radio immediately. Repeat, Mayday. Alert Lusaka that Cliff Bishop is badly hurt. Accident with lion … evacuation today … lost too much blood already … in serious pain … has to be taken out, tonight if at all possible.'

Tomorrow will be too late, was the unspoken subtext, although the radio didn't say that.

The airstrip at Waka-Waka was no more than a swathe of cleared and levelled bush and a windsock hanging limp from its post. No radio, no runway lights. In the hour before it grew dark, the camp staff parked a Land Rover at the end of the runway and, finally hearing the drone of the plane, switched on the headlights. Somehow, and against all rules of aviation, the pilot managed to put down his plane and take off again in the dark with his broken cargo.

The ambulance was on standby at the side of the runway when they landed in Lusaka late that night. Professor John Jellis,

the orthopaedic surgeon from Lusaka University Teaching Hospital took one look and made his immediate decision, right there in the moving ambulance as it swerved through the late Lusaka traffic towards hospital: amputate. Now.

When Cliff arrives back at Chibembe a few months later, there is no apparent change in him, other than a pronounced limp resulting from the artificial leg under his trousers. If there is any self-consciousness at all, it is that he avoids wearing shorts, even in the hot weather. But at the swimming pool, he shows no shame or self-pity. He unstraps the plastic leg, peels off the sock-like bandage that protects the stump below his knee from its hard edges, and dives into the water.

The surgeon had been first class, Cliff tells us, but the nursing at the hospital was outrageously bad. 'They steal medicines on the way from the dispensary to the ward. Nurses hijack drugs and sell them in the street, patients who don't have beds lie on the floor, and if they're lucky, their family brings them a blanket. If it's a good blanket, it will probably get stolen.' Cliff shrugs. 'There were no bandages, no disinfectants. My girlfriend had to run around to all the pharmacies in town, trying to find fresh bandages.'

As a result, the slow-healing wound contracted gangrene, and Cliff had to go under the knife for a second time and lost another part of his leg.

He climbs out of the pool and hops over to his yellow and red striped towel. The fist-sized stump below his knee is gleaming whitely, drops of water drying slowly on its pallid-looking skin.

'Mummy, Cliff says he will teach us to swim,' giggles Tamara. 'He says he can only teach us to swim in circles, cos he's got one short leg.'

Cliff is grinning, the Wyatt Earp moustache under his nose quivering in complicity. Pam laughs too.

'But Mummy, does that mean we'll only be able to swim in circles for the rest of our lives?'

At the breakfast table, the manageress stares at Cliff. Again, he was the first of the morning drives to return to camp. Again, he ignored her instructions. Yesterday a message arrived from the new airport at Mfuwe. While picking up arriving guests, Cliff had driven over the newly planted lawn and parked the Land Rover smack in front of the entrance. Airport security had complained. She looks across the table at Pam and lifts her eyebrows. How on earth do you control these guys?

Apart from female tourists, Pam is the only other white woman she can talk to. The only trouble is that although Pam is beautiful and has all the exterior attributes of a woman, in her ways and attitudes she can at times be more of a game ranger than the men in camp, and not particularly interested in girl talk. Besides – perhaps because of it – she is popular with the boys. On *their* side, not hers.

The manageress seems out of her depth. I wonder if she really likes living here. Her ex-game ranger husband is no

help, either. He is a competent manager, albeit a reluctant one. He wants to be out in the bush, not behind a desk or in the storeroom. One of the guys, too.

She calls the waiter and points at the stack of toast on a plate in front of her.

'This is stale. Bring some fresh toast.' To demonstrate, she takes a piece and breaks it in two, like a piece of chalk. 'And my eggs are runny. Look!'

The kitchen staff aren't used to taking orders from a woman. It never happens in the village. The white woman orders them around as if they were children. Chiding and reprimanding. Shouting sometimes. And she always seems to know *everything* that goes on in the kitchen. Any mistake is immediately picked up. *Makhuntu*, they call her. 'Ears.'

Well, at least they obey her. They have to. But not the guides. And especially not Cliff. Cliff only ever does exactly as he pleases. For the game drives, he would climb into the Land Rover nearest to him, not the one assigned to him. When he was told to stay on the east bank and drive to the saltpan, he crossed the pontoon to the other side and went game-viewing miles down the west bank and came back late. Or he would do the quick saltpan trip and be back early when the clients had been promised an extensive outing on the other side.

He infuriates her by blatantly ignoring her instructions. She thinks it is out of spite. She hates it.

I feel sorry for her. She doesn't seem to see that it's just Cliff, that it simply doesn't occur to him to do things any different from the way he wants to do them.

That evening Lester finally accepts Patrick's challenge to a drinking competition. A number of volunteers among us sponsor the drinks, a total of thirty-two shots each, plus a beer and a glass of red and a glass of white wine. At the end of it they try to toast each other by clinking glasses but miss, lose their balance and tumble towards each other in an unsteady embrace. They both have to be escorted home, vomiting all the way.

The next day is another airport day, and of the five guides the manageress picks Lester and Patrick to do the trip, pale green and still puking, two hours each way in open Land Rovers in the boiling sun.

The season has grown hot and the sun has moved further west, and all the dining tables have lost their shade and have to be moved. It makes no difference at dinnertime but at breakfast – and especially at lunchtime – the sun beating down with its October-force heat melts the butter, and knives and forks feel like they've been touched by electricity – too hot to handle.

Cliff is sitting between Pam and Ishmail at lunch. I'm on the opposite side of the table with three clients and the new guide. He arrived a few days ago to help out until the end of the season. We don't really know much about him yet. We can only guess at why he's here; at his private reasons for running away from his job, his comfortable life, maybe his girlfriend. But we know this: On his way down to the Valley in his short-wheel base Land Rover, he found God.

'God spoke to me on the escarpment,' he tells us. 'He spread light into my life.'

We listen to his sermons for the first few days, but grow slightly alarmed when it transpires that God has given him a particular mission: to convert one of us and lead him or her into the fold of the Christian faith.

Pam is polite, even interested in an academic, theoretical sort of way. 'I'm definitely prepared to listen to you,' she says, 'but you'd better have some convincing arguments.'

Ishmail says, 'Well, I'm a Muslim. But I'm ready to abdicate my faith on one condition.'

'Oh, good. I'm sure Jesus will not disappoint you. What's the condition?'

'Do you guys eat bacon? I love bacon.'

Cliff has listened to the man's zeal silently without comment. But now the guy is at it again. He ignores Ishmail and turns to Pam.

'Pam,' he says, sensing no doubt that she is a soft target. Pam hates disappointing people. She will go to great

lengths to make people feel comfortable and good about themselves. She hates bullies and always sticks up for the underdog. This, if ever there was an underdog, is him. 'All I ask is give Jesus a chance. Read a few pages of the Bible, and I will talk to you about the deeper meaning.'

The tourists have been listening politely. One of them even joins in the conversation. 'That seems fair enough.'

I notice Cliff is shifting in his seat, his eyes broodingly on Pam. I can see he's getting irritated.

'Okay, I'll think about it,' Pam promises.

'Give Him a chance, open your mind to Him,' the new guide repeats.

Cliff takes his eyes off Pam and stares across the table. He says, levelly, 'Hey! Don't ever try that shit with me. If you do, I'll fuck you up.'

The manageress has had enough. She's had enough of all this male energy buzzing around camp; all these egos trying to outdo each other, score points against each other, against her. She has taken to her bed and hasn't been seen in four days. Not feeling well, says the manager. Female problems. When at last she shows herself at the breakfast table, Cliff asks her with genuine sympathy how she's feeling.

She turns on him with unconcealed loathing: 'Well, how would you feel if you just had a miscarriage?'

Cliff looks down at the stump of his missing leg and says nothing.

His success with girls is undiminished. If anything, it reaches new heights. Perhaps his handicap brings out maternal feelings in them – some kind of nursing instinct … Or perhaps there is something intoxicating in the combination of his rugged masculinity and the helplessness of a little boy.

When Ellen arrives in camp late in October, she immediately has all the guides' attention. Her heart-shaped face is framed by dark glossy hair and her almond eyes and fine-boned body suggest a mixed European and Oriental ancestry. She seems shy and polite, and totally inaccessible. Robin and Patrick have been following her surreptitiously, trying to make eye contact with her for several days now. They spin coins to decide in whose vehicle she'll go game viewing, they try to move themselves into position *early* to sit near her at dinner. But so far, neither of them has found the courage to actually speak to her.

Time is running out. Tomorrow she is leaving, and tonight at the bar will definitely be their last chance. They wait for the right moment and climb onto bar stools on either side of her – safety in numbers. They order drinks for her, tell her funny stories, each of them trying to catch her eye in that special way, before the other can. At dinner they flank her again, draw out each course with charming anecdotes, and don't notice Cliff sitting opposite. After dinner, they invite her back to the bar for a nightcap, but she declines politely. With a quick smile at each of them, she excuses herself, says goodnight, and walks away to her room.

I have followed the two safari guides' progress – or lack of it – sporadically during the evening, and now, as I am talking to a client, I can feel their disappointment sliding towards me along the bar counter from the corner where they are sitting with their double whiskies.

At ten o'clock, the generator splutters briefly in the distance, the lights flicker and go out, and we sit in darkness. We finish our drinks and our conversation, and when my eyes are used to the night, I grab my torch from the counter, say goodnight to the tourist, and leave the bar. I notice that Robin and Patrick have already gone, but on my way home I pass Ellen's hut and see them both lurking in the shadows outside her window, and hear them calling softly.

'Ellen. Hey, Ellen. There's a beautiful moon out here.'

No reply.

'Ellen, have you ever seen the Southern Cross?'

Silence.

'Hey, Ellen!'

Nothing, and then suddenly Cliff's gravelly voice from inside her hut, 'Hey you guys. Piss off!'

The new airport is still under construction and the entire area surrounding it is a rubble-strewn building site. Someone, however, is planning ahead and has planted a lawn between the proposed parking lot and the terminal building. Driving over the newly planted grass – repeatedly – has not endeared Cliff to the security guards, and today he does it again. While the guests are climbing down from the Land Rover, a man approaches, walking briskly.

'This lawn is trying to grow. You can't drive here. Or park here.'

'What lawn?' Cliff looks around him.

'This grass that you are standing on, you can't park here,' the man repeats.

'So why don't you put up a sign?'

'Well, I'm telling you!'

'Okay, I'll try to remember. Who are you anyway?'

'Eh-eh! I am a policeman.'

'Oh yeah? So how'm I supposed to know that? Why aren't you wearing a uniform, if you're a policeman . . .'

'No, I'm in plainclothes.'

Cliff eyes the man's threadbare T-shirt, his dirty brown trousers, and grins. 'Very plain, mate, if you ask me.'

Zambia Airways is about to land. Although part of the terminal building is still under construction, the runway has been open for some weeks, and there is a makeshift check-in counter in the hall. There is even a functioning PA system. But no one quite knows how to use it. Or what to say.

I hear Robin explaining to a lady from Zambia Airways. 'You press this button, I think. When the plane is about to land, you say that Zambia Airways announces the arrival of flight number so-and-so. Or the departure, whichever it may be. If the plane is late, you say that Zambia Airways regrets to announce . . . and so on. You got that?'

'Yes, I think so.'

The clients have all checked their baggage and are milling around between the unpainted walls of the building. Some rooms have doors, some don't. The toilets have doors and are fully equipped but there is no running water. Anyone who needs to empty their bladder before the flight has to go and find a bush outside.

The overhead lights have not yet been connected, but in other parts of the hall electricity is already working. Suddenly, there is a metallic screech, and the sound of an amplified female voice.

'Zambia Airways regret to announce the arrival of flight QZ 008 from Lusaka.' The voice sounds startled by its own unexpected loudness.

I notice Cliff, out of the corner of my eye saying goodbye to his new friend, and it looks like the goodbye kiss is getting out of hand and leading to other possibilities. But there is no privacy between these bare unpainted walls, and I wonder where they're headed as they disappear round a corner, holding hands.

Robin is standing at the check-in, explaining to the Zambia Airways lady that the word 'regret' only goes with 'delay'. I see her nodding earnestly. Our camp manager is standing next to him, shaking hands with some of the departing tourists. I can see the Hawker Siddley on the tarmac through the big windows. A man in blue overalls is wheeling the luggage trolley towards the plane. A policeman comes and stands next to us, shuffling his feet. He clears his throat.

'Excuse me, Mr Berry.' The manager turns to face him. 'May I please speak to you?' the policeman says, his eyes un-smiling. 'It concerns one of your workers. It is serious business.' He speaks slowly, emphasising each word, as if trying to give weight to the importance of the occasion. He motions with his hand, and the manager follows him to a pile of cement bags against the far wall, out of earshot. Their conversation lasts only a few minutes, and when he walks back towards us, the manager is shaking his head, frowning and smiling at the same time.

'What was that all about?' asks Robin.

'Cliff. About Cliff.'

'What about him?'

The manager lowers his voice, trying to sound serious like the policeman.

' "We found your employee, the one with the leg, inside the radio room," ' he intones slowly. ' "We found him with a lady. They were having intersection." '

I see Cliff that evening, sitting at one of the low coffee tables under the high thatched roof of the *chitenje*. Again he is back early from his drive.

'Hey boy, come and join me for a beer.'

'Sure. How was the drive? See anything special?'

'Nah, just the usual stuff.'

A client disagrees from the bar counter.

'Oh, we thought it was exciting!'

'Yes, lovely. Those elephants climbing

up the steep riverbank!' his wife adds.

'And that … what was that eagle again? A Marshall Eagle?'

I turn towards the bar. 'Martial Eagle,' I tell them. 'You spell it M-a-r-t-i-a-l. They're impressive birds, aren't they?'

I notice that all five tourists are staring at Cliff, who has his beer mug in his hand and is taking slow sips from it, eyes on the river. One of the guests whispers something that I cannot hear, another is shaking his head. I look back at Cliff and I suddenly see what has caught their attention: Cliff is sitting with one leg crossed over the other, but something looks wrong. His feet should be pointing forward, both in the same direction. Instead, one foot points the wrong way, straight back. I realise he has strapped on his leg back to front. He grins at me across the rim of his beer mug but says nothing.

He came back for another season the following year and another one after that but finally Cliff decided that his bush career was leading nowhere. He went home to the Copper Belt, where presumably he sits in some bar at sundown, eyeing his beer for a while, teasing himself before he takes the first sip.

6 *Kudu*

People often ask me if there is one animal I like painting more than others. The answer is that the subject of a painting is not really what makes it succeed or fail. Once the subject is decided and the initial composition drawings have been made and I have started painting, the picture usually takes on a life of its own. I am far too busy juxtaposing shapes, balancing colours, arranging light and shade, thinking about perspective and focal point, to worry much about the subject. There *is* no poor subject; in fact it can be an interesting challenge to make a successful painting out of a subject that might initially appear unpromising.

Still, there was a time when I particularly enjoyed painting kudus. I felt that their striking facial and body markings, their corkscrew horns and their angular yet elegant shapes gave me opportunities for dynamic designs and suited my particular painting style. I probably painted several dozen kudu pictures, large and small, over a period of ten years or so.

I walked and drove all over the Park with sketchpad and camera, looking for them. My eyes became aware of the telltale signs: the flash of a white tail, irregular vertical stripes on sandy-grey skin. Large ears that turned ceaselessly into the wind like miniature satellite dishes, tuning into frequencies only they could hear.

I learned where to search for the big bulls, which thickets they preferred and what kind of country they avoided. Where I could find them in the early morning and where they hid in the heat of the day; where and when they came to drink. I learned that in the cool months of the early dry season they could usually be seen near the cows, while the rest of the year they preferred solitude.

I painted them standing alone, in pairs and with cows. Browsing, drinking, and running. I once saw seven mature bulls on an anthill at sunset and when I painted that picture nobody believed me.

As I returned from one of these searching-for-kudu trips, I saw a flash of white-tipped spiral horn as I drove past a *Combretum* bush that stood near the side of the road. I stopped the car, grabbed my camera from the passenger seat and got out. Unless you are prepared to be stealthy, even to crawl on your hands and knees, it is usually advisable rather to stay in your car and drive as close as you can to wild animals. They tend to tolerate an approaching vehicle, but are much more wary of a person on foot, and once they have seen you, it is usually impossible to get within photographic range. But this kudu was standing in thick cover and the bushes were too dense to allow the vehicle to approach.

I walked slowly towards him, a warm breeze blowing into my face, pausing every few steps to watch him watching me. I kept my eyes on the ground, taking care to walk quietly, and every time I looked up he was still standing behind the bush, eyeing me, only part of his head and neck showing. The white chevron between his eyes blazed like a flag among the dark green leaves. I raised my camera and took a quick shot. The shutter made a loud noise, like a twig snapping, but he didn't move. I took three or four paces to my left, looking for a clearer field of vision, and saw his head turning a fraction, his eyes following me.

I circled the bush slowly, aware of insects in the air and of small beads of sweat breaking out on my forehead. Through my lens his muzzle looked wet and the one eye I could see was shadowy and dark and had the stillness of a deep well. The muscles in his neck tensed but he stood his ground and I suddenly realised that I had come to within five paces of him and still he had not moved.

His horns were magnificent: thick at the base and curling up and out in perfectly symmetrical curves. His tongue flicked, wetting his muzzle, but his body looked thin; ribs showed in his chest, his skin was dull and lifeless, the hair matted, and the stiff white mane along his spine lay flat. He stood perfectly still, the deep eyes scrutinizing me with a steady solemn gaze.

I said quietly, 'Hello Kudu. You're sick, aren't you?'

He raised his head a fraction and flicked his tail, not taking his eyes off me.

A yellow-billed stork from the nearby breeding colony drifted above us in lazy circles and for a moment I visualised the two of us from several hundred metres up in the air, as if through the eyes of the bird. A man and a wild animal facing each other just a few feet apart, both standing absolutely still. Somewhere close by I heard the sounds of other animals going about their business. A group of impala, perhaps, or a flock of guinea fowl scratching the dry ground. Still the kudu did not move.

I looked at his eye again, trying to penetrate the oily sheen of its surface, to bore deeper, as if this would reveal the secrets of his life and the reason for his sickness. Was it old age? The length of his horns certainly indicated an animal at the end of his life. I imagined what those eyes had witnessed – things that I would never see – and I felt a sudden sadness. Not for him and his poor condition, but for myself. For the fact that I knew so little about him and his kind. For the fact that millions of wild creatures are born and live out their lives without touching ours; for our lack of curiosity, our lack of caring.

Kudu: how many offspring have you sired in your life? How many times have you had to fight lions that wanted to devour you? The ebony tips of his horns still looked hard and sharp. You can defend yourself against a lion without help, without guns – which is something that I cannot do. Now you're old and sick. Perhaps, if I were a hunter, I would shoot you. Perhaps not.

I took another silent step towards him. Did he know I was not armed? Could he see my hands and see that they were empty? Did he sense my friendship? He could kill me with one quick sweep of those horns but it would never enter his mind. I have never heard of a kudu that has tried to harm a man for no reason. It is strictly a one-sided thing.

I stayed with him over an hour, not quite touching but close enough to see the slow pulse in his neck and the flies settling on his ears and taking off and settling again.

Finally I left. I drove back to camp and asked the guides if they had seen a sick-looking kudu along Riverside Drive, but no one had. I asked them to look out for him but the days passed and no one saw him.

I painted this particular kudu several times, on his own or as part of a group, but I never quite managed to capture the solemnity of his eyes.

7 Wooden Owl

'Daddy, will you call the wooden owl tonight? Pleeeese?' Miranda smiles, a glint of anticipation in her eyes. 'Please, Daddy?'

'It's not a wooden owl,' Tamara corrects her, 'it's a Wood Owl.'

'I know,' says Miranda, irritated. 'I *know* that.'

Tamara raises her eyebrows. 'So if you know, why do you call it wooden owl?'

'Cos.' Then, turning serious, she says, 'Daddy, why *is* it called a wooden owl? It's not made out of wood, is it?'

'No, it isn't. But Tam is right, it's called a Wood Owl. I suppose because it lives in the woods.'

'Oh.'

'See?' says Tamara. 'Told you.'

A pair of wood owls have their nest somewhere in camp, or possibly just outside it. We haven't found it yet, but every night we hear them call, a deep but slightly surprised sounding *Whoooo*, the female's at a higher pitch than the male's. The eerie sound drifts back and forth through the trees for an hour or more, until they launch into their other call, an excited, breathless series of *wooo-hooo, woo-hoo-hoo, woo-hoo*.

It is an easy call to imitate, and I have spent much time practising it. (Artists apparently have nothing better to do.)

If it's a slow night at the bar, one of the guides might say, 'Hey, we haven't heard the wood owls tonight.' He'll look at me. 'Maybe you need to call them.'

I step outside and I cup my hands in front of my mouth to give my voice resonance, and go *whoooo, whooooo*, and then *woo-hoo, woo-hoo-hoo, woo-hoo*. After ten minutes of this (by which time any client who has seen me has decided that I've lost my mind), I have usually convinced the male owl that there is a rival bird in his territory, and he starts responding in the distance. I call again, and when he replies, he is closer. Sometimes we hear the soft whoosh of his wings, and when we next hear him calling, he may be in one of the trees right outside the *chitenje*. The barman shakes his head and looks the other way.

'Daddy, it's getting dark. You promised!'

'Yes, I did. Well, let's try.'

I cup both hands to my mouth to form a hollow shell and make that high drawn out sound, '*Whoooo*', rising and falling.

'Again,' urges Miranda. Tamara has heard us and comes up from behind.

'Shhhh, Daddy is talking to the wooden owl.' Miranda puts a small finger to her mouth. Tam is giving her a look. '*O-kay*, Wood Owl then. It's coming. Listen.'

After the fourth try, we hear a soft *whoosh* and then the reply from a nearby tree. '*Wooo-hoo! Woo-hoo-hoo, woo-hoo*.'

'See?' Miranda beams.

We have been playing this game for several months now, and we often hear him coming after our first call, trying to investigate, trying to identify his rival. But now it's September and the pair seem to have started breeding. We have seen them fly in and out of the same tree, not far from our grass hut, all soft ghostly wing beats and silent turbulence, and always in the half-hour of dusk when the light among the trees has turned grey and visibility is compromised by moving half-shadows.

We think they are breeding because the male has become aggressive. He suddenly appears and tries to chase anyone who walks between the trees. Especially, it seems, me. Has he seen me, standing with my hands cupped, mocking his call? Does he think I'm an owl? Does he think I want to steal his girlfriend? Have I irritated him so much that my size doesn't scare him? Several times now he has made a low pass at me in the last twilight of dusk, twice I have heard the sudden soft rush of wings behind me and felt his talons at the back of my neck.

I am reminded of a poem by Goethe

about the sorcerer's apprentice who is left alone by his master and decides to try his luck. When he has called up the spirits, he is pleased with his success, but dismayed when they start creating havoc in his master's house. He asks them to leave, but they refuse. *Die ich rief, die Geister, werd' ich nun nicht los.*

I feel like that sorcerer's apprentice. The trouble with Africa is that the fine line between scientific explanation and mystical flights of fancy is easily smudged. I know there is a sound reason for the bird's aggressive behaviour, but it is all too easy to be sidetracked into the transcendental – the *non*-rational – and let my mind wander to the world of totem animals, of shamans, of the interconnectedness of all living things.

The Zambians know this and when they see the owl coming, they whisper and glance at each other under lowered brows and shudder.

I try to stay under our roof in that twilight hour, and when I have to go outside, I walk slightly bent with my head pulled between my shoulders and a hand clamped to the back of my neck. The last few rounds have gone to the owl; I imagine him gloating in victorious satisfaction, his yellow eyes round and staring. Inscrutable.

But he is not finished with me. One night I relax my guard. Darkness has crept up from the river and is almost complete. I approach our house with my hand to my neck, but as I step under the roof of our veranda and drop it, I feel a ghostly prickling of my skin the instant before he strikes. This time he draws blood, I feel it running down my neck, my glasses fly off my face, and I shout in pain and surprise just as I see his dark shadow dip under the low roof and vanish into the darkness outside.

Game over. The owl has won.

8 Baked Beans

First things first: Baked Beans is a dog; we're not talking legumes here. He is quite an ordinary dog, no different from dozens of others that live in the villages near Chibembe camp. We drive through these two villages often – raggedy mud huts under sagging thatch roofs that huddle on both sides of the dirt road to Chikwinda Game Gate. Some shady dark green mango trees and a few grain bins woven from split bamboo and elevated on stilts to keep the rats out. The bigger one, Mukasanga village, has a makeshift football field with crooked poles for goalposts.

The little yellow dogs stand under the mango trees and in the dirt between the huts and stare at us with crazy eyes as we drive past. They are all skinny with protruding rib cages and curly tails. There is a lethargy about them, a resignation to a life of near-starvation, a silent acceptance of their fate.

Patrick Ansell is one of Chibembe camp's most popular guides. He is twenty-four but his sense of responsibility is closer to that of our daughters Tamara, who is seven, and Miranda, who is four. He likes to play with them, and play practical jokes. He is quick with words. When the manageress found a small snake hiding in her cash register, he asked her innocently if it was an adder.

One day Patrick drives past Mukasanga village and sees a small yellow puppy standing between two huts. Something in the puppy's innocent expression and his cocked ears makes Patrick stop, negotiate a price (expensive even at fifty cents, I later thought), and buy him. He arrives in camp with a bundle under his T-shirt, convinced that our two girls would like a dog. In fact, a dog is the very last thing in the world we need. A dog is about as useful to us as a bicycle to a mole snake, but it's too late.

You shouldn't look a gift horse in the mouth, or a dog, for that matter (if you try, he'll probably bite your nose). Oh my God, I think, we're stuck with him – probably at the same moment that Tamara and Miranda are thinking, Yay! A puppy!)

So the dog stays, and Patrick names him Baked Beans. Why, nobody knows, least of all Patrick himself.

It isn't a very good name, all things considered, but then he isn't a very good dog. He is selfish, undisciplined, and not very bright. And we have found out by now that he is totally untrainable. He is a shameless opportunist of the most hard-bitten kind and I can't say that I ever really warm to him.

I usually like dogs, and have known some good ones. Most of them had a sense of self-esteem, a kind of animal dignity. Some were affectionate, some protective, some even had a sense of humour. All of them had that quality we subjectively and condescendingly call faithfulness.

This puppy has none of these attributes and I suspect from the start that he will be nothing but trouble.

He is not big – the size of a fox terrier – and quite plain-looking, an even dusty yellow colour with no marks or distinguishing features. His eyes are yellow and mean. Even the puzzled puppy-frown that makes most young dogs lovable, is in him a spiteful grimace. His teeth are needle-sharp and he uses them to good effect on the kids' shoes, clothes, toys and skin. After his first week, he hasn't endeared himself to anyone. Tammy and Miranda still love him, sort of, but no one else does, least of all the camp manager.

Of course it hasn't taken Baked Beans long to figure out that there is delicious food to be had at the guests' lunch table in the main camp. He is strong and agile enough to leap and snatch anything edible off the edge of a dining table, and small (and cowardly) enough to run and hide between the clients' legs, which makes it impossible for me to catch him without making a complete fool of myself. On the rare occasion when I do manage to corner him (muttering indistinct words like *bad dog … shouldn't be here … excuse me please, oh, I'm so sorry …*) and carry him back behind the kitchen fence, his outrage is monumental. I stand there behind the grass fence, holding the writhing, howling puppy, and wait for the yelps to die down, alternatively whispering desperate endearments and clenched-teeth threats. For such is the force of his frustration that I have to wonder what the tourists think I am doing to him to provoke such fury. Strapping him to the kitchen table and torturing him with kebab sticks? Setting fire to him in the bread oven? (Not that such thoughts don't occur to me.)

When the convulsions have finally subsided and the tantrum has died down, burnt itself out like a petrol fire, I let him drop to the ground, both of us exhausted. I barricade him somewhere where he cannot escape and walk back through the gap in the kitchen fence, red-faced, short of breath and with bleeding hands, into the stunned silence of the dining area. I take my seat at the table, trying to avoid the other diners' eyes.

When I go to free him from his banishment, he is not happy to see me. He stands there trembling, ears flattened, upper lip drawn up in a snarl, sharp teeth gleaming, and stares at me with demonic eyes.

*

There is a family of honey badgers that lives in the bush downstream from the camp. We see their tracks in the morning in front of our hut, evidence of their nocturnal raids on the garbage bins and food containers in the kitchen. Sometimes we hear noises from the kitchen at night: banging of dustbin lids, breaking glass. Occasionally, we get a quick glimpse of them: dark furry creatures with sharp glittering teeth and a swathe of white bristles along their backs.

The manager has been complaining about disturbed sleep; his is the first house behind the kitchen. When your day begins at 5am you value your sleep, and the sounds of a party from further down the line of staff houses doesn't help, particularly on Thursdays when all the walking trails have returned from the bush and the guys feel like a drink or two. That's when the manager glares at me the next morning and says, one day I will burn that guitar of yours.

But the honey badgers are even worse. The music has finally stopped, there has been an hour of blissful silence with no sound at all, except for the wood owl and the occasional hippo – sounds he enjoys and sleeps through anyway – and then he is wide awake again because these bloody honey badgers are banging around the garbage again.

But Phil Berry is a resourceful manager. I will get you, he says to himself as he lies in his bed pondering, his teeth clenched. He has visions of bear traps, electric fences; of walls with metal spikes running along their tops. But they all turn out to be impractical or expensive in the sober light of day. One of the ideas might work, he thinks; one of his night time frustration-born plans might just bear fruit. He orders a *big* bag of white pepper from HQ in Lusaka over the radio. (I imagine the radio conversation, the storeman's disbelief, and Phil's insistence, no, I'm talking about *kilo*grams!) It arrives two (sleepless) nights later, and that evening Phil is seen skulking through all the known badger hangouts with his sack of pepper, sprinkling handfuls against the walls of the store-rooms, on the lids of garbage cans, around the refrigerators. Of course it does nothing to curtail their foraging; but on this night at least, Phil knows the sweet flush of revenge. Lying in bed, awake and alert, he listens raptly to the familiar cluttering, and smiles every time he hears a sharp *pitt-chooo*, *pitt-chooo* as four or five honey badgers sneeze in the dark outside his hut.

As the season advances and the weather turns warmer, the honey badgers become bolder and start venturing into camp during daylight hours. One lunchtime, three of the trail leaders, Ishmail, Cliff, and Charlie Mardy, sit at their table and talk. I have just got up from the same table and am on my way to my hut when something makes me look back. Lunch is over, the clients have retreated into their chalets for their siestas and the waiters have cleared the tables. The three of them are lingering over coffee and cigarettes, talking about nothing in particular, when suddenly a honey badger, a big black male, struts into camp, the swathe of white fur

bristling on his back. He looks around with the casual confidence of a big male and makes straight for their table. His rolling gate is reminiscent of a sailor on shore leave. The three guides look at each other, then at the badger, and it seems that the badger is not the only macho male around.

'I'm not scared of that thing,' says Charlie.

'That'll be the day when a little bugger like that drives me from my coffee,' adds Cliff and drags on his cigarette, eyes on the badger.

Ishmail nods in agreement, but says nothing.

'Brazen little bastard, though,' says Charlie, his voice suddenly quiet.

'He's got balls. Look at him swagger,' whispers Cliff. 'Looks like he's coming straight for us.'

'Anyway,' says Ishmail, and slides off his chair, plainly all too aware of the honey badger's reputation for fierce courage, tales of attacks on adversaries many times his own size, and, furthermore, of his reported habit of going straight for a man's testicles.

Charlie seems about to follow suit and shoots a quick glance at Cliff who stares back at him in unspoken challenge. I watch, fascinated, from where I stand and recognise the spark of testosterone flicker into life; the macho pride that can turn an ordinary situation into a dare, a matter of honour, in a split second.

But the flame is short-lived. While the waiters watch, speechless, from their safe distance, the badger leaps on to the table and stares at the two men, head held low, issuing a challenge more powerful than any machismo pride. Charlie leaps to his feet and knocks over his chair as he sprints for cover while Cliff, mustering a last shred of dignity, withdraws more quietly but not without haste. The honey badger, unconcerned, capsizes the jam jar with a sharp butt of his nose and starts licking up the spilled contents.

Secure in their absolute hegemony of Chibembe camp, the honey badgers have begun to bring their young with them. During the first few weeks of their lives, the recent litter has been kept hidden in their burrow under the thicket but now that they have grown into two compact black bundles of energy with a pure white stripe of springy fur on their backs, they have started accompanying the adults on their nightly dustbin raids. They always approach from the south, along the riverbank, and as our hut (last in the row of the staff houses) is the first they encounter, we usually see them first.

So does Baked Beans.

At night he is not so eager to follow us to the dining room. There are many strange sounds and smells lurking in the bushes, and most of them must be quite alarming to a small dog. He is usually content to stay behind and lie on the sparse lawn in front of our hut, within easy sprinting distance of his blanket. Often we are at dinner in the dining area of the main camp, but some nights I am tired of the social life at the bar and come home to read my book under the bare light bulb

and to the faint throbbing sound of the generator. That's when I see them arrive, always around nine o'clock. They amble along the riverbank in single file, the cubs following the adults, their shorter legs moving a little faster.

Baked Beans sees them coming too and rushes for cover behind the low grass fence that surrounds our veranda. He squats behind the fence on his haunches, his body tense, only his eyes and ears showing above the fence, his eyes following the badgers' solemn procession.

I watch him and smile at the internal battle that must be going on inside him, between the two well-developed instincts of curiosity and caution. One night I see curiosity gaining the upper hand, if only for a few seconds. I see him leave the safety of the veranda and take a few tentative steps towards the badgers on the bank, only to think better of his newfound bravery in mid-stride and bolt back behind the fence.

Two weeks have passed and the sausage tree between our house and the river has begun to lose its leaves. It has been a quiet night with few guests in camp. Pam is already in bed, and I am on my way back from the campfire to finish my book before the generator shuts down at ten. Preoccupied with my thoughts, I approach the house in the moonlight. I may have heard a rustling in the dry leaves under the sausage tree; I may have half-registered the presence of the honey badgers and I look for Baked Beans at his observation post behind the fence.

He is not there.

He is nowhere.

He has vanished, it seems. I turn around to look behind me, at the rustling near the riverbank. A group of several adult badgers have halted under the sausage tree. I can scarcely see them in the deep shadows but they appear to be looking back at their two youngsters who are playing in the dry leaves. It isn't hard to imagine a slightly impatient expression on their faces, of parents indulging their children who are dawdling at the playground. For there, ten metres behind them, their cubs are rolling in the dirt, bouncing up and down in mock attack, running around in tight circles, almost catching their own tails.

And with them is Baked Beans.

My first impulse is to run to his rescue, save him from a mauling by these two savage creatures. But I instead I stand and watch the game they are playing. A badger pounces on Baked Beans and pins him to the ground. The dog wriggles out from underneath and drops into a crouch. His curly tail is erect now, his head low, ears flattened against his skull. The badger stands still and waits for the dog to catapult himself towards him. They engage for a brief moment, then the dog breaks loose and runs as if in flight. But he stops in mid-stride, spins around and launches himself like a missile at the other cub. The first cub jumps high in the air and lands on both their backs, and they roll in the dirt again in a tight knot.

And suddenly, as if the cubs have noticed their parents' impatience, they stop and run to join them, and together they disappear into the darkness.

I feel the smile spreading on my face as Baked Beans trots past me without looking at me to his place on the veranda, curls up on his blanket, and falls asleep.

Late in the season, when his lack of domestic graces have made a mockery of the traditional master-dog relationship, we realise that a harmonious camp life with this dog is impossible. Not very reluctantly, we turn Baked Beans over to one of the game guards to join his pack of hunting dogs during the rains. This new career will probably suit his temperament better, we think. Although it will be a harder life with none of the amenities of the spoilt camp dog, we feel that Baked Beans was never really cut out for the tame decadence of domesticity.

But dogs in the bush have to be careful. I know of several who were imprudent and became easy meals for a leopard, or who strayed into shallow water for a splash and were caught by crocodiles. Others have had hunting accidents of some kind or other. I find it hard to believe that a dog of Baked Beans' temperament will die peacefully of old age.

Phil Berry says, 'Are you going to play your guitar at his funeral?'

I say, 'I have never seen or heard of another dog that plays war games with wild honey badgers. I wish him luck.'

74

9 Interlude

Pam's brother Adrian had spent the Zambian off-season hunting in the Congo and brought home a small civet for Pam. Civets are common in the Valley, although their nocturnal habits make them difficult to see. When we do encounter one in the grass along the side of the road, it is usually quite unperturbed by our spotlight and goes about its business of sniffing the ground and foraging for fruit, grubs and small insects. Civets are often mistakenly called civet cats, but there is nothing catlike about them. They look and behave more like badgers and are in fact members of the viverrid family that also include mongooses and genets. Weighing up to thirteen kilograms, they move about alone with arched backs and long sleek tails, their black and grey body markings helping them blend into the night.

Adrian's present to Pam was a juvenile female. Presumably because she was young, pretty, and somehow beguilingly feminine, Adrian named her Lolita. She certainly bewitched us all with her elegant bearing, small pointed face, and the stillness in her deep round eyes. But the most striking thing about her was that she was black. Anyone who has ever seen a black leopard – or panther – in a zoo, knows that there is something different about them, and it's more than merely the colour. They possess an aura of the rare, the exotic – the almost magical.

Melanism is not uncommon in the jungles of the African equator. In the constant twilight world where the sunlight rarely reaches the ground, many animals are born with an over-abundance of black pigment in the skin and fur. Like the black panther, Lolita vibrated with the secrets of the rain forest.

'My God, she's gorgeous,' said Pam and held her to her face, nose to nose, the civet's dark eyes staring back at her. 'How on earth did you manage to get her here from the Congo? On a commercial flight?'

Adrian grinned. 'Flew from the camp to Kinshasa in a small Cessna, so no problem there. Before I checked in for the Lusaka flight, I took her out of my shirt and put her in my suitcase. In a small box I had prepared so that she wouldn't get squashed. When the suitcase came off the plane in Lusaka, I quickly stuffed her back in my shirt, so when the customs people opened my case, all they found was an empty shoe box.'

During her first week at Chibembe, the civet almost got lost. Pam and I had gone fishing in a nearby lagoon. Lying stretched out and fast asleep between us, Lolita wasn't about to go anywhere and we concentrated on the surface of the water. When we looked again, she was gone. We were surrounded by sparse bush country. Dappled sunlight fell on a carpet of dried leaves, shadows shifted in a soft breeze. We searched in a radius of thirty metres or more, but there was no trace of her.

We looked at each other and silently shook our heads.

The game scout Mwenda was resting against a tree trunk, eyes closed in the deep shade. His rifle was leaning against the side of our Land Rover where we had parked it under a trichelia tree. He had come with us in case we wanted to take a walk in the game reserve, and now his bush craft and tracking skills were our only hope.

Pam squatted down next to him and said, 'Mwenda. We have a big problem.'

How he found her, I have no idea. The ground was hard and covered in sparse grass and fallen leaves and gave away no clues. Yet it didn't take him long. Instincts honed by a lifetime spent in the bush, coupled with small signs that neither Pam nor I could see, told Mwenda where she had gone. He beckoned us from a dense thicket fifty metres away, and we walked over to see her lying fast asleep in a tuft of thick grass.

Shortly afterwards, we had to fly to Johannesburg. It was a long journey: the drive to Mfuwe, a flight to Lusaka in a small plane, an overnight stay in Lusaka. From there, the only flight to Johannesburg was via Blantyre, Malawi. In Blantyre, the plane stood on the tarmac with unspecified problems all afternoon, and we finally arrived in South Africa late at night, tired and travel-worn. Pam was carrying a handbag, a woven basket in which the civet was hiding under a bed of sweaters and scarves. We approached the customs desk, Pam with surface confidence; me, I thought, visibly apprehensive.

'Anything to declare?'

'No, just personal effects.'

'Okay, you may proceed. Hey, wait a minute. What's that there in your basket?'

'What?'

'That thing there. I saw something move.'

'Oh, that's just my cat. My small kitten,' Pam said and looked the customs man in the eye.

'Lady, don't you know you're not allowed to bring live animals through customs. Do you have vaccination certificates for it?'

'Well … actually, no. She's just a small kitten, I thought it would be okay …' Pam managed a smile.

The customs man looked tired and seemed on the brink of waving us through. 'Well, maybe I'll turn a blind eye this time as long as you … hey!' He stared at the basket. 'That's not a cat!'

'Yes it is.'

'No it's not. Not like any cat I've ever seen. *Jissus,* lady, what the hell is it?'

'Well, it's a civet. A civet cat. Different kind of cat …' Pam said lamely.

'But it's a wild animal?'

'Well, no, it's tame. It's my pet.'

'Ja, but it's a wild animal. No lady, I'm sorry, I really can't let you through with that. I have to confiscate the thing. Sorry.' Under his breath he added, 'Whatever it is.'

The veterinary quarantine station near Johannesburg airport was housed behind the blank walls of a dismal run-down government building. When we came to visit the next day, dogs and cats were lying listlessly in the corners of the small cell-like concrete stalls. Others paced up and down along the soiled dirty-grey walls, their eyes blank, filling in the time until the next low-cost meal. The whole place smelled of urine, animal excrement, and quiet desperation.

We found Lolita crouched in a back corner of her stall, her black body coiled tight and facing the wall. Somehow we knew she was not sleeping. I looked at Pam and saw tears forming in her eyes.

Pam's mother had contacts in high places and made some phone calls. Telephones rang in Pretoria government offices, interdepartmental orders and directives made their way down the chain of command, and two days later, Lolita was released.

But Pam's mother had a big dog. A

Great Dane. Nervously we introduced them. The dog was interested, sniffing and licking, the damp flaps of his great muzzle slobbering excitedly. The civet raised her small head at him, her black eyes neither friendly nor hostile, and walked away. We watched them anxiously, ready to grab the civet in a heartbeat, but they seemed to tolerate each other. After several days of tense but uneventful co-existence, we relaxed our guard.

Late one afternoon, the civet walked through the open kitchen door into the garden where the dog was waiting. The suburban sun was sliding down behind the red-tiled roofs on the hillside. Maybe he wanted to play, or maybe some ancient dog-instinct suddenly clouded his brain. It took only one bite to kill her.

Back at Chibembe, we pondered, not for the first time, the wisdom of adopting an orphaned animal. Once a wild creature has been taken out of the expected path of its destiny, the odds are stacked heavily against it. What do we try to do? Play God? Meddle with predestined fate? Some of these creatures manage to stay their death sentence and adapt to their new situation. But their lives become artificial, like astronauts stranded on the moon.

A zoo leopard bears a close outward resemblance to his wild brother but his soul has been irrevocably altered. And perhaps death is a better fate. Still, for a long while we felt Lolita's absence with the pangs of recently bereft lovers. She had survived the loss of her mother, emigration to a new country, the scrutiny of a scary customs official, the desperation of solitary confinement in quarantine, only to surrender her life to a dog with jaws too big for his small brain.

The following rainy season when Chibembe camp was wet and inhospitable and cut off from the outside world by impassable roads and rivers in full flood, we rented a cottage in the farming district of Mazabuka in the Southern province of Zambia.

The rainy season is not a time of continuous rain. The weather alternates between periods of torrential downpours that can last a week at a time, turning roads and fields into slush, and calm sunny summers days that never seem to end and cause the farmers to cast worried looks at the white sun in the hot sky. Farmers are a pragmatic lot not usually given to superstition, but as the grass turned brown and the mealies were drying on their yellowing stalks, there were times when even the most hardened of them happily slaughtered a sheep to encourage the local population to begin the festivities of the Rain Dance.

It was during this time, when the sky remained clear despite the nightly drumming in the villages, that our neighbour found a civet lair in one of his maize fields. The nest had been abandoned by the adults who had presumably been disturbed by the sound of farm machinery and human voices. But they had left behind their litter of three tiny kittens. When the adults had not returned after several hours, the farmer took the babies home and offered one of them to Tammy and Miranda.

In memory of Lolita, we named him Humbert.

As so often happens, the radical change of diet – from mother's milk to human baby formula – had its consequences, and Humbert immediately slid into an alarming decline. His eyes were bright with fever, and spasms convulsed his body, leaving him limp. Luckily we were surrounded by farmers who were familiar with veterinary medicine. With the help of saline solutions, antibiotics, and a slightly modified milk dilution, he survived the crisis. It took a week of dedicated nursing while his small body struggled for life. Our alarm clock rang at three-hourly intervals throughout the night and we all took turns feeding him and forcing medicines past his sharp teeth down his throat, but at the end of it, he began to prosper. He gave up his nocturnal lifestyle and slept through the night (at least we think he did) and woke up in the morning when we did. He wanted nothing to do with beetles and grubs but preferred to join us for a breakfast of fruit, toast and boiled eggs.

Especially boiled eggs. He preferred them hard-boiled, so that he could carry them away without messing. He'd leap from table to chair to ground, shake the egg in his mouth vigorously from side to side, as if to make sure it was really dead, making small growls deep in his throat. Then he'd carry it off to a safe corner of the veranda to eat it.

The Rain Dance finally brought success. Whether the rain clouds marching up on the horizon one morning were a direct result, no one could be quite sure. But even the most cynical among the farmers had been frightened enough by the drought not to proclaim otherwise.

The rain washed the haze out of the sky, and the hills at the rim of the valley seemed to come closer, as if drawn by curiosity – as if trying to look over the farmers' shoulders to observe the bucolic bustle of the planting season.

It rained and it rained. And soon the fields had become swamps and the roads resembled rivers and we couldn't tell any more where the road ended and the ditch began. And the same farmers who had cursed the endless blue skies of the previous months, cocked their heads at the heavy clouds and said, 'Jesus Christ, when is it gonna stop?'

'Miranda has a problem,' said Tamara.

'Oh yeah?' said Pam.

'Yes. You said we're going away for Easter, but she doesn't want to miss the Easter Bunny.'

'Well, that's easy. Why don't we tell the Easter Bunny to come on Monday when we're back?' Tamara smiled knowingly, but Miranda was near tears.

'How? We never see him, so how can we tell him?'

'Hmmm,' said Pam, 'let me think.'

At that moment our tame oribi, whose name was Biltong, ducked under the fence at the edge of the lawn and walked up to the edge of the veranda. An oribi is a small African antelope, one of the smallest and most delicate, only slightly bigger – as a matter of fact – than an Easter Bunny. Ours was only a few months old. His mother had been killed by some of the farm labourers, and we had nursed and raised the small orphan who had turned into a surprisingly tough little creature.

'I know!' I said. 'Why don't you write a note to the Easter Bunny and tell him your predicament. Tam can help you. Then we'll tie the note to Biltong's neck.'

'That's a good idea,' Tamara said quickly. 'And when he goes walkabout,' she pointed at the fence, 'the Easter Bunny will see him and read the note.'

'What if they don't meet?' Miranda looked at me sceptically.

'Oh, of course they will,' said Pam. 'All

the animals meet at night.'

And she was right. We returned late Sunday night, and on Monday morning we found proof that our plan had worked. As was his habit every morning, the oribi stepped out of the tall grass where he spent the nights and came skipping up the lawn to sniff at the breakfast table. The note around his neck was gone. And there were Easter eggs hidden all over the garden. When the girls had found them all, Miranda patted the oribi on the head, peeled the foil off a chocolate egg and stared thoughtfully at the rustling grass beyond the garden fence.

When the sky finally cleared and took on a hard cerulean hue, and the evenings grew colder and the wind blew dust across the ploughed fields, it was time to pack up and head back east to Luangwa. Humbert was quickly growing into adulthood and was spending more and more time on his own in the pathways and tunnels he had made for himself in the tall grass beyond the garden fence. Often he would stay away overnight or even several nights in succession, and when he did come home he would eat, spend the night on the couch or on one of the children's beds and be gone again in the morning. We thought he was independent enough to be left to his own devices, and one day in late May we packed the Land Rover and left.

A month and a half later I was back in Lusaka on business. I had a couple of free days and, since we had kept the lease on our cottage, I drove down to Mazabuka on a whim to spend the weekend.

I asked at the farm whether anyone had seen Humbert. The kids in the staff compound shook their heads. Gerard, the farm manager, said he had seen him once, soon after we left, one evening just before dark. A short while later, it appeared that he stole some eggs from a farm labourer's chicken coop, and there was a distinct possibility – Gerard gave me a long look – that the man had killed him. There had been no sign of him since then.

I went out that evening to visit friends in the district, stayed for dinner and came home late – just before midnight. A high three-quarter moon reflected in the water of the dam as I drove up the track that led across the dam wall, past the cattle pens and up to the cottage. A wind had come up, rattling the fronds of the banana tree as I stopped the car and opened the door. As I was about to flick down the light switch I noticed a dark shape silhouetted against the back wall of the house. Humbert was standing at the kitchen door, blinking in the glare of the headlights.

He stayed for the weekend, eating his meals with me – not always by invitation – sleeping on the couch or on the corner of the sitting room rug, and presenting himself often to be scratched and tickled. When I opened the door on Monday morning, he walked out on to the lawn and across to the fence and was swallowed up by the high grass and bushes behind it. When I started the car an hour later, he had not reappeared. I threw him a casual

salute, wished him luck, and drove down towards the dam wall, not expecting ever to see him again.

What is it about wild animals? What is the power they wield over our imaginations, our dreams? What is it about a wild mustang, with its flowing mane, that ennobles him above the domestic carthorse? The wolf – despite its reputation of evil and cunning – assumes an exalted position in our souls that the yapping poodle can never hope to achieve. The romantic notion of friendship with a beast untamed and perhaps untameable: why do we feel so humbled and at the same time so honoured when this creature – he of the feral temper and the wild look in his eye – turns trusting and submissive in our presence?

Any scientist will tell us that the 'love' of an animal is an anthropomorphic notion that should be banned from our vocabulary. An animal cannot love us. A dog may get used to its regular meals and will regard his owner as the pack's alpha male. It submits to him and it might respect him, but it does not love him. The imprinted goose, the horse that recognises his rider as he walks across the stable yard, the cow that anticipates the milk maid, or the circus lion that correctly reads his trainer's mood – they don't love us. Yet something touches our souls when a wild animal, free and unrestrained and with no reason to seek out our company, does exactly that. Could it be the ancient memory of a time when we ourselves were part of that wildness, when we communicated in the same way, without language?

It was late August when we all visited the farmhouse again for a short mid-season break. If any of us thought of Humbert, it was as a memory – *remember the time he fell off the window sill?* – but none of us seriously expected to see him. Gerard confirmed that he had not been sighted at all, and it made sense. He must be almost fully mature now and, if he was still alive, he would be looking for a mate and had perhaps wandered far away to find her.

The evening passed, we were all tired after the long drive, and Pam and the girls finally went to bed. I left the kitchen door open, telling myself that I was being foolish and sentimental, while I showered and brushed my teeth. It was more of a subconscious gesture, I told myself, than any realistic expectation. I dried myself and wrapped the towel around me. I took my half-drunk whisky from the dining table and walked into the kitchen to lock the door.

Distant stars were framed in the dark rectangle of the doorway. Whisky in hand, I lowered myself to the floor and sat on the cement step with the damp towel around my waist, and watched the dark shape of the banana tree moving against the night sky. I heard a faint sound from the direction of the dam, an owl perhaps.

I took a deep breath, drained the whisky, and got up. I drew the curtains, and as I turned back to close the door, Humbert strode in. He walked straight towards me without hesitation, paused to sniff at my leg, and arched his back while I bent down and scratched him. Then he purposefully walked into the lounge, looked around, continued into the bedroom where Pam was asleep, and jumped on to the bed.

I held my breath. A fully grown civet was standing on our bed, astride my wife; it was not something that happened every day. He must weigh ten kilograms at least, I thought to myself. His fur was wiry and slightly erect, his eyes intense. Slowly he lowered his head and licked Pam's face.

Anyone else I know would have screamed. Pam opened one eye. She blinked, slowly focused on the animal's head inches from her face, and stared for long seconds.

Then she said softly, 'Hello Humbert.'

10 Kapani Ruins

We had some unseasonal rain today. It wasn't very spectacular; not the great cloudbursts of the rainy season when lightning tears up the sky and thunder rolls off the escarpment like distant artillery.

It started as an unusually sultry day; by mid-afternoon the air felt heavy and humid, and there was an ominous build-up of clouds in the shimmering sky, and at sunset it started raining. Gently, hesitantly at first, in slow big drops. A low salmon-coloured cloud covered the entire western half of the sky, with furry pink outlines turning vermilion where the sun was setting. Gusts of wind blew up from the river, then the rain settled into a steady drizzle, turning our dusty paths into slippery chocolate-mousse mud and raising that peculiar fecund rain-smell, like a freshly watered graveyard.

Our new house is made of wood, not grass. We have definitely come up in the world; the house is roomy and solid but inside the rough wooden walls it gets dark early. Pam has lit a hurricane lamp, and outside, too, the light is draining from the sky and the pink cloud has turned grey-brown. The wind gusts again and sends the hurricane lamp swinging on its hook, casting unfamiliar shadows against the dark walls.

Rain rattles on the roof like a tambourine, and this is the moment the frogs appear. They come out of their hiding places behind the bookshelves and from the cracks in the walls. They hop along the polished cement floor, not skidding like the cat does but gripping the slippery surface with the sticky pads on their feet. Bouncing purposefully in short leaps, they jump up on to stools and chairs. My guitar, leaning in a corner, suddenly seems to strum itself; I see a frog has landed and is clinging to the strings.

They fall from the ceiling and land on the table and on top of the cupboard and the desk with soft thumps. One lands on my shoulder; I feel his cold sticky feet soft against my neck.

I don't know enough about frogs for a positive ID. I think the bigger ones are tree frogs, *Leptopelis* something or other; the little ones are reed frogs. Painted or tinker reed frogs. I'm not sure and don't really care. They come in sizes from thumb-

nail to matchbox. One of them has, in fact, found a matchbox and made itself at home on top of it. Another is hunched at the edge of the porch, poised to leap off like a suicide off a bridge. A big greenish-coloured one is slowly climbing the table leg, long legs scissoring. I have to be careful where I sit so that I don't squash one.

Pam is making tea, but there is a frog perched on the kettle lid. It sits there unblinking until the water boils and it is covered by a thin film of steam.

Outside it is dark now and a big yellow moon hangs low in the sky.

In the bedroom, frogs are all over the place. I see three of them lined up along the curtain rail, ready to jump. Three more squat on the piano like ornaments on a mantelpiece. (Yes, we have a piano now, an old one inherited from the doctor at the clinic. But no one here can play it very well.) The bed is covered in frogs, and I scoop up a handful and toss them out. One is left behind, staring at me from the folds of my pillow.

It soon becomes clear that they are all heading in the same direction, towards the veranda – for the rain outside.

It never rains in August. The months between May and October are supposed to be our dry season. At the height of the rains, yes, we have the frogs in our house, and they blend so well that we hardly notice them. (Except for the ones that have found a *really* ridiculous perch: Look, Ma, there's a frog on your lipstick.)

When the rainy season ends, the frogs slowly disappear. Where to, I have never really asked myself. Now I know: they don't go far.

I have never seen such a sudden migration before. I suppose they will realise that today's rain was a false alarm and go back into hiding until the real rains come.

Several families of squirrels live in the roof of our new house. They are noisy creatures and we hear them scurrying along the roof beams at night. They chirp their shrill alarm call whenever they hear a snake. Or our cat. We like them and would like to keep cordial relations but it's an uneasy truce. Occasionally I throw something at the roof to shut them up, a shoe perhaps. It doesn't help. A couple of weeks ago I threw a book and a baby fell out of the roof and landed on our bed, stunned. I felt bad about it, but Miranda raised it by hand and took it to school.

At night, bats drop out of the *mchenja* tree under which our house is built and find their way into the bedroom. I don't mind them flitting around the porch but when they come into the house and start their dogfights above our bed, they keep me awake. On such nights, I have dreams of being a fighter pilot.

I tried to block the gaps under the eaves where the bats find their way in with cut-up pieces of grass mat but I fell off the ladder and cracked two ribs. I happened to run into the doctor the next day (the successor to the one who sold us his piano) and he examined me standing under a sausage tree by the side of the road, and told me I had cracked some ribs.

As if I didn't know.

'It only hurts when you laugh,' he said. 'Or sneeze or cough.' As if I didn't know. Or *breathe*.

The bats still play Battle of Britain above our mosquito net.

Once a porcupine gnawed a hole through our bedroom door big enough to squeeze his body through to get at a bar of chocolate. They have big strong teeth, and it didn't take very long.

The rain is falling heavily now. The squirrels in the roof are quiet. All the frogs have gone. They are probably sitting out on the *dambo* in the pouring rain thinking mating thoughts.

A wind has come up and drives the rain through the open sides of our veranda. I have to roll down the blinds against the rain, and two snakes fall out. One has a frog in its mouth.

Tomorrow it will be Full Moon.

Our new camp is near the new Luangwa bridge, a couple of miles from the new tar road that connects the bridge to the new airport. Norman has been sensible and has decided on convenience over charm and remoteness. The new site is not even along the river.

'I've had enough of this river eroding my camps away. I don't trust it any more.' Although the Luangwa is only a stone's throw away, and we can see it shimmering through the trees from our new *chitenje*, our main view faces an oxbow lagoon. During the rains, the lagoon flows again and turns into the river it once was. It takes its water out of the Luangwa at one end, and we hear it rushing in all night. The muddy water can rise over a foot a day and quickly spreads over the banks of the channel that runs down its centre. Within days the entire *dambo* in front of us, the size of several football fields joined end to end, is flooded. Hippos and crocodiles move in and all day we see storks and sacred ibis fishing in the shallow water.

In the dry season, when all the water has gone, the place becomes a green lawn, from the edge of our camp a hundred metres across to the trees opposite. Baboons and puku come to graze and shy bushbuck step gingerly from between the trees at dusk.

'You know we could have a golf course here,' muses Norman. 'The Lusaka golfers would love it.'

'Or a motocross track,' I tell him. All my Lusaka racing friends can bring their bikes and ...' Norman gives me a look.

'Model aeroplanes,' says Lester. 'We could fly model aeroplanes here.'

'*Ja, ja.* Remote controlled aeroplanes.' Patrick is instantly excited. 'We'll paint

them like eagles and dive-bomb game drives from other camps.'

'Oh, shut up, all of you,' Norman says wearily. 'I am surrounded by children.'

When Chibembe camp was sold and Norman looked around for somewhere new, it was the two survivors of the drinking competition, Patrick Ansell and Lester Shenton, who chose to leave Chibembe as well and follow Norman. Or perhaps it was Norman who chose them but not, I suspect, for their capacity for alcohol.

Robin Pope has started his own operation at the old Nsefu camp. He is busy rebuilding it. The manager Phil Berry is now divorced and runs the neighbouring camp of Chinzombo. Lester's girlfriend has come to stay and is helping Pam teach the kids, but it's almost time for Tam to go to boarding school.

Our new camp is strictly residential. Norman swears he will never run a lodge again. 'People want to come and see the great Bwana for his bush knowledge,' he says, 'not because he runs a good hotel.' In an ironic twist of fate, Norman has come full circle and accommodates his safari clients at Mfuwe lodge, the same place he left fifteen years before.

'But I don't have to run the place,' he grins. 'Let someone else worry about food and catering and supplies. I just do the thing I'm good at.'

Every morning Norman, Lester and Patrick start up the Land Cruisers and drive the three miles to the tar road, across the new bridge, to meet their clients at Mfuwe lodge at the first hint of dawn. To do this, they get up at five.

I am still in awe of the man. I am blinded by the aura that surrounds him like a bullet-proof vest, and do not yet see the chinks in his armour, don't see that he has his small faults like the rest of us, that he is human. I am shocked when someone makes a disparaging remark, like, 'Jesus, Norman is as stubborn as a bloody warthog.' Phil Berry says, 'If you want to get Norman to agree with you on anything you have to suggest the opposite.'

His children share the view that he is a hero. Pam talks about his quiet masculinity as a quality every other man should aspire to, including her husband. I grudgingly agree, not knowing that a time will come when the competition between us will grow and threaten the harmony of our camp. For now, the man can do no wrong in our eyes.

'I thank my stars that I'm no longer a lodge owner.' Norman shudders. 'But,' he adds, 'I used to do it a lot more efficiently than that chap who now runs Mfuwe.'

I know he has become fed-up with the management of Mfuwe lodge. His guests have been complaining – politely – about the sub-standard food, the inefficient service. When they leave, they enthuse about the outstanding wildlife, the fantastic game viewing. They praise Norman's knowledge, Patrick's playfulness and Lester's calm authority. But they don't say anything complimentary about the food or accommodation.

Sometimes I see Norman walk to the top end of the property and draw lines in the ground with his stick. I see he has marked out large square shapes and he paces out the distances between them.

'Norman, you said you'd never build another lodge in your life.'

'Did I? Well, then I suppose I shouldn't.' And he walks away with a secret smile, swinging his stick. But one day I hear him tell Iwomba, our cook, to go and find Manduna, his chief builder from the Chibembe days. And I've seen the drawings lying on his desk.

But building a lodge takes time. And money.

Sunday morning, Pam and the girls are redecorating the schoolroom. I am sitting on Norman's veranda, drinking tea with him and discussing the plumbing problems in our bathroom. Norman is dead-set against burning wood in our hot-water boiler and insists on trying various home-made solar heaters. None of them has really worked so far, and our showers are always more cold than hot. His new plans involve a criss-cross grid of black-painted water pipes on the corrugated-iron roof of the bathroom.

'But how much water can they heat?' I say, playing devil's advocate.

'Enough for a quick shower, I'm sure.'

'Norman, remember there're eight of us, all sharing the same bathroom, the same two showers.' I start counting them on my fingers. 'Lester and Sheri, Patrick ...'

'I'm aware of how many people live in our camp,' he mutters irritably. He hates it when I'm negative.

'Pam and I want to build our own bathroom, attached to the house, sooner or later.'

He looks at me. 'That's rather a luxury, I'd say. I think we have other priorities for now.' He turns back to his desk, his back to me, and starts drawing on his page of plumbing plans with a pencil stub. I drink my tea and look across the *dambo*. The baboon troop is at the far end, in full strength, it seems. There must be thirty or forty animals there, but they are hard to count because the young ones are always on the move. I pick up Norman's binoculars from the low table. A very small baby with bright button eyes has strayed too far and the mother is yanking it back by the tail. The baby strains against her grip but she holds firm, scratching in the ground for edible roots with her free hand.

I put the glasses down and look at Norman. I see he has pushed the plumbing plans aside and is leafing through a sheaf of bank statements, staring intently at each page before turning it over. He puts them down on the desk and now I see him open an ancient, scuffed briefcase and take out a dog-eared cheque book. He picks up the pencil again and slowly pages through the cheque stubs, licking his thumb and making notations. He turns and looks out at the *dambo*, shakes his head and drops the cheque book back into the briefcase. He seems to have forgotten that I'm sitting in his armchair.

I take the last sip of tea. Norman gets up from his hard-backed chair and walks into his bedroom. It is a very rare sight but this Sunday morning, after a hard week with a demanding group of international

clients, Norman is still not dressed. He has been comfortably shuffling around his house, barefoot and in his underpants, since he got up an hour ago. He comes back through the open doorway and sits at his desk again. I see he has a stack of dollar bills in front of him now. I smile ruefully when I realise what they are.

During the penultimate year at Chibembe, before it was sold, the company finally made some money. All the revenue came from the hunting side, not the walking safaris, and it was a big surprise when one of the other directors came to see Norman in camp and placed a wad of hundred dollar bills in his hand.

'It was the first time in my entire career that I had some money at the end of the season,' he said at the time.

But easy come, easy go. The floods were particularly severe that year, and the little hideaway safe lay submerged for three months before Norman could even get to it, the money – the only money he had ever saved – rotting inside. When he finally opened the safe, the bills were stuck together in a solid brick and covered in dry mud. All the paperclips that held the individual stacks together had rusted, and when he tried to dislodge one of them, the bills disintegrated in his hands.

Now he eyes them, lying on the desk in front of him. Slowly he picks up his Swiss Army knife, opens the long blade and carefully tries to insert it between two of the bills.

'Oh bother,' he mutters as the brittle banknotes turn to confetti between his fingers. He tries again, then closes the knife and pushes the stack away. He reaches back into the briefcase for the cheque book but seems to change his mind and lets it fall back. He turns in his chair.

'Oh Vic, I didn't realise you were still here.' He is smiling ruefully, and shaking his head.

He says quietly, more to himself than to me, 'I haven't a bloody clue how much money I've got.' He reaches for the teapot. 'Any tea left? Oh, look at the baboons.'

Meantime, even our own residential house project seems ambitious. Pam and I have designed a grand (by Norman's standards) family house for ourselves. The foundations are built, and to look at them on the ground, it seems indeed excessively large. What's more, the camp has spread in both directions and our foundations have somehow ended up in the very centre of camp. We don't want them there, we want our house to be at the end. So, heeding the adage of every successful estate agent, 'location, location, location', we abandon the project and build a different, more modest house at the far end, under a tall ebony tree.

But the foundations remain. They cost money, and after fifty years of living frugally in the bush, Norman is not happy about breaking them down. Norman's house, like ours, is made from prefab-ricated hardwood that comes from the factory in the north of the country in easy to assemble four-by-eight panels. The houses are quick to construct and the indigenous wood finish blends in well with our surroundings. The rest of the camp is a different matter. A red-brick kitchen with a tin roof, a cement block bathroom with two showers and two toilets. Two grass-and-bamboo huts for our visitors, an experimental mud hut (village style) for Lester and Sheri; a wooden schoolroom and a strange contraption that Patrick has built himself from asbestos panels. Our camp is not going to win any prizes from *Garden and Home*. And the abandoned foundations of our would-be dream home remain in the middle of it all.

One day, though, they come into their own.

Norman's son Adrian has given up hunting. It's not that he's grown tired of the hunt itself, for nothing else brings you as close to the wild animals as hunting them. It's the clients, he says. As a gentleman in his father's mould – of the old-fashioned English school – he dislikes the nouveau-riche vulgarity that most of them bring into his camp. Gone are the days of the true sportsman, he says, who doesn't care whether he bags the record trophy but understands that the important part is skill and endurance, and the thrill of the chase – for whom *being there* is enough. Nowadays it's all about killing, and the tyranny of the record book.

Adrian plans to catch tropical fish in Lake Tanganyika – as far from the Valley as he can get – and to raise crocodiles for export. He has a permit to collect two thousand croc eggs along the Luangwa River, on condition that he will release a number of the crocs when they reach a certain size. Most young crocodiles don't make it through their vulnerable first few months, when they are easy takeaway snacks for eagles, hawks and other predators, and the proportion of young crocs he will return to the wild will be greater than the natural survival rate.

Patrick is part of the collecting team who comb the beaches and sandbanks along the river for signs of crocs' nests. As female crocodiles never stray far from their nests and usually keep a close watch over them, we are surprised that he has so far avoided being eaten by a mother crocodile. Female crocodiles lay forty or more white eggs the size of goose eggs in shallow depressions that they have excavated in the dry riverbanks and covered with sand, to be incubated under the burning October sun.

Conditions are almost identical inside our foundations where, months ago, a team of workers with shovels and an old Land Rover deposited load after load of soft building sand from a nearby river, in anticipation of the construction of our brick house. When Adrian's team return from their day's work, they bury the eggs forty or fifty centimetres deep in the sand, just like mother crocodiles. Each clutch of eggs is buried separately in our sandpit, a metre or two apart, and every day when Patrick, Lester and their helpers return from their expeditions, they add new nests.

How long till they hatch, Tammy and Miranda want to know. But there is no way of telling exactly when the eggs of each nest were laid, or when their three-month incubation time will end. In the wild the female crocodile, sometimes assisted by the male, will dig the new hatchlings out of the sand and carry them to the water. Miranda watches the mounds of sand and checks them for movement a dozen times each day. 'How long now?' she asks as she sits on the edge of the low wall with her eyes on the white sand.

When the first crocs hatch it is at night. They push their hard little snouts against the leathery shell of the eggs until a hole opens large enough to accommodate their heads. They greet the outside world with high piping sounds, as if they are surprised. Their squeaks alert the others still inside their shells and within minutes the forty or fifty crocs of this particular clutch start struggling out of their eggs. By the time we realise what's happening and get out of bed with our torches, a scene out of Jurassic Park greets us: a corner of the foundations is covered with writhing creatures, seemingly from a distant age. Tiny reptile heads with big yellow eyes stare at us; small feet claw at the sand, trying to find purchase, some still trailing the shells of their eggs which glow dully in the torchlight. And all of them chirping – a thin whistling *cheep*.

We help the stragglers to the surface and out of their remaining shell fragments and carry them to a far corner, for fear their calls might set off other nests prematurely. We wash them in clean water to rinse off the sticky slime clinging to them and do everything a mother croc would do – except carry them in our mouths to the river, although I can see that Miranda would like to.

As the days pass more and more eggs hatch.

'Miranda, Tam. Where are you going?'

'To the crocs. They might need help hatching.' Tamara soon gets bored staring at the sand and goes back to her room to read. But Miranda waits.

'I was scared at first,' she tells me. 'But now that I know how sweet they are I'm not scared any more. But their teeth are sharp. Look.' A baby croc clamps its jaws around her finger. I leave her there and when I go past an hour later her patience has paid off. Another group of hatchlings is struggling to the surface, cheeping weirdly. Miranda is crawling among them on her hands and knees, a busy midwife.

One day the gardener comes and fills a wheelbarrow of sand to cart away to somewhere, and he forgets to remove the wooden plank that he has placed under the wheel, one end resting on the wall. Unnoticed by anyone, a baby croc walks up the plank as if it were the gangway of a ship that will carry him to freedom. He hops off the high end into the dirt and shuffles across the camp, heading for the trees. A little while later, another croc follows. As no one is there to see, we can't be sure how many crocs escape this way, when they escaped, at what intervals, whether singly or in groups, but by mid-afternoon a large number are missing. The

first sign that something is amiss is when a man arrives at our kitchen, holding a baby crocodile, and asks: 'Is this yours?' Through the afternoon more and more babies are returned to us by passing fishermen, workers on their way home, and others who come across the little escapees scurrying across the road and through the mopane forest.

I imagine that a fair number make good their escape and find their way to the river. With more than a thousand croco-diles now living in our foundations, there is no way to tell how many got away. With the little creatures swarming all over the sand, it is impossible to conduct an accurate head count.

When nearly all the crocs have hatched we put them in cardboard boxes padded with crumpled newspaper, tape up the boxes and take them to the airport. The last of the unhatched eggs go too.

'What's in these boxes?' the man at Zambia Airways wants to know.

'Crocodiles.'

'Ha ha,' he says.

In Lusaka, Adrian's assistant, a wandering Kiwi who came to Africa three years before to watch the All Blacks play a test series against the Springboks in South Africa and then cycled north, drifted around Zambia and hasn't yet managed to leave (it will take quite a few more years), picks the crocs up and takes them to a rented warehouse before sending them north to their new home on Lake Tanganyika.

The boxes, when he opens them, are a mess. Soggy newspaper, baby crocs climbing all over each other, some still inside their shells, some free, some with bits of shell clinging to them, most covered in slime.

Some of the hatchlings haven't survived the journey. For no reason he can explain, Kiwi takes one of the leathery carcasses and puts it in the pocket of his shorts. I see him in Lusaka that week, and wherever he goes he likes to surprise people by pulling the crocodile out of his shorts, and saying something along the lines of: 'There's something here inside my pants ... feels like ... oh, it's a croco-

dile ...'

At the Longhorn Restaurant – the regular hangout of farmers and safari people – Kiwi orders a plate of soup for lunch, an unusual choice where the standard order is rare rump or T-bone steak. But his plan becomes clear when he calls the waiter to his table.

'Waiter, look. There's a crocodile in my soup.' The waiter stares at the plate. 'What are we going to do?' asks Kiwi.

The waiter's face is expressionless, his eyes never leaving the plate. The crocodile's head is hanging limply over the edge, its spine showing yellow under the soup. He shakes his head. 'I don't know.'

Norman has decided that when he builds his new lodge, he will call it KAPANI, after his old lion camp. The foundations are dug and the first walls are rising, and every morning at seven Norman stands impatiently by the piles of bricks, leaning on his stick, waiting for the building crew to assemble. He's had a busy morning already and is impatient to get the builders to start.

On our side of the property, progress has ground to a halt. Any available money and all the workers have been put to work on the lodge project; even our gardener keeps being called away to help. Our camp looks a mess, and the ruined appearance of the unfinished foundations gives it the appearance of an archaeological dig, especially now that all the crocodiles have gone.

I don't remember whether there is a connection between Adrian's crocodile plans, if it is a copycat enterprise (someone looking at someone else's new business and saying, oh *that's* a good idea) that is so common here, or whether it's purely coincidental. Maybe there is something in the air, because soon after the last of Adrian's crocs have been moved north, a couple of Zimbabweans show up in the Valley and announce at the Chinzombo bar one night that they've come to start a croc farm. They have a backer in Lusaka, a silent partner whose main advantage over Adrian seems to be that he has money. They've acquired a stretch of river frontage upstream of the bridge, and with the cash flowing in from Lusaka seemingly limitless, they start building. Reception buildings, a restaurant and bar, staff houses, row upon row of crocodile pens, a huge freezer room, a snakepit, an aviary.

They have just finished a massive concrete archway over their entrance, presumably to evoke a sense of Roman grandeur. Foot-high copper letters are set into the stucco and proclaim LUANGWA CROCO-DILE FARM. Charl and Basil look upon our modest progress with pity, and at the state of our domestic conditions with disdain. At the bar, they have started calling our camp Kapani Ruins. I can't blame them for feeling superior.

One morning, at breakfast, we notice two camera-laden tourists standing under the sausage tree outside our kitchen. They have arrived quietly; perhaps they parked their car some distance away and approached on foot. I get up to greet them.

'Morning, can we help you?'

There's a puzzled expression on the man's face. He looks around him. 'We're looking for the ruins,' he says uncertainly.

'Ruins?'

'Yes. Someone told us there are some old ruins here …'

The name has stuck. On the eastern end of the plot, beyond the combretum thicket, the Valley's first luxury lodge is growing, but our residential site is from that day known as Kapani Ruins.

11 Nido

Every morning and every afternoon, a flock of Crowned Cranes flies over our camp.

In the local language, they are called *owani,* in perfect imitation of their call.

Nyanja is a language full of expressive exclamations, and it's easy to follow the gist of a conversation simply by paying attention to them, and their inflections. 'Eh, Eh. Aaah, uh-uh. Ah-ah is different from a-a-a-a; oh-oh has an entirely different meaning from ooooh, or o-o-o. The language is musical, too, with unexpected lyrical sounds and onomatopoeic incantation. Mosquito is *mzuzu.* A hippo is *mvu*, after its deep resonant grunt.

Mvula means rain. The word even smells of rain, and it blows with the wet wind that brings it, as anyone can testify who has ever been exposed to the power of an African rainstorm with no shelter. It speaks just as eloquently of being trapped inside a mud hut, of the dull sound of rain drumming endlessly on to a thatch roof, soaking it, when all the world outside is dampness, puddles, sticky mud and dripping trees; and has been so for three months. *Mvula*.

The *owanis* come over our camp east to west in the morning, from their sleeping place in the mopane forest to the beach, where they stand in the shallow water of the river's edge all day and peck at the mud with their long grey-black beaks. When we walk on the beach, they keep their distance. If we come too close, they run along the hard sand next to the water on their long legs, flapping their wings – wingspans the size of ironing boards – and sounding their shrill but melodious tune: *owani owani*. As soon as they gain enough speed to take off, they cease looking ungainly. Seeing them float effortlessly above the sand, their slow wing beats seem to bridge the chasm of time and space to older civilisations, as if they have this moment arrived from the Bosporus, messengers from ancient Byzantium.

In the late afternoon they take off and leave their feeding grounds by the river and cross our camp again, this time in the opposite direction. When they hear their call, our monkey and our warthog sometimes look up from what they are doing and follow the birds' passage with their eyes.

This is how it usually happens. Most animals drop their young at the beginning of the rainy season when food and water will be plentiful in the coming months. Warthog babies are the first to arrive, a month before the first rain clouds roll up on the horizon. November brings the first impala fawns along with the first storms, and when the rains have set in properly a month later, there is new life everywhere. Baby monkeys and baboons leap in the trees and play on the ground, their mothers always watching. Civets and genets and mongooses give birth in the grass and under bushes, yellow-billed storks gather in their breeding colonies in the tops of guano-covered ebony trees to lay their eggs (although we don't see the fledglings until later).

And the local people go hunting. Armed with wire nooses, slingshots, spears and fishhooks, the sharp-eyed village boys scour the newly rich countryside for small animals hiding in the grass, fledgling birds in their nests, anything that moves. The villagers are permanently hungry for protein, and most of their quarry ends up in village cooking pots. But a baby monkey or baby warthog can always be sold to a *mzungu* for some extra kwacha. Be careful of baboons – *ayeee*, they can bite! But it's easy with those smaller things, monkeys, genets, baby bushbuck. You kill the mother and sell the babies.

We discourage these little hunter-entrepreneurs. 'Don't ever do this again. It's bad. We'll never buy an animal from you again. In fact, we should report you to the ranger.' They nod, their faces serious, holding a limp baby monkey in one hand, the other hand open, palm up, waiting. The monkey's frightened eyes stare at us unblinking. We know the creature is orphaned, starving, and traumatised.

'Plee-ease,' says Miranda, a light in her eyes. 'We've got to.'

We place a few kwacha notes in the boy's hand and he runs off with his friends, giggling and squealing. 'Don't do it again!' we call after them. Fat chance.

So we have a warthog called Widdle (Norman's name for him), and a monkey named Nido because he spent his first days in a cardboard box stencilled on the sides with Nestlé's NIDO powdered milk labels. There is an uneasy alliance between the two. They have realised that they have to share the same resources of food and affection that their new life has brought them, but they are two very different creatures.

Although Patrick recently managed to get himself, the two girls, plus the warthog and the monkey on Pam's motorbike for a trip to the neighbouring camp, you couldn't call them friends. Widdle is close to the earth. He has short legs, and for the most part of each day, his front legs are folded under him and his snout is digging, in direct contact with the soil, often *in* it. His character, too, is down to earth: predictable, solid, unsurprising.

The monkey is at the opposite end of the spectrum. While his earth-bound companion plods along on the ground, Nido is given to sudden flights of fancy, both physical and metaphorical. He spends a good portion of his life airborne and has the flighty arrogance of a fighter pilot to go with it. He leaps unchallenged from one person to the next, snatching food out of our hands and off our plates, jumping on to the breakfast table and disappearing, in the blink of an eye, with an orange clutched in his hand. He will sit in a tree above our heads, unaccountable, un-admonished, *un-admonishable*.

'I swear that monkey is grinning at us,' Norman says.

Of the two, Widdle is the good guy.

Nido is the anarchist, the bandit. When he does something bad, he knows it. But he is too quick to be caught, and too smart to be lured by feeble gestures. If I try to trap him by holding out a biscuit or piece of chocolate, he will weigh up the situation with raised eyebrows and in-stinctively make the right decision: Don't touch it. Not yet, wait. Wild monkeys don't survive by acting impulsively, and his natural caution always wins out over greed or curiosity.

But he can be affectionate too. For no apparent reason, his mood will suddenly change and he lands on my shoulder and snuggles into the hollow of my neck. Then I can handle him, scratch between his large ears and pick at his soft fur as if looking for ticks and lice. He will close his eyes, luxuriating in the attention. I stroke his head with the tip of my finger, from his forehead down along the bridge of his nose; I tickle the soft hairs under his chin, and he stretches his lips in perfect imitation of a smile.

He opens his mouth and gently bites down on my fingertip. Eyeing me through half-closed lids, he begins to exert pressure, clamping his small jaws with surprising strength. When it starts to hurt, I pull my finger away and reprimand him: 'Nido!' But he is already gone, watching me intently from the top of the cupboard.

Miranda has malaria again. The biggest problem of living in a remote bush camp like ours – and Pam's biggest worry – is the absence of medical facilities. There is a small missionary clinic an hour's drive away but the medical staff there are not equipped to handle anything but the most rudimentary illness. For anything more serious than a throat infection, we would have to fly or drive to Lusaka.

Luckily, we are all acclimatised to bush-life by now, and have probably built up immunities to most local viruses. But not to malaria. Both our daughters have been raised on a steady diet of chloro-quine, Maloprim, Deltaprim, or whatever prophylactic is available in the Lusaka pharmacies. It can't be good for them in the long run, we think, but malaria is worse.

The trouble is, they still get it. 'Mu-um? I'm not feeling well. My back aches and there's a pain behind my eyes.'

'Uh-oh, better get some Fansidar into you right away. And better go straight to bed.' We can't take a chance with blood smears and lab tests – it would simply take too long to drive to the clinic at Kamoto and sit there waiting for results. The doctor in Lusaka hates us.

'You people in the Valley,' he fumes, 'every time you have a headache, or get the flu, you think it's malaria. This self-diagnosis and self-treatment is dangerous! Malaria strains become immune if they're exposed to the same drug too often; every time you take the treatment, you're weak-ening its effectiveness. Bugger it, some of you probably never even had malaria.'

But the doctor is wrong. We do know

the symptoms (we've all felt them often enough), and we know that time is of the essence, and that if you wait too long, malaria can kill you.

That night, Miranda's temperature climbs to just below the red. Her sheets are damp and crumpled; sweat pools in the hollows of her body, and there is a fire of unnatural brightness in her eyes.

Half an hour later she will be shivering under a mound of blankets, her whole body gripped by freezing spasms, an arctic chill deep in her bones. The fever will die, and then it will rise again; die and rise again until, after two or three days, her eyes will clear, and her body will stop aching.

'Miranda, I'm glad you're feeling better. But, you know, you need to be a little more careful. Your mozzie net is there for a good reason, and it kinda defeats the purpose that there's a great big hole in it.'

'Dad,' Miranda looks at me with the patience of a nun. 'You *know* the cat likes to sleep with me. How else could he come in and out?'

'And the warthog too, I suppose.'

Miranda nods.

The monkey has stolen Norman's shaving cream and taken it away with him.

'That monkey is a complete bastard,' growls Norman. Miranda grins. Patrick says, 'You sure? I didn't think he was old enough to shave.' He winks at Miranda but Norman is clearly not amused. He seems distracted these days, preoccupied with the building of his lodge.

Our small kitten, named Generator for its loud purr, has become Nido's reluctant friend. In the manner of two passengers

thrown together in the same compartment on a long train journey, they have no alternative – or at least, one of them hasn't.

The cat, pushed into the role of the passenger who is content to look out of the window or perhaps read a book while the other wants to chat, is at the receiving end of this one-sided friendship, and it literally doesn't have a choice; every time it tries to slink away from the monkey's attentions, Nido grabs it, slings his long skinny arm around its neck, and drags it back to his fluffy towel in the corner of our bedroom.

There he wedges the cat tightly into the corner to prevent its escape, leans on it for comfort and closeness, and begins sucking its left ear.

Sometimes, when the monkey relaxes his grip and closes his eyes, the cat manages to get away. Sometimes it is halfway across the room, or has even made it out the bedroom door on to the veranda, before Nido notices its absence. But there is no place to hide, and we get used to the sight of this ill-matched twosome inching across the carpet towards the corner by the piano. Sometimes the cat uses its paws to slow the passage but soon learns that any resistance is futile. It is too small or too polite, or perhaps too smart, to fight and we never once see it hiss at the monkey or use its claws in anger.

During daylight hours the monkey rules supreme, but when dusk begins to settle, he grows nervous, as if apprehensive of the night. Although he is safe and snug in his corner on the towel, the collective monkey memory of nights in the high branches of the trees, with the leopard prowling below, unsettles him and makes him uneasy. Evening is always the best time to handle him, when he most needs the comfort of someone's hands and reassuring words.

It is also the time when the cat suffers most of its abuse, and after the first few weeks of their acquaintance, the fur on its left ear begins to disappear.

'Look, Dad,' says Tamara. 'One ear is almost bald.'

Nido continues with his airborne attacks on our lunch table, and Norman's patience is at breaking point. 'I'm not going to let that little bastard spoil my meal.'

Patrick comes into the dining room and sits down at the table.

'Oh. Looks like I'm late. Had a few beers with the clients.'

He glances at the sideboard where the bowls and dishes stand. 'What's for lunch?'

'Chicken,' says Pam. 'Don't know if there's any left. Go and have a look.'

Patrick suddenly sees Iwomba standing in the corner, holding a slingshot in his hand.

'Iwomba, what the hell are you doing with that *catty*?'

Iwomba clears his throat. He looks at Norman with his usual expression of deep worry.

'Bwana told me,' he says.

Patrick looks at Norman.

'Patrick,' says Norman. 'We're being overrun here. These *bloody* monkeys and baboons are ruling our lives.' Iwomba coughs uncertainly, and Norman continues: 'Of the three loaves of bread that Iwomba baked this morning, two have already been stolen. Look!' He points to the *dambo* where a group of four baboons sit around an unrecognisable white blob that might once have been a loaf of bread. They are screeching and baring their teeth at each other, and the white lump keeps changing hands.

'So if any of them come near the *chitenje*, Iwomba has instructions to shoot them with that catapult.'

'Well, I hope he's a good shot,' says Patrick.

'And that goes for your bloody monkey, too.'

'Oh no, not Nido!' Patrick is standing between the table and the sideboard. 'Anyway, Norman, it's not my monkey,' he says in an Inspector Clouseau accent, nodding at Miranda.

'I don't care whose monkey it is, he's got to learn to behave himself. Sorry, Miranda.' Miranda knows that Nido is far too quick for Iwomba, and smiles at Norman.

But Patrick is like a terrier with a rat. 'Poor Nido, it's not his fault that the baboons have stolen the bread.' He looks at the monkey clinging to one of the roof beams. 'Poor little boy.' Then he looks at Norman and laughs. 'I'm not being much help, am I, Norman?'

Norman shakes his head.

'In fact, more like a hindrance, hey?' He turns to the sideboard. 'Damn. Chicken's finished.'

We have new visitors. As is so often the case, no one seems to know who they are. They arrived a few days ago, a young couple with backpacks, after a few days' hard travelling no doubt, and greeted us cheerfully.

'Oh, we're looking for Norman Carr.' And then to Norman who has been resting after lunch and has got up drowsily and is not particularly interested: 'We met a friend of yours in Lusaka, Peter Miller, who said to look you up.' And Norman, who knows Peter Miller well but hasn't a clue who these two are or what their relationship is with Peter, decides to err on the hospitable side and offers them accommodation, food, even game viewing.

'We must always help people who are stranded in the bush,' he says with typical generosity. Next door, visitors pay a hundred dollars a day or more, but the magic words 'I met a friend of yours' seem to ensure Norman's hospitality free, every time.

As it turns out, these two are nice, and they really seem to appreciate the little bamboo hut. They are on honeymoon, they tell us. Instead of two weeks in Mallorca or on a Greek Island, they decided to spend their money on two backpacks and two air tickets to Africa instead. They have planned an extensive itinerary, from the South and Zimbabwe, through Zambia, Malawi, Tanzania, Kenya, and possibly even the islands of Zanzibar and Lamu. They will avoid the big towns and stay in game camps, rest houses, camp sites. We are only their third stop on a long journey and what promises to be a memorable honeymoon.

On their last evening, I see them sitting side by side on the stone step in the doorway of the round bamboo hut. Generator the cat sits between them, his bald left ear gleaming whitely in the last light of the setting sun. Nido, inquisitive as usual, has been hanging around in the mopane trees. He is always interested in people, and he suddenly jumps out of the tree on to the roof of the hut and, in one fluid movement, on to the girl's shoulder. I see him grab something she is holding in her hand. She starts and tries to grab it back, but he is already sitting on the roof. He is holding the flat shiny object, sniffing at it and biting it.

They both jump to their feet, and this arouses the monkey's suspicions. He jerks his head and raises his eyebrows at them. The girl reaches for him, slowly, her hand inching towards him with the deliberate stealth of a snake. He lets it come closer, blinking at it, but at the last moment, when she has almost touched the shiny object, he clamps it between his teeth and jumps in a long lazy leap to the nearest tree trunk.

He shins up the trunk and sits on a horizontal branch, high in the tree, examining his prize, turning it over in his long fingers. But he is soon bored with it and opens his hands. I see the thing spiralling slowly down and disappearing somewhere in the dense foliage of the tree. 'Well, you'll never find that again, whatever it is,' I think to myself as I walk slowly towards the couple who are still standing outside their hut. They haven't moved.

Nido comes flying out of the tree and lands on the ground at my feet, blinking.

The honeymoon couple look stunned.

'What was that?' I ask.

He has a wide-eyed look on his face but the girl looks slightly more composed. There's even a tentative smile tugging at the corners of her mouth.

She says in a small voice, 'That was . . . my birth control pills.'

A month later, while Pam and the girls and I are away, another young couple show up, this time hitch-hiking from Malawi, also on the cheap, also with the idea that having met an acquaintance of Norman's somewhere along their travels must surely entitle them to a free holiday in Norman's camp. They arrive after dark and find Norman, who is relaxing with his whodunnit, deep in his scuffed armchair, almost ready for bed. He hasn't a clue who they are. So-and-so said they should look him up, they say, but he doesn't know who so-and-so is. Maybe friends of Pam and Vic, he thinks, and finds the key to the guest rondavel.

'I think there'll be clean sheets on the bed,' he says, 'and the bathroom is that grey building over there.'

The next morning he tells Iwomba to make them breakfast, and then he takes them game viewing. When we return from Lusaka, they have already been there for three days. We still don't know who they are. They have the annoying arrogance of some backpackers who have seen the world at others' expense and think themselves vastly superior to their hosts because of it. They are critical of everything, they eye our primitive kitchen with suspicion, they kick at the dirt floor of our *chitenje*. The girl is a little less obnoxious but it is her boyfriend who really irritates me.

'I don't understand the way you treat your staff,' he says to me. 'I mean, why do you make them call you *Bwana*?' I start to answer, explaining that I don't *make* them, that they are free to call us anything they like, that if they choose to call us Bwana, it's their way of showing us respect, and wouldn't he address *his* employer as Mister or Sir, and what does he know about African customs and the finer points of African *language* anyway? But of course I stop in mid-sentence. What is the point?

Before they leave, after another breakfast of porridge and bacon and eggs, and after we have asked around the camps and found a lift to Chipata for them and arranged for them to be picked up, he opens his backpack, reaches into the bottom, and pulls out a pineapple.

He says, 'Do you eat pineapples?'

I eye the dented fruit – its black bruises. 'Yeah, sure.' He holds it out to me.

'Oh. In that case we would like to leave this with you, as a thank you gift.' He is still holding the pineapple, seemingly reluctant to let go of it. 'I just wanted to make sure you like them. Didn't want to waste it.'

I nod. As they wave goodbye, I look for Nido, thinking, 'Why didn't you steal *their* birth control pills?'

At every mealtime now, the cook stands in a corner of our little dining room with a catapult in his hand. We eat to the rattling of small stones in his pocket. So far, he has shot at the flying monkey a dozen times, but never yet hit him.

Norman says, 'Have you seen the monkeys at Mfuwe Lodge? They're a complete pain in the arse. Thieves, each and every one of them.'

It's true. Pam and I sat at the Mfuwe bar the other day, waiting for Norman's game drive to return. A monkey landed on the bar counter in front of me, next to my gin and tonic. One eye on me, he calmly reached into the glass, took out the slice of lemon and began to eat it. His eyes never left mine in case of the need for a quick exit. But I knew I had no chance.

Some of the big males can be aggressive and threaten us with drawn-back lips that expose long teeth, and raised hackles and guttural growls.

Back in our own camp it's not only Nido who keeps us alert. The wild monkeys are no better, and we seem to be engaged in a continuous battle to outsmart them. The war starts early in the morning when they drop out of the trees on to our house and run across the roof ridge like galloping cavalry. It continues all day, around the vegetable garden, at the pantry window (barred and wired), on the sideboard in the *chitenje* where tea trays with milk jugs and sugar bowls are sometimes left unattended.

We throw thorn bushes on top of the roof and put chilli powder in the sugar bowl, but the monkeys don't care.

My studio is under a big tamarind tree. For many months (too many) when the fruit ripens, the tree is alive with monkeys and baboons from dawn to dusk. They drop twigs and half-eaten tamarinds on my roof; they break branches off the tree and let them fall, and sometimes a baboon or monkey lands somewhere above my head with a thud. All day the roof reverberates with the animals' presence, and I am tense, waiting for the next noise. It's not the ideal environment to concentrate. I tell myself it doesn't matter, the animals belong here more than I do, and just when I begin to relax and think that they've moved off to the next tree, a baboon lets go of a branch high in the tree and crashlands on my roof, and I jump out of my skin again.

But the baboons are the lesser evil. When they are in the tree, they feed quietly – seriously – breaking the fruit off at the stems and pushing them into their mouths without haste or greed.

Monkeys, however, are chaotic feeders. Like everything else they do, there is no order to their lives, no system. They jump all over the roof, chase each other back and forth, in and out of the tree, back again on to the roof, looking into the windows, screaming. At first I think it's funny but after a while I tire of the sight of an upside-down monkey peering in at the window.

They drive me crazy, and every deterrent I think of has failed. But then one day I paint a leopard, and the monkeys go berserk. They cackle and screech, they bob their heads and flick their eyebrows up and down. They run towards the window in short mock-attacks, and finally they flee.

The baboons handle the crisis differently, more maturely. When I come back from lunch, they are sitting in front of my studio in a shallow semicircle. I stop behind a tree to watch them. They are ducking their heads from side to side to get a better look through the window. Tree shadows on the glass shift and change, obscuring what is behind.

The leopard sits on the easel. It doesn't move. Is it asleep? Is it perhaps dead? Why can't we smell it? Is it really a leopard? They look as if they are trying to discuss sensibly what to do about the problem. I can almost imagine a baboon conversation.

'Is that what I think it is? You bet it is. It's not real though. If you're so sure, why don't you go and have a look. What, you think I'm crazy?'

For a few days, the monkeys and baboons stay away from my studio, but of course the peace doesn't last. Soon they begin to see that this particular leopard is harmless, and they come back into the tree (and on to my roof) with new vigour.

Patrick made Nido drunk. And while they

were both drunk, Patrick gave Nido a haircut. With his big ears, Nido is not the most handsome creature in the first place, but this new Mohican hairstyle makes him look downright ridiculous.

'Patrick, I know drunks like company, but a monkey?'

'We were bored.' He is talking in a Cornish accent, which he sometimes does when the booze of the night before is still busy in his system.

'Both of you?' I ask.

Patrick is at the dining table, elbows on the polished wood, his head resting on his palms. He looks at the monkey sitting on the table in front him.

'Yeah, Nido was looking bored. So what's wrong with having a drink?'

Patrick stretches out his hand and tickles the monkey under his chin. 'You liked it, didn't you Nido? Being all wobbly. You missed the pole, trying to jump into the roof, didn't you?' The monkey stares at Patrick with round eyes. 'And you skidded on the table. But look,' he turns to me, 'he's okay now though, isn't he? Look, he can walk straight again.'

So far this season, Patrick has fallen out of a tree into a thorn bush. He nearly dropped a Land Cruiser off its jack on to his foot. He cut both arms in long red gashes while stumbling through a scrap heap looking for an old Land Rover spring, but collided with a broken windscreen instead. Afterwards, he sat in the

chitenje with bleeding arms and a bottle of Scotch, moaning and rocking back and forth on his chair.

Patrick says, 'Can I have a go on your bike?'

'No.'

'Come on.'

I shake my head.

'No way, this one's not like my other bike.'

He is grinning at it, running his hand over the tank.

'Patrick, this is a full-on motocross bike, a racing bike.'

'Ja, I know. That's why I want to ride it.'

I should have taken heed of the slow glint in his eye, but I didn't. My mistake.

I shrug. 'Okay, but be careful, all right? It takes a while to get used to the power band, don't rev it too high at first.'

I turn the throttle to show him, and the sound from the exhaust is like a chainsaw: deafening, metallic. Patrick grips the handlebars and climbs on to the high saddle. He kicks the Yamaha into first, drops the clutch. The back wheel spins, throwing clumps of earth. I have to duck so that they don't hit my face. Then the chunky rubber knobs of the tyre bite the ground and the bike is thrown forward along the uneven stretch of grass along the riverbank.

'Keep your weight forward,' I shout after him as he disappears in a rain of flying grass and mud clods. Pukus grazing in the distance raise their heads in alarm and gallop away. I am not surprised when the front wheel hits a bump and lifts off. Patrick, who is sitting too far back like a road racer is suddenly airborne, unable to control the bike's balance, and man and machine come down with a jarring thud on the hard ground, somersaulting and bouncing off in different directions.

'I'm going to kill him this time,' I mutter to myself. My new motorbike has twisted handlebars and the front fender looks like something from Star Wars, sharp red plastic splinters that point like weapons.

The dull abrasions along the tank concern me far more than those on Patrick's face. He says he has broken his collarbone but I'm not sure that it's true. Still, he wears his arm in a sling for the next week.

The locals shake their heads at Patrick. Their nickname for him is *Malo wa ngozi,* the place of the accident.

Norman is standing next to Patrick, who is slouched on a bar stool. 'Patrick, I hope your drinking isn't interfering with your work,' he says. Next to Patrick, several clients sit on the bar stools or stand with drinks in their hands.

'Patrick, can we buy you a drink? That was an absolutely phenomenal drive this afternoon,' says one. 'Pure bloody magic ...'

Patrick shrugs. 'A beer, please.'

'How on earth did you know that leopard was there?'

'Told you. I saw a puku look up and snort.'

The client turns to me. 'This guy is unbelievable. He just knew the leopard

had to be there somewhere, in all that grass.'

'It took us an hour to find it,' enthuses his wife, 'and that must have been the most exciting hour of my life.'

One of the others says, 'I was so absorbed by the hunt, I didn't even feel the tsetse flies.' Patrick has lit a cigarette and sips his beer. He appears bored by the conversation.

The client looks at him. 'But Patrick, what was the final clue? I mean that was a big area, he could have been hiding anywhere.'

'Do you remember that flock of guinea fowl? Well, I heard one of them give a short alarm call. The others obviously hadn't seen the leopard but that one did. So I knew he had to be right there. Then I saw his ear twitch.'

'Unbelievable,' says the client.

Patrick looks at his empty beer mug and says, 'Anyone know who won the rugby?'

Next door, the new lodge is under construction. The main buildings are almost finished, and the carpenters are busy with the interior finishes: doors, wardrobes, window frames, everything wooden is made of *mukwa*. The long bar counter in the main *chitenje* is solid *mukwa*, as thick as my wrist, and gleams under the oiled polish.

We're having breakfast. Nido sits in the rafters under the thatch, following each of our moves. He has just made a successful assault on the bowl of sliced mango and

sits chewing, juice on his face and three mango slices still in his sticky fingers. This does not stop him from planning the next strike.

I push my empty bowl aside and look across the round table at Patrick.

'You're not looking too good this morning.'

He doesn't reply but stares at the untouched bowl in front of him, his face as pasty and pale as the porridge inside it. He pushes the plate away and lights a cigarette.

'I think I'll give up drinking for a while.'

'Oh yeah?'

'Mmm.'

Pam says, 'That'll be the day', and does a quick Buddy Holly jig at the table, complete with air guitar.

'No, Pam. I will. You don't believe me.'

Pam shakes her head.

Patrick looks at me. 'She doesn't believe me,' he says.

I shrug.

'No, I'm serious. I came back from Mfuwe last night. After drinking with some clients. I parked the Cruiser and walked to my house. I don't remember it but I must have done 'cause I woke up in my bed this morning.'

Nido has let go of one of his mango pieces and it drops wetly on the table in front of Patrick.

'Oh, Jesus.' He frowns up at the monkey. 'Anyway, this morning I couldn't find my cigarettes. Or my lighter, or my sunglasses.' He pats his shirt pocket. 'So I went looking for them.'

He glances up at Nido again. 'Don't bloody look at me like that! So anyway. I found the cigarettes on the path between where I parked the Cruiser and my house, so that's okay. But then the lighter was on the floor of the workshop. I mean, that's a hundred yards away.' He pauses and shifts his cigarette pack around on the table.

'And my sunglasses I found over there on the *dambo*.' He turns and points behind him, into the middle distance. As he turns back to the table, the monkey lands with a thud on his head, tousling his hair.

'Oh Jesus, Nido. My head! That hurts.' Patrick reaches up with both hands and gently lifts the monkey off his head and places him on the table in front of him. Nido trusts Patrick. They are drinking partners, after all, and who knows what secrets they have shared in the lonely dark hours of the night, what confidences Patrick has entrusted to the monkey that he would withhold from us.

Patrick takes a slice of mango and extends the yellow fruit towards the monkey. Nido reaches for it and carefully takes the slice out of Patrick's hand with delicate fingers. His eyes never leave Patrick's. He sniffs the fruit, then opens his mouth and stuffs all of it inside. His cheeks bulge.

'Nido,' says Patrick, 'I'm going to give up drinking.'

12   Widdle and the Silver Sow

'Mum. Mu-um!' Miranda's voice, never exactly quiet, is even more forceful.

'The warthog is trying to climb into my bed again!'

'I thought you liked him in your bed.'

'I do, but he's just had a mud bath, and he's all wet and yucky.'

Warthogs lead a hard life, or so it would seem from our human perspective. On their knees for most of the day, digging in the dirt with their snouts for roots and tubers, under constant threat from some of Africa's fiercest predators – lion, leopard, and hyena – and of course they are not exactly blessed with good looks. Lacking the grace of impalas, the elegance of giraffes, or the sleek power of cheetahs, only other warthogs could be attracted to a warthog.

And evidently they are, for when the days turn hot in October and nothing moves in the bush once the sun has climbed into the leaden sky, it is a common sight to see a warthog sow followed by four or five young in single file, all running with their tails straight in the air like radio antennae. But as the weeks progress, the lines get shorter and the litters shrink from five or more to two or three; we start seeing females with only two babies following them, or one, sometimes none at all.

Warthog babies are pathetically easy to catch. They can run fast but they tire quickly and when they are out of breath and out of strength to run and zigzag, they just stop and turn, put their heads down and stand and await their fate. If even a human can outrun them, how easy it must be for a leopard. And leopards make full use of the October glut of piglets. They are such easy pickings, and there are so many of them in the Valley, that leopard sightings drop drastically – the cats no longer have to venture out into the open to hunt puku or impala but can afford to hide in thickets or trees for most of the day and night. Photographers seldom see them at this time, and hunters find it hard to attract them to their baits.

Yes, even a human can catch a piglet, and as a result many a warthog ends up as a pet.

The wildlife authorities don't like it. The ranger tries to pounce on those of us who keep wild animals as pets. We point out to them that they are usually orphaned and have been rescued from a fate of starvation and death. That they were not caught by us but by village kids trying to make some easy money. We tell them that we do not confine them in any way, that they are free to leave. Hundreds of animals die in snares and are poached, and what difference could one habituated warthog possibly make. The poachers and those who set illegal snares go unpunished; often they are known to the ranger and the scouts and seem to have their silent complicity.

The trouble with Africa is that authority seems to bring with it its own wilful arrogance. People in positions of power often tend to lose sight of their objectives, the real demands of their jobs, and lose themselves in side issues of petty jealousies and vindictiveness.

Widdle is even-tempered, predictable, tolerant, but he can be obnoxious. He can be stubborn. Digging in one's heels takes on a new, literal, meaning when he gets hold of something he loves and somebody tries to take it away. Someone's shoe, for instance. Or a loaf of bread.

His long snout is equipped with mobile lips, tough and rubbery, and a blunt muzzle that he uses to dig up the hard dirt like a plough. His eyes are small and buried in a bed of deep wrinkles. The long slope of his forehead is hard and bony under the tight skin and covered with short hairs. If I rap a knuckle on its hardness, he slowly closes his eyes, the long lashes twitching in contentment. A strange creature, indeed.

The one thing he really seems to hate is not being able to reach the food on the dining table. The folds in his thick neck bulge in tight rolls as he strains to raise his head higher, but the tabletop remains just out of his range. He stands under it, rubbing against our legs, knocking the chairs, and squealing loudly. The more delicious and tempting the smells from the table, the louder he squeals. It's a big mistake to give in and pass a titbit to him because once he has tasted it he wants more and the squeals turn into screams.

As he grows older, Widdle becomes more independent. He stops being a pampered pet and starts behaving more like a warthog. He walks out on to the *dambo* in front of camp every morning and spends his days rooting. Hour after hour on his knees, his head pivoting in a semicircle, digging in the ground.

Occasionally something frightens him, the shrill call of a dive-bombing plover or the sudden grunt of a hippo in the reeds, and with a start he jumps to his feet and runs back to the safety of camp. When the danger has passed, or when he realises that there was no danger after all, he trots out again and continues his foraging until dark, seemingly oblivious of time. As twilight falls, he suddenly, with no warning and for no apparent reason, stops feeding. It is never a gradual process; he doesn't start looking towards camp as it gets darker, doesn't slowly shuffle nearer while still rooting. It is always sudden. One minute he is feeding contentedly, the next second he jerks back his head, almost as if to say 'Ohmygod, look at the time!' and comes trotting back and jumps up on to our veranda and settles down in his corner.

The zoologist down the road suggests that we remove his tusks. 'They can do a lot of damage when he gets older. I've got some M99. We can knock him out and I'll extract the tusks. No problem.'

Widdle lies stretched out unconscious on the ground in front of our kitchen. Patrick, the girls, and the zoologist kneel beside him, the zoologist holding a pair of pliers. I stand behind them with Iwomba and Alefer. I try to imagine what might be running through Iwomba's mind. 'Okay, they've killed the pig. Good. There'll be plenty of meals for me to cook; the deep freeze will be stocked for a long time. Maybe there'll be some *nyama* for me to take home.'

The zoologist twists and pulls and the tusks come out easily. I look at Iwomba. Is he thinking: 'I wonder why they have to do that before they cut him up. Probably another one of those incomprehensible *mzungu* rituals.'

But when the antidote is injected and Widdle slowly opens his eyes and looks around him, Iwomba and Alefer are still as stones, their bodies rigid, their own eyes wide open as they stare at the pig. Iwomba turns slowly towards me, speechless.

At first Widdle looks a little silly without his tusks, but slowly they start growing back. Even the zoologist hadn't expected that. They grow into handsomely curving, formidable weapons but Widdle never ever uses them against any of us, not even in play.

Towards the end of his first year, when he is almost fully grown, Widdle becomes the subject of a prolonged legal battle. Someone in the local game department offices has taken it into his head to enforce the letter of the law, and begins writing overzealous letters to his superiors. Letters arrive in our post box at the airport from Chilanga, the Game Department headquarters near Lusaka. They are addressed to Norman and request the release of the pig. Norman answers patiently, saying that the pig is free to go if it wants to.

One day a government Land Rover arrives at Kapani. Two uniformed wildlife officers step out and present Norman with a letter which instructs them to confiscate the warthog and take him to an animal park in distant Ndola in Zambia's Northern Province. Norman is speechless. Then he explodes.

'We need dedicated scouts who go out on patrol. We need people who are concerned about our wildlife. Who are willing to stop the illegal hunting. Our parks are run by poachers. I never see you people organise any patrols. Only my friends do: a few honorary rangers who don't get paid and who do all the work *you* should be doing.'

The two scouts look at each other.

'Wait,' Norman's voice rises a few decibels, 'I want to show you something.' He turns and storms into his house, walking quickly with his cane swinging. I

112

see him through the big window, bent over his desk. He is muttering, 'Where is the bloody thing?'

The scouts stand in front of his house, looking at each other, looking at the ground. The warthog comes rushing from the direction of the kitchen and stops, his mane bristling.

'Here, look at this!' Norman marches towards the two wildlife officers waving a yellow file in his hand. 'This is the correspondence I've had with your superiors. Your department has nothing better to do than waste its time – and mine – creating a useless war of words, a paper war! We lose thousands of elephants each year to poachers, and what are you doing about it? Nothing. You sit on your backsides writing letters.

'The roads in our National Parks are full of potholes. I've never, *never,* seen anyone mending them. I have to get our own people to repair these things if I want them done. I see more and more sick animals in the park every day, animals caught in snares, animals dying. No one does a thing to stop it. But here you are. You have nothing better to do than come a thousand kilometres, wasting time and government funds, to take a small animal away from my grandchildren! An animal that was orphaned and would have died if they had not looked after it.'

Norman waved the file again. 'I have written to your superiors on countless occasions. This animal is not confined. It is free to go if it wants to! Look around. Do you see a cage? A fence?' He took a breath. 'Tell your superior I said *No*. Tell

him Norman Carr said *No*. Years ago, I was in charge of this whole outfit. I'm not now, I know that. But I know what's right and what's wrong. And you are not taking this animal to Ndola. Because that is wrong.' Norman waved his stick in the air.

'Tell your superior that he can take me to court if he wants to, but this warthog stays here in Luangwa. Now please leave my camp. Goodbye.'

It is the last Norman hears of the matter. The letters stop coming. Evidently the matter is closed.

At the eastern end of the plot, behind the combretum thicket, the lodge is nearing completion. Norman is fed-up with the shoddy catering at Mfuwe lodge and I can see he's getting impatient.

The new lodge is dominated by a big thatched *chitenje* that houses the dining room, lounge and bar. Behind it, a kitchen and storerooms, and off to one side there is a reception building and an office. Four double chalets face the lagoon, dry now but waiting to be filled again when the rains break. At the far end of the property is a large swimming pool.

But the finishing touches take time: wiring, plumbing, painting – installing the kitchen, office equipment, a cold room. We are reminded daily how far we are from the nearest town. Still, Norman has set a deadline: two more months, and the lodge will open. The first visitors have already booked.

Widdle has started straying further and further from camp and we often don't see him at all during the day. We have never spotted wild warthogs in the vicinity of the camp or along the river and if he is looking for company, he has to explore the area behind the camp, in the bush around Kalawani pan and on the plains beyond. Several times people have spotted a warthog there that they thought was behaving a little strangely. Instead of running for cover, it stands and stares at them, or sometimes comes rushing towards them.

He is now a fully mature warthog, strong, healthy, and obviously capable of taking care of himself. He often stays out overnight, sleeping somewhere in the bush; his visits to Kapani become less frequent, and finally he stays away altogether.

Lester and Sheri have left us, too, to try their luck at being farmers, get married and make babies. Lester's younger cousin Rolf has taken his place.

Patrick, too, has moved out. He says he wants to be independent and has started building his own camp in the trees on the other side of the *dambo*, half a kilometre away. He lives in a tent while building the foundations of his house. His closest neighbours are bushbuck, leopards, and the resident baboon troop. The deep gully that runs through the middle of the *dambo* prevents access by vehicle, which makes commuting to and from work difficult. It's a long walk back after a night at the bar, and sometimes he stays over at the Ruins. He finds an empty grass hut and throws himself on to one of the beds. Or

he'll sit in the *chitenje* most of the night, finally catching a few hours' sleep on one of the wooden benches. In the morning, he tells us of the leopard who came in the middle of the night and stared at him.

The leopard often comes through the camp, we see the tracks of his insomniac prowling in the mornings; I wonder what he makes of the man talking to himself under the thatch roof, staring into the night sky at Orion's Belt.

'Patrick, you should cool it with the booze.'

'Why? Alcohol gives us insight into what life would be like if it weren't for the intrusion of reality,' he says ponderously.

'You read that somewhere?'

He shrugs. 'I'm looking for the truth.'

'Oh. *In vino veritas* . . .'

'And I'm experimenting. I want to see what lies on the other side of rationality. Anyway, God gave us booze. I drink it. Be rude not to.'

His new house, he tells us, will be double-storeyed. A steep thatched roof with walls made of brick. He has constructed the oversized brick mould and will start burning the clay kiln later this season, he says. Upstairs will be a bathroom and his bedroom. The bedroom window will open into the trees where he can eavesdrop on the baboon headquarters. Downstairs, he will have a ten-seater dining table with hand-carved chairs. He is looking forward to the time, he informs us, when he will give large dinner parties. People won't forget his parties in a hurry, he says, because the pipe from the upstairs toilet will descend down the centre of the room and through a hole in the middle of the dining table. It will be made of clear plastic. This, Patrick feels sure, will stimulate dinner conversation and encourage lively debate among his guests. His parties will not be boring. Patrick has a fear of being boring. Is this a recognised phobia, we wonder.

Early one morning, he leads me to his yellow Land Rover, which is parked at our workshop, and points. It looks as though he has dismantled the wing mirrors on the front mudguards and replaced each one with a baboon skull.

'Look,' he says, jumping behind the steering wheel. I take a closer look and see that thin wires run from under the bonnet to each skull, and into each eye socket, Patrick has wedged a small light bulb.

'Watch!' he shouts, and flicks the indicator switch inside the cab. The baboon's eyes start blinking.

'I'm going to patent these,' he says. 'Maybe London taxis can use them.'

Our second warthog is a female and we call her Miss Piggy.

She was caught by one of the professional hunters in the area, but word had got out that this man was keeping a

wild animal without permission and the pig was confiscated. The ranger decided to make a case against the culprit and keep the pig as evidence, court exhibit A. But he wasn't keen to look after it in the interim, and in a logic-defying move she was handed into the temporary custody of Tam and Miranda, who were by now experienced in the care of small orphaned animals and eager to have her.

The court case somehow never happens, and Miss Piggy stays. Like Widdle, she grows up as part of the family and soon thinks of herself as one of us. And not merely one of us but, specifically, she thinks of herself as a woman.

Like Widdle, she discovers a fondness for *mzungu* food, and spends entire breakfasts or lunch-hours under our dining table squealing and chomping her teeth in frustration. When someone drops her a morsel, she chews it noisily and clacks her jaws when it's finished. Miranda once fed her a piece of chocolate, and Miss Piggy has never forgotten it. She stood stock-still, letting the chocolate melt slowly on her tongue, savouring the moment. I swear she even closed her eyes. She sighed. Then, of course, she wanted more.

The memory of that day seems to live on in her pig-brain, and it seems to be a great disappointment to her that not all the bits of food that fall from the table taste like chocolate. The vexation is plain to see in her body language but she will eat the piece anyway. Some of the things that we *mzungus* eat are hard for a pig to handle, even a person-pig. But manners do not seem to be a concern. And she does love her saucers of milk, although milk is not easy to drink either, at least not elegantly. The slurping noises that accompany each saucer are not ladylike.

Norman's Lodge is up and running. The food there is far better than ours. Miss Piggy is fully grown now, a year and a half old, and she knows when it is lunch time. She will trot the few hundred metres along the path through the combretum thicket, and arrive in the Lodge dining room just in time for lunch.

She is confident. She *makes an entrance*, like a lady who is accustomed to the maitre d' showing her to her favourite table with fawning deference in view of the whole room. And the eyes of the room are indeed on her.

She singles out a table, pushes under

it, between the legs of the diners, and screams. There really is no other word for the noise she makes. Some diners think it's cute and make the mistake of feeding her bits of their lunch from the table. She eats noisily and raises her head for more. If nothing happens she squeals again, and if that doesn't elicit a response, she might bite their ankles.

She is generally more tolerant of men; she likes men, I think. But not women. Curiously, she seems to hate women. Once she has passed her first period of oestrus, her hatred becomes more intense, as if the frustration of being a pig, a second-class citizen in human company, is just too much to bear. She tolerates Pam and the girls but any stranger in her territory spells trouble.

Her territory includes the Lodge, and none of us can think of a way to stop her daily raids. Several tourists have been bitten. We have to warn them now. Careful of the pig. She may be cute but, boy, she can bite!

We sit at the low table between the bar and the riverbank under the stars. Pam and I, Rolf and Patrick and two of the clients. The others have finished dinner, had their coffee and whisky nightcaps and gone to bed. Pam has her feet on the table. Patrick is smoking.

Chitumbe calls from the bar, 'I'm closing now. Goodnight.' He is busy lowering the iron grille on to the bar counter, ready to lock up for the night.

'Wait,' says Patrick. 'Chitumbe. We need some more beers.'

Chitumbe shakes his head. 'No. I am closing. I already said *last round*.'

I nod at Chitumbe, then turn to Patrick. 'Chitumbe's had it, let him go to bed.'

'Just one more round,' says Patrick querulously, but Chitumbe has already snapped the lock shut. Patrick's eyes follow him as he leaves the bar. He looks at me, takes a fresh cigarette out of his crumpled packet, and lights it. Then his eyes drop to the table, to the paraffin lamp standing there. He leans forward in his chair and reaches for it.

'Well in that case,' he mutters, and lifts the lamp off the table. He unscrews the lamp's fuel lid and shakes it. We can hear the paraffin sloshing in its belly. Then he looks at me, raises the lamp to his lips and begins to drink.

'At least you could turn the wick down,' says Rolf.

Patrick coughs and goes red in the face.

'Mmmm, very nice,' he says, his breath stuck in his throat.

Both the girls are at boarding school now. Tam is fourteen, Miranda eleven. Home schooling has been a success. It has given them the unique opportunity of growing up in the bush, learning secrets of the animal world that no city child can ever know. The company of their friends from the village has enabled them to learn the local language, and Pam's patient teaching, the intensity of the one-on-one teacher-pupil relationship, has prepared them well academically.

But it's time to meet other kids, to enter the topsy-turvy, give-and-take world of social interaction with their peers that is part of growing up. There is a good school, run on British public school lines, across the border in Malawi. It's a long drive in our new short-wheelbase Land Cruiser but we make the trip once or twice a month to see them at weekends.

We take them to the Lake or up Zomba mountain, and they come home for every school holiday and half-term weekend. And when they're home, along with the secret language of their new boarding school vocabulary that no one but they can understand, nothing has changed.

'Maybe she's bored,' suggests Miranda.

'We need to entertain her more,' Tam nods.

'Or give her something to do, a sense of purpose.'

We have a friend staying at the Ruins again, an anthropologist from South Carolina who is writing his PhD thesis on the politics of the local tribespeople. The pig, being a person too, presumably falls into his sphere of expertise.

'Why don't you train her?' he suggests. 'Make her learn a skill.'

'To do what?' Tam appears sceptical.

'Don't know. Maybe a showjumper.'

Miranda is instantly enthusiastic. 'Yes! She could be the first warthog showjumper in the whole wide world.'

'An equestrian pig!'

'Do you think they'll let her enter one of those snotty horse events though?' asks Tamara. 'You know what those horsy people can be like.'

'She'll need a name,' suggests the anthropologist. 'A show name.'

'True. What should we call her?'

'How about *The Silver Sow*? How does that sound?'

After lunch, I see them practising. The girls have levelled a bamboo stick between two metal oil cans, and are trying to chase the pig across it. Of course, the pig doesn't get the point and keeps knocking the stick down. As I approach them, I notice that her mane has been plaited and decorated with pink ribbons, and she has been freshly brushed and groomed.

Norman says, 'You don't think sending the girls to school is a waste of time?'

13 Mr Guzzie

Whenever I rode past a village on my motorbike, a horde of children would gather in the dust by the side of the road and clap and cheer and shout. I sometimes entertained them by popping the front wheel in the air and accelerating past, balancing on the back wheel. This never failed to produce wild shouts of amazement and celebration.

I have no idea where they learned the word; I can only assume that one of our staff overheard me and passed it on to his family in their village, or perhaps Miranda taught it to some of her play-mates who took it back to their friends. In any case, before long, the children in every village along the airport road would come running to the road when they heard the bike approaching, shouting,

'Pull a wheelie! Pull a wheelie!' Sometimes I was going too fast and couldn't oblige but it didn't seem to matter. They knew I had to come back eventually, and when I did I could see them from a long way off dancing and jumping, and as I passed the screams came again, pullawheeeeeliee!

Our camp was growing slowly. The tents and makeshift huts of the early days had been dismantled, and an air of permanence had taken hold. Now we needed some real furniture. There was a small carpentry workshop in the hills west of the airport, an hour and a half's drive along the road that led past Chief Kakumbi's old palace. Perhaps the word 'road' is misleading. It was little more than a track, and even in the dry season a motor car made slow progress – there were long stretches where a bicycle would be the vehicle of choice. Once past the Chief's palace (again a word that needs to be qualified: the palace was really little more than a ramshackle collection of mud huts surrounding a slightly larger, square red-brick house with wooden shutters over open holes in the wall), the road got even worse.

But the villages got prettier. Suddenly the ubiquitous drab, brown mud huts were left behind us and we drove past villages where the houses were decorated in bright colours, children sang and danced and even the yellow dogs seemed to look happier where they lay in the sand under the shade of the mango trees.

There must have been some unusual pigments in the earth that had inspired the villagers to decorate their homes in such bold designs and cheerful looking murals. I asked Alefer about it, and he replied, 'Yes, these people are very lucky. There are some very different soils in this area, clays of different colour. There is the usual red but also black and pure white. The black they make even blacker by adding charcoal.'

Finally the track climbed out of the valley into the foothills, and the soil changed and the vegetation of the valley gave way to the trees of the hill country. Amongst these, the *Mukwa* tree (*Pterocarpus angolensis*), which grows here in abundance, is sought after for its valuable wood. The heartwood is a beautiful reddish colour, it is easily worked and can be polished to a glowing shine. It has long been used by Africans for building canoes, making mortars, drums, and even spears. Apart from its quality and beauty, the red heartwood is also resistant to wood borers and termites.

In other parts of the country, these trees were being cut down in vast numbers and the wood used for building or furniture manufacture, or it was exported, and even in these remote hills *Mukwa* trees were becoming rare.

The carpenter's workshop was a large shed with a corrugated iron roof standing next to a group of mud huts and some pawpaw trees. A wire fence surrounded the compound and a faded sign said CHIPAKU SAWMILLS. I saw the carpenter emerge from one of the huts as I drove the dusty Land Cruiser through the opening in the fence late one morning. He was barefoot and wearing blue jeans and a T-shirt. He smiled as he walked towards me. I was standing next to the Cruiser, stretching my back. I greeted him and asked about the progress of my order.

'Well,' he said.

'Well what?'

'Well, it is difficult.'

I waited.

'You see, we experienced some difficulties. That we had not anticipated.'

I nodded. 'Yes, I understand things aren't always easy, but I placed my order well over a month ago. I paid you a deposit. This is now the third time you promised it would be ready, the third time I've come all the way from Kapani to find it's not so. Come on, you even sent a message to say everything would be ready today!'

'Yes, I know. I'm sorry, I made a mistake. Things did not go as planned.'

I sighed. 'Well, all right. I'll have to come back. Let me at least take the things you *have* finished, so that this trip wasn't a complete waste of time.'

He shook his head again. 'Well, eeeh …'

'You mean there's nothing finished, not one bed, not a table, not even one single chair?'

'But we have cut most of the trees now. Problem is, they are still in the bush.'

'So you haven't even *started* on any of the furniture! Then why did you send the messenger to tell me it would be ready today?'

'As I said, I miscalculated.'

'Please,' I said, 'we have to understand each other. I do not want to get angry with you for wasting my time, but you have to understand that every time I come here it is a long journey for me.' He nodded his head, and I continued: 'It wastes fuel, but above all, it wastes my time. I'm very busy and I cannot just take a whole morning off work to come and visit you.' He nodded again, but I wanted to press the point

home, make sure he really understood.

'Don't send any more messages until the stuff is actually standing here in your workshop, completely finished and ready for me to take. I don't want to waste another trip.'

He eyed me guardedly.

'You see,' I said, 'I'm not like *mzungus* who can delegate – tell others to do the work. They have people in their employ, but I don't. I have to do all my work myself and I have to work every day. So it's difficult for me to take time off.'

There were not many white people in the area and they were all objects of

curiosity among the locals. I thought he might have heard what I did for a living.

'Yes,' he said, 'I will try next time. I understand you are a famous motorcyclist.'

Several weeks later, I finally collected my furniture, paid the outstanding balance, shook hands with the carpenter, his assistants and most of their children.

A few days after this, a man on a bicycle arrived at Kapani and handed me a folded sheet of paper that had been torn out of a school exercise book.

I read, in faultless handwritten English:

To: Mr Guzzie
Kapani Lodge

Dear Mr Guzzie
The directors of Chipaku Sawmills would like to invite you to attend their next board meeting on Wednesday to discuss the possibility of your financing the purchase of a second-hand truck.

M Chulu
(carpenter)

PS When you come please bring a cassette tape and a pack of twenty Peter Stuyvesant.

14   Everything is Broken

It takes a worried man to sing a worried song
— Traditional Negro work song

'Everything is broken,' said Iwomba, our cook. 'Everything.' His voice shook as if he was about to cry. He is a man with a permanently downcast expression but now he looked even sadder than usual.

'What do you mean, everything in the country?' asked Patrick Ansell, deadpan.

'No, no.' Iwomba was literally wringing his hands (the first time I'd seen a grown man do that), Patrick's humour lost on him.

'In kitchen. Everything is broken. It's *fisi*,' he said, and then, struggling with the word, 'Aheena.

Come, you see.'

Now I remembered hearing a noise, or a series of noises in the middle of the night, too far away to wake me fully but loud enough to register in my sleep. Like something at the edge of a dream, barely perceived, just out of reach. I must have dismissed it as another of those un-identified night sounds and drifted back to sleep.

So we all followed Iwomba into the tin-roofed red brick hut that is our kitchen. He stopped in the doorway and pointed.

'You see. Terrible.'

Yes, it was a mess. The kitchen floor was a battlefield of broken plates and coffee mugs, and pots and pans lay scattered about.

'And look here! No good.' Iwomba pointed accusingly at a cooking pot which was punctured by two large holes, side by side. 'Teeth,' he said and shook his head. 'No good.' I felt an urge to comfort him but there was really nothing I could say.

'And fridge, look in fridge!' He averted his eyes as he stepped over a puddle of orange juice and some soggy bits of wrapping paper and opened the door of the refrigerator. The shelves were empty. The hyena had somehow opened the fridge and eaten the week's supply of fresh meat and groceries that Pam and Patrick had brought back from their shopping trip to Chipata the previous day. The only hint that the fridge had been full the night before was the streak of a congealed egg yolk down one side and a chewed plastic margarine tub.

'And look!' There were teeth marks in the corners of the deep freeze, too. Unable to bite through the metal, the frustrated animal had opened the wooden sideboard instead where the pots and pans and plates were stored, and scattered the contents everywhere. It looked as though the hyena had been in a frenzied rage because, as Iwomba had correctly observed, everything was broken.

Spotted hyenas are not the cowardly scavengers they were once believed to be.

True, they wander the bush searching for leftovers – the remains of someone's kill, a shred of skin, a dry bone, things even the vultures won't touch. They hang around hunters' camps and African villages, they try to steal the kills of smaller predators. But scavenging is not always an easy business and when dead flesh is scarce, they are perfectly capable of killing live food. Most of the guides in Luangwa have seen hyenas kill, and the most obvious reason they don't witness it more often is that hyenas tend to be most active in the hours around midnight, long after the night drives have returned to camp, and in the early hours before dawn when the tourists are still asleep.

There are exceptions, of course. One of the Nkwali guides told how he saw a pack of eight or nine hyenas chase a healthy adult buffalo bull into the shallow water of Mfuwe lagoon at midday. All afternoon they took turns at harassing the buffalo, running at him, splashing in the muddy water, whooping and snapping. Every time the bull tried to move, they were at him, snarling, biting, and blocking his escape.

As night fell, their yipping attracted others of their clan; hyenas started appearing from between the trees and out of the shadowy grass, ten, fifteen, then twenty. In the end there were over thirty of them milling around in the moonlight, and Simon watched as they tore the buffalo apart, right there in the thigh-deep water of the lagoon, until there was nothing left of him.

But generally hyenas prefer to sleep during the day, lying up in the cool places, on the bare trampled mud around water holes, in the tall grass, under shady thickets. When night falls, they begin their nocturnal raids, often covering vast areas foraging, scavenging, killing if necessary.

They are opportunists. Like most predators they prefer an easy meal, something that can be obtained with a minimum of effort and risk to their own lives. Perhaps more than any other predator they have the instinctive ability to seek out the newborn, the lame, the sick and defenceless.

Doug Skinner, Norman Carr's assistant during the early Wilderness Trails days, was asleep under his mosquito net one night. He was alone in camp, his bed under the open sky, tucked behind a man-high grass fence. He had dosed himself with chloroquin tablets in order to get rid of a bout of malaria, and when he felt something tugging at his pillow in the middle of the night, he put it down to a feverish dream. But a foul smell made him gag and he awoke with a sudden jolt, finding himself staring into the face of a spotted hyena just a few inches away. He

felt paralysed for a second or two, then his involuntary shout made the animal turn and hurry away into the night.

'He must have known I was sick,' Doug said later. 'I don't know if he smelt the fever or what kind of vibes he picked up, but he definitely knew. Otherwise he would never have dared to be so bold.'

In African folklore, hyenas are the outcasts of the bush, the lowliest and most loathsome of all creatures. No other animal is as reviled as *fisi*. They are widely believed to be the accomplices and willing tools of sorcerers. Persons suspected of being witches are known to ride on hyenas' sloping backs at night, cackling maniacally, in order to pursue their victims. Witches carry out much of their nocturnal work in the guise of hyenas, assuming the animal's form in order to kill their victims, and often devour them.

Only owls carry the same stigma, the reputation of being go-betweens, messengers between this world and the one beyond. But owls accomplish their missions in secret, away from curious observation, and only their ghostly cries in the night announce their presence. The way they appear and depart unnoticed, in total silence, leaves no doubt that they have arrived from, or are departing to, the world of the dead.

'Owls are very bad,' Iwomba maintains, his face darkening.

But it is the hyenas that do the dirty work.

They eat mostly dead meat killed by others, and they don't seem to care how

long dead. They come in the night and bite the faces of unwary sleepers. They seek out the sick and they skulk around village huts by moonlight to ambush their victims and drag them away into the bush, sometimes never to be seen again. They are the undertakers: in parts of East Africa, certain tribes leave the bodies of their dead out in the bush for the hyenas to dispose of. Their dental arrangement – sharp incisors, strong canines, and powerful premolars that can crush the bones of a buffalo – coupled with a highly efficient digestive system, ensure that nothing is left of the carcass, human or animal; nothing except perhaps the teeth and parts of the skull, the horns and a few scraps of skin.

Their very appearance brings shudders of uneasiness and mistrust. The short hunchbacked body, the misproportioned legs, the large head with its shadowy eyes. And the misshapen strange-looking genitals, at pains not to reveal the owner's true gender: *are you male, are you female, or are you something else entirely?*

Anyone who has heard the strange giggling, the mournful lowing and the long, drawn-out *whoooo-ooop* of spotted hyenas on a starlit night will understand where these superstitions come from. The sound alone makes you pull your chair a little closer to the fire and look uneasily over your shoulder at the dark whispering bush behind you. The sound alone haunts your dreams.

One night I rode my dirt bike on the old Lukuzi airstrip, looking for owls. As I balanced the bike, riding slowly along the trees lining the runway, one hand on the handlebars and the other shining the powerful beam of my Maglite into the tree-tops, the sloping back of a spotted hyena suddenly appeared in my headlight. I stuck the Maglite into the waistband of my shorts, steered the bike in its direction, and followed. The country was flat and open, the air smelled of dry dust and the remnants of the day's heat still hung in dense pockets above the ground. After riding in the hyena's footprints for a hundred metres or so, the hyena loping in its curious see-sawing gait in my headlight beam, I accelerated and drew level.

From this position, no more than two or three feet away and only slightly higher than his head, I suddenly felt a strong connection to this strange beast, as if the physical closeness had momentarily bridged a much larger gap than mere distance. It was as close as I'd ever been to a large and active and alert wild animal and for the briefest moment I could imagine, I had a *sense* of what it was like to be a hyena, as I loped along in tandem with the creature through the dark night. He flicked its head sideways once or twice; a swift glance, its eye in shadow – but made no move to break away.

Alefer had a story.

When he was a child in the sixth form, he remembers, a hyena terrorised his village – the big village behind the Indian store. All the boys knew something strange was going on. There was a lot of furtive talk amongst the grown-ups that excluded the children, but they soon pieced it together anyway. It seemed that a certain woman went missing every night, just before the hyena made its appearance. The hyena then proceeded to cause havoc, opening doors to huts, stealing food, and scattering pots and pans left by the fire. People lay huddled inside their huts, terrified, while the demonic beast shuffled through the village and kept everyone awake with its maniacal cackle. While this was happening, there was no sign of the woman – she seemed to have disappeared like smoke. There could be only one explanation. A hunter was contacted, a specialist who travelled from another village, to kill the hyena. And when it was dead, there was the irrefutable proof: it had around its neck a bead necklace such as the one worn by the missing woman, and a bracelet round its foreleg. Alefer clamped his left hand around his right wrist to demonstrate.

I nodded. 'But you were a child, so maybe a trick of your memory ...'

'No no no.' he shook his head emphatically. 'There was the proof, the beads. Hard evidence. We all saw it.'

'Has anything like this happened more recently?' I asked, trying to conceal my scepticism behind a mask of curiosity.

'Oh sure. Of course, yes. It happens all the time, everywhere. People can turn into any kind of animal. Often they become bush pigs and go to people's gardens at night and eat their maize.'

'Bush pigs? Not warthogs?'

'No, never warthogs.' He gave me a look. 'Warthogs don't eat maize. And also ... don't you remember last year when that fisherman was killed by a crocodile? That was in fact a man, his enemy, who turned himself into a crocodile and killed him. Actually there were two crocodiles involved.'

He looked grave for a moment then gave a short laugh.

'True. It happens a lot. A lot. Everywhere, even in Lusaka. But especially here. That young boy who was killed by a lion? In Aaron Banda's village recently? You know that village with all the decorations which you liked. Don't you know what happened there?'

I shook my head.

'It was the headman himself who killed the boy. This is true because he confessed when he was confronted. It happened like this. He became a lion and killed the boy right there at Mfuwe Basic School where he was boarding. The parents suspected something and called the *sangoma,* and the headman became frightened and came forward and confessed. He went to the boy's parents and apologised and said yes, it was me. I did this thing, and I am truly sorry. Please forgive me but I assumed the form of a lion and killed your child.'

'And what happened? Was he punished?'

'Of course! He was stripped of his position as headman and was removed from the chief's palace. He had been a chief's *induna* but he was relieved of his duties.'

'Do you know why he killed the boy?'

'It seems he was jealous. The boy was very clever and did well at school and would benefit from his education, while the headman's own sons did not.' Alefer shrugged. 'Just a stupid mistake.'

'But do you really believe all this? You do, don't you?'

'Of course, yes, there is plenty of proof,' he said dismissively.

'In our culture this would be impossible. People would never believe such a thing.'

Alefer laughed a sad laugh and shook his head, and as so often in conversations with him, I had the fleeting sensation of doubt. A sudden need to question my own values, as if a curtain had been drawn aside to reveal a window through which I could see into a world where all this was possible. Where witches riding hyenas could coexist, on some intriguing level, with computers and sophisticated jet engines; a world that allowed us to dream, a world not so exclusively materialistic that all magic, all mysticism, had to be firmly shut out.

'But especially *fisi*,' Alefer continued. 'There was, a few years ago, another documented case; a certain lady, a very powerful businesswoman who owned a bottle store outside Chipata. She was well respected in the community but then one day she died and immediately, *immediately*,

turned into a hyena.'

'And what happened?'

'No, nothing. She ran into the bush and has not been seen to this day.' Alefer nodded his head gravely several times.

*

The hyena had almost reached the end of the runway. Riding next to him, a few feet away, I couldn't help thinking how ordinary he looked. There was certainly no discernible magic about him; he was just another nocturnal animal going about his business. I suppose if he had suddenly gathered speed at the end of the runway and taken off, I would have had to reconsider. But he didn't. He merely glanced at me once or twice, a sidelong glance with the deadpan innocuous expression of an animal that appeared at peace with itself, with no evidence of the demons that were said to torment it.

Just before we reached the end of the runway when the bushes were about to swallow him, I had the sudden urge to extend my left arm and touch him, remembering a zookeeper I once saw patting a tame hyena on the head and scratching behind its ears, just as you would with your Labrador. I resisted the impulse but had the strange feeling that had I reached out, I might have been welcome.

Then again, he might have bitten my hand off.

15   Lion Man

If you ask people what their favourite animal is, you usually end up with the same half dozen or so candidates. Leopard is always a big star, followed by elephant and lion. The fish eagle has a strong following, and so does the giraffe. And then one of those two magnificent antelope, kudu or sable, depending in what kind of country you are.

Ask Arthur Ansell, and he'll say lion. He'll take a drag on his cigarette and say, 'Yeh, lion.'

Arthur is the son of wildlife biologist Frank Ansell, who served in the Northern Rhodesian Game Department and wrote the definitive book on Zambian mammals, and older brother to Patrick. He is a biologist himself by training but at heart, and in his demeanour, he is a soldier. He is stockily built and his hair is always neatly combed. Everything about him looks square: although softened now by middle age, you can still see the hard angles and planes of his face, the set of his shoulders; even the frames of his spectacles are rectangular. He always wakes up at dawn, smokes a couple of cigarettes, drinks a few cups of tea by the fire, and is ready for anything the world wants to throw at him.

He is a farmer in Cornwall from November to May, but comes out to Zambia every year for the safari season to work as a guide for one of the camps. Not for the money, which is negligible and barely covers his bar bill, not for the usual reason – one or two years in the bush before going out into the world to look for a serious job – he's too old for that. Not even out of curiosity or to look for adventure, he's been there and done that too. But because it has become habit, a routine in his life.

Despite his extensive knowledge and experience, Arthur is not always an asset to the safari camp that employs him. While the younger guides are keen to follow the management's instructions, are conscientious, diplomatic with clients and eager to please them, Arthur has none of those qualities. He is his own man, he has paid his dues in the safari world, and he likes to do things his way.

If you're interested in wildlife and the things he can show you, and if he likes you, you couldn't wish for a better guide. But not if you're boring or ordinary. And not if you're a foreigner.

As a soldier and veteran of the British home guard, Arthur is a patriot, and he seems to view it as a necessary tradition to be suspicious of anything not British.

As anyone in the tourist industry will tell you, the national characteristics of people from different countries are always more pronounced outside their own borders. When abroad, Americans tend to be loud and insensitive to the customs of their host countries. Germans focus their interests mainly on the dinner table; the Swiss expect precise timetables for all their activities and do not tolerate any divergence from them. And the island mentality of the British often manifests itself in a haughty arrogance and fierce xenophobia.

Camp managers have learned to take Arthur's prejudices into account, and to avoid potentially embarrassing situations they try to shield problem clients from his lack of tact and diplomacy. But sometimes the best efforts can be in vain.

The radio crackles into life.

'Arthur from Kapani. Arthur, please take the light green Cruiser and collect some clients who are stranded at the airport. They arrived unexpectedly. Someone messed up their booking, and they've been waiting at the airport for an hour. Please apologise and explain the situation.'

'Okay, no problem. I can be there in forty-five minutes. I'll take a cold box, give them some drinks.'

'Yes, good idea. Be nice to them.'

'Of course. You got their names?'

'Not sure. Miller, I think. But it could be Moller or Muller.'

Arthur's eyes narrow.

'They're not German, are they?'

'Don't know, could be. Why?'

'No, just wondering. Okay, I'll get them. Then what?'

'Take them on a night drive. Get Craig to spot for you, he should be back from Nsolo. He'll be at his house.'

Arthur is driving, Craig Doria is in the front seat next to him with the spotlight at his feet. Right now Craig is a passenger, another pair of eyes. Later, when night falls, he'll be the 'spotter'; he will shine the spotlight into the trees and the tall grass and try to pick out the leopard's eyes from those of the genets and hippos and impala and all the other eyes glowing in the darkness. Behind them, on the two bench seats, the six tourists sit with their cameras and binoculars. There is a low hum of voices with foreign accents.

Arthur stops at a colony of carmine bee-eaters. It is late afternoon, the sun is hanging low in the sky, just touching the trees on the far side of the river and casting its slanting light on the bank below them where hundreds of the blue and crimson birds have dug their tunnels into the steep river bank for the females to lay their eggs. There is a flurry of activity as the birds chirp and chatter and flutter around the car and in and out of their nests in a last burst of energy before their day ends.

There is another flurry of activity – the clicking of camera shutters in the back of the Land Cruiser. Arthur, trying to ignore the insult of the foreigners' presence, has given his little talk on the breeding behaviour of the carmines – 'they are inter-African migrants who arrive in the Valley in September and start these large breeding colonies that you see here below us …' and he sits behind the wheel,

impatiently drumming his fingers and waiting for the clicking to stop.

After a few more minutes he puts the car into gear and, without turning around to the clients, moves off. They haven't gone far before he hears a voice behind him.

'Excuse me plees. Can ve go back, I dropped ze lens cap.'

'Collaborators,' whispers Arthur.

I'm spending a night at Nsolo camp. Nsolo is built entirely from local bush materials with great attention to detail. It is Kapani's luxury bush camp and Craig and Janelle Doria, who are managing it this season, are justly proud of the place. It is situated in a grove of *Khaya nyassica* trees in a bend

Arthur stops the car and reverses to where they had been parked. He sighs, gets out of the car and bends down to pick up the plastic cap and holds it up to the man, unsmiling and muttering something that sounds to Craig like, 'Be a bit more careful ze next time …'

As they drive off, Craig leans across and whispers, 'Arthur, what are you doing, man? Why are you being so rude?'

'Bloody Germans,' hisses Arthur.

'So what?' says Craig. 'But actually I don't think so. I think they're Belgian.'

of the Luwi river, a two-hour walk downstream from Luwi Camp, another of Kapani's small satellite camps inside the park. The guests tonight are a young American couple and two middle-aged men. During dinner, I notice that one of them has an accent, possibly German. Over coffee and cheese we suddenly hear the sound of a Land Cruiser bumping along the track into camp. Craig and Janelle look at each other, then at me.

'Any idea who that can be?' Craig asks. I shake my head.

'Unusual to get visitors at this time of night, out here in the middle of the bush,' Craig explains to the Americans.

'Oh, it's probably Arthur,' says Janelle. She turns to the two men sitting beside her. 'He's the manager of Luwi camp this season. I think it's empty tonight.'

Craig nods. 'Must be him, looking for company.'

The motor has been switched off, and in the light of the paraffin lamps that line the sandy path, I see Arthur walking towards us. He is wearing an army parka and is carrying something in his hand, something long, slim and black. He enters the dining room and says, quite loudly, as he reaches the table, 'Hey Craig, look at this!' and slams a five-foot cobra down among the plates and dishes and coffee cups. The American woman jumps off her chair, nearly overturning it, and stares.

'Jesus Christ, Arthur! What the hell …' Craig is on his feet too.

'Is it alive?' asks the American woman, her voice shaking.

Craig shakes his head. 'No, it's not, don't worry … but … Arthur, man!'

The snake lies still, looking very black on the white table cloth among the silver cutlery. Arthur reaches down and grabs it by the neck and starts pushing it around the table. 'Well, I'm not sure …' he cackles.

The American girl has both her hands to her cheeks, eyes wide, muttering, 'Oh my God I do not believe this.' The German says something. Arthur stares at him a moment, takes the cigarette out of his mouth and puts it between the cobra's fangs.

'Oh, just ignore him,' Janelle looks at the American girl with a suppressed chuckle. I can see the secret amusement in her eyes. 'It's just Arthur. You've heard of English eccentrics, haven't you? Well, you're seeing a live one …'

Her husband has put his arm around her shoulder. He is looking at Arthur in frank amazement.

'Where did you find it? Was it dead or did you kill it?'

'When the Germans marched into Stalingrad …' says Arthur, and Craig shoots him a look that is both steely and pleading at the same time.

'Hey, Arthur, take the bloody thing away, man. We were just having coffee when you arrived. Anyone for more coffee?' He holds up the coffee pot.

'Kill it?' says Arthur, suddenly looking serious. 'I would never kill a snake. Never. Would you, Craig?' He knows Craig is mad about snakes and keeps some in a fish tank in his hut.

'Well …' Craig pauses a few seconds, 'under certain circumstances I probably would … I mean some of these things are dangerous. If a cobra or a mamba threatened one of my kids, yeah, I'd kill it. Before it killed them.'

'You'd try and catch it first, though, wouldn't you? Before you killed it?'

'Don't have any kids yet,' says Janelle.

'No, Arthur, what I'm saying is … if it's a situation where I'd have to act quickly, where there's no time to mess around …'

Arthur shakes his head. 'Hm-mm, I'd hate to kill a snake. I'm sorry this one's

135

dead, poor thing.'

All four clients are staring at Arthur, who has lowered his eyes to the snake.

'Poor bloody snake.' he says softly.

The German, confusion all over his face, mutters: '. . . Stalingrad?'

Arthur and I are sitting on bar stools at the Kapani bar, drinking beer. All the clients are out in the bush on their evening game drives and the camp looks empty. Arthur is playing absent-mindedly with his packet of cigarettes and box of matches. Chitumbe is hunched on his perch behind the bar, his eyes staring past us into the distance.

'If what you're saying is true,' I say, 'if all art, architecture, music and so on is rubbish, how come it has all survived for so long?'

'Marching music's all right. Bagpipes . . . Chitumbe, bring me another beer.' Arthur looks at me over the top of his glasses. 'You want one? No?'

'Arthur. Listen. You're telling me that only science can explain the mysteries of the universe, that any attempt to understand ourselves through art, literature, philosophy, is crap. Is that right?'

'Just one, Chitumbe. Yeh, something like that.'

'So you would be quite happy living in, say, Moscow?'

He pours his beer into the mug and takes a long sip. 'When you look at a herd of eland,' he says, 'what are you looking at? Just saying to yourself, oh look at all the pretty antelope.'

'Yeah, I look at their colour, the shape

of their horns. At the way their ears rotate and try to pick up sounds on the wind. I look at the way their muscles tense when they're about to run.'

I grin at him. 'I know what *you* do. You count them. You see how many males, how many females. How many calves and sub-adults. And you think you understand them better than I do.'

Arthur shakes his head in an exaggerated manner, his whole upper body weaving back and forth on the bar stool.

'Nooooo,' he says patiently, in the tone of voice he might use to a backward child. 'I also pay attention to the habitat, I notice what type of grass they're eating, see if the area has been overgrazed. I look at the trees around the area. What kind of trees, whether there is a browse line. Which animals made the browse line. I note the condition of the animals. I may go and examine some of their droppings.' He gives me a look of patient disgust.

'Oh look-at-all-the-buck. All the pretty, pretty antelope. He lifts his beer mug and drinks deeply from it, and a look of boredom passes over his face. We have been here before, many times.

'The Victorians had a need to classify everything,' I say. 'They went around the world collecting specimens . . .'

Arthur has taken a handful of peanuts from a bowl on the bar counter and is throwing them, one by one, at his match box. 'These are Allied bombs falling on Cologne,' he mutters.

'. . . and then they took them home to their museums . . .'

'And this is Hamburg.' More peanuts.

'... and then they tried to put everything into neat categories and labelled everything.'

Arthur has set fire to his matchbox. 'This is Dresden burning.'

'But the old Romans had a saying ...' I gaze at the burning matchbox. 'To name is not to know.'

He watches the fire go out, takes a long sip of beer, and lights another cigarette from his last one.

'I know you're not a true German any more but you were born there, so that makes you one. In my opinion there are only two good Germans in the world. You and that model, Claudia Schiffer.'

demarcates Jake's own square of privacy, wedged in between the ablution blocks and overland trucks of Flatdogs Camp on one side, and the general shambles of the Luangwa Croc Farm on the other. In front of his house is the river.

A year or two later, Arthur has teamed up with Jake da Motta for the season and has put up a small tent in the enclosed yard in front of Jake's little house. This is where he sleeps. Jake can hear him moving around inside in the early morning, then the sound of the zip opening like tearing cloth, and Arthur's head emerges along with a cloud of cigarette smoke. The head looks all around, mongoose-like, and then Arthur climbs out, stretches and walks over to the blackened wood stove in the corner of Jake's veranda for his first cup of tea.

The purpose of the wire fence surrounding the yard is to keep the dogs in and the crocodiles and hippos out. It also

Jake has made a deal with Charl Beukes, owner of the Croc Farm, to use some of the Croc Farm's land for his new camping site. There has never been any budget accommodation or any camping facilities in the Valley before, and Jake's new venture is to address that need and fill the gap. The site occupies two hundred metres of the Croc Farm's river frontage and is appropriately named Flatdogs Camp.

Arthur talks a lot about his farm in Cornwall, about the lambing season, getting up in the middle of the night to assist a ewe in a difficult birth, taking the runts (do you call them runts?) into his own bed and bottle-feeding them three times a night. 'Do you know some of the names he gives them?' asks Jake. '"Mrs Chicken-head". And "No. 84". And of course the names of his girlfriends.'

Arthur looks up briefly from his computer. Wood smoke is rising from the stove where a tea kettle is hissing. Milo, Ranger and New Dog are chasing each other around the porch, then out to the fence and back again. The rickety table is laden with books, scribbled notes, an empty tequila bottle, a sugar bowl, some tea mugs.

Arthur's love life is an enigma. He hasn't had a girlfriend for years, it seems, but each season he falls in love. Each season the object of his affection is more unsuitable than the last. He gets older, the girls get younger (Arthur, wake up man … she looks on you as a kind old uncle, not a potential lover. What are you thinking …) and with each passing year the possibility of romance, of an actual affair, becomes more remote. But Arthur will not be deterred. He buys presents, he writes letters, he says, 'Just give it time, she'll see me for what I am, and it'll work out …' And when the season ends he will go home to the farm and name a new lamb after her.

'Charmaine,' says Jake. 'Zoe, Katie …'

The sun reflects briefly off Arthur's glasses as he looks up at Jake. His gaze settles back on the computer screen. 'Now if I move my artillery over here, behind this rise …'

'Want some tea, Arthur?' Jake has lifted the kettle off the smoking wood stove and is holding it up in the air. Arthur is engrossed in his game. 'Now the Germans are over here, in front of this forest. But I can't go there because of the tanks. What? Yeh.'

An overland traveller from the camp-site has come up to the fence and is leaning over it. He has spiky hair and an untidy beard and wears sandals and pink shorts that cover his knees. Three small earrings shine in his left ear lobe.

'Jake. Hey, Jake!' Jake is pouring hot water into the tea mugs he has lined up at the edge of the table. He looks over his shoulder. 'Oh, it's you again. Yes, what is it now?'

'Jake, listen. There are four of us in our group, we all want to book a night drive. Any chance of a discount? There's four of us, we thought you …' Jake sighs, shifts the hot kettle to his left hand and cocks his thumb at a yellowing hand-written sign stapled to the wall. Then he turns back to the table, puts the kettle down and starts spooning sugar into the mugs.

The overlander is peering at the sign. It says: 'FLATDOGS camp offers the most affordable accommodation in South Luangwa National Park. Quibbling about our prices makes you the biggest cheap-skate in 9050 square kilometres.' The camper clucks his tongue and walks away, shaking his head. Jake, too, shakes his head and snorts. 'These people,' he says. He puts a tea mug in front of Arthur's computer. 'Do you want this, or what?' Arthur nods absent-mindedly. Milo comes and lies down in the shade under the table and lifts one eyebrow at Jake. Ranger and

New Dog are still patrolling the fence, looking for mice.

'I've never seen anyone drink as much tea as you do. You drink the stuff from morning to night.'

'Till six o'clock,' says Arthur.

'And then?'

'Then I drink beer.'

Jake nods.

'How is your brother these days?' he asks. 'Does he ever want to come back to Zambia, do safari work again?'

'Naw. He talks about it a lot. About the good old Chibembe days. But he thinks the place has changed too much and he won't fit in any more.'

'Well, it has.'

'Yeh, but it's still the Valley. The animals are still here. Just got a bit busier that's all.'

'He'll be back, I'm sure. I hear he's upset with you because you wanted to shoot him.'

Arthur looks up from his computer and tilts his head skyward. He rolls his eyes. 'That's such crap. Someone overheard a conversation I had with him, and suddenly there's this rumour going around.'

'But you did say you would shoot him.'

'No, man. That's completely out of context. We were talking about a war situation. I explained to him that, in war, deserters had to be shot. And, typical Patrick, he asks me if I was his commanding officer and he was deserting, would I have him shot.'

Jake nods.

'And what did you say?'

'I said yeh, I would have to. And I would.'

'Oh.'

'And he gets all upset and goes around telling everyone that I want to shoot him. His own brother would shoot him.'

'Well, that's Patrick.'

'Yeh, that's Patrick.'

'But you *would* shoot him. Your own brother.'

Arthur stares at Jake, exasperated. 'I told you, it's a hypothetical situation. If we were at war. What do you know about war? Nothing.'

'Quite.'

We were parked at the edge of an open pan with dark trees around its rim. Dusk was gathering around us. The sun had glowed briefly through the trees like burning coals and lined the branches red-gold and then quickly disappeared. A breeze stirred in the leaves and bent the tall yellow grass that stood in patches on the open ground.

Five of us, in two vehicles. Hugo Jachman, the biologist from Chipata, and Katinka de Balogh, a Dutch wildlife vet based in Lusaka, in my Land Cruiser; Arthur in an open Toyota HiLux with Robin Pope. Our mission was to try to remove the radio collar from a lioness that had been one of the subjects of a research project conducted by a Japanese biologist. When the project ran out of funding, Koje Yamasaki went home but neglected to remove the lions' collars. They were young animals, still growing, and a year or two later the collars had become so tight that they were threatening to choke them.

The lioness had been seen that afternoon in the area around Mwanalunga and Baka-Baka lagoons, a network of oxbows east of the Luangwa river in Nsefu sector. One of Robin's drivers had spotted her lying up under a thorn thicket, and as dusk fell, we were ready for action. Each vehicle had a powerful spotlight; Hugo Jachmann had a dart gun loaded with immobilising serum. Katinka, the beautiful vet, had a case of injectable penicillin and various other drugs and ointments. We had wire-cutters, pliers, pens and notepads and hand-held radios.

We waited until darkness settled and moved off, driving slowly around the perimeter of the *dambo* in opposite directions, Robin going east, our car turning west in the direction of the river. Hugo was in the back with the dart gun, Katinka in the seat beside me holding the spotlight and scanning the dark trees that stood at the edge of the pan. The beam picked out the eyes of impala and puku between the tree trunks and the occasional twin catseyes of genets glowing in the branches.

After ten minutes, perhaps less, we found the lioness lying under a combretum bush in some tufts of grass. We called the other car on the radio.

Hugo spoke softly into the mike, 'Arthur, we've got her. She's under a bush near that steep gully at the northwest end. You can probably see our light.'

'Roger, I see it. We're less than a couple of k's away from you, coming over.'

A dart gun is only effective at a range of twenty to thirty metres. I put the Land Cruiser into first gear and slowly moved closer, listening to the tyres crunching over the hard ground, breaking chunks of bone-dry clay under our weight. Katinka kept the spotlight beam away from the lion's face and we eased up to her metre by metre until we were in a position for Hugo to have a clean shot. I heard Robin's vehicle pull up behind us, and then heard the swish of the dart and saw it hit the lion's haunch. She jumped and started running.

Hugo nodded urgently at me, 'Quick! Don't let her get away.' I had the car in gear and let out the clutch. Hugo had another dart ready and was reloading the gun as the car bumped across the uneven cotton soil. The lioness picked up speed and we followed. I tried to keep a distance that was not too close to spook her and chase her into thick cover, yet close enough not to lose her. As long as she stayed on the open *dambo*, we had no trouble keeping her in sight.

So far, so good.

She was running at a steady pace. Robin's vehicle was behind us; their spotlight flashed in my rear view mirror and momentarily blinded me, then I saw the lioness change direction and head towards a clump of bushes and winter thorns in the middle of the pan. She circled a bush and then abruptly lay down beside it.

I drove slowly to within twenty metres of her, and as the car came to a stop, Hugo fired. The dart hit her again, and again she jumped up and ran.

I felt the rear wheels spinning on the dry ground as I quickly let out the clutch.

'Do you think we misjudged the dose?' Katinka said next to me, turning towards Hugo. 'Surely she should be going down now.'

'Ja, it's strange. According to her body weight we should be on target.'

'Maybe we misjudged her weight? A hundred kilograms – maybe she's heavier. Look at her run, I can't believe it.'

The lioness had changed direction again and was now heading towards a dense wood on the far side of the dry lagoon. The ground got rougher under our wheels and the Land Cruiser bounced on its springs. I shot a quick glance at the speedometer in front of me: 25 kph.

'Maybe there's something wrong with the drugs; I've had them in the fridge but maybe they got too hot somewhere else.' Hugo held up the handset. 'Arthur, do you still see her?'

During the chase across the open pan, I noticed the HiLux had fallen back, its headlights dimmer in the dark night behind us.

'Roger, roger. Hope she's not going for that forest, we'll never follow her in there.'

'Damn right,' said Hugo into the mike. 'Why don't you try and pass her and outflank her. Then you can try to cut her off if she heads that way.'

'Roger that.'

But it was too late.

'Look out! Jesus Christ!'

The lion had suddenly broken to the left in mid-stride like a rugby player, and was running straight for the forest. I jerked the wheel sharply and we bounced after her. Dozens of pale trunks loomed up in our headlights and, as we came closer, I saw that they were not mature trees but the springy trunks of half-grown trees no thicker than my arm. I suddenly remembered that I had been here before; I knew these trees, this dense field of immature rain trees.

'Thank God they're young trees,' Hugo shouted from the back, 'maybe we can make it.'

I felt Katinka's eyes on me. 'Such a shame if we lost her now.'

We all knew that if the lioness escaped us and collapsed somewhere in the thick of this woodland, we'd never find her again before morning. But the hyenas would, and sometime during the night they would lose their fear and sidle closer and one of them, emboldened by the whooping of the others, would take the first jabbing bite, and the others would crowd in and they would start feeding on the immobilised cat.

The lioness had entered the forest at a flat-out run. I saw her shape amongst the trees in the beam of our spotlight. I pushed down hard on the accelerator. 'Hold tight!'

She was more shadow now than cat, difficult to make out among the boles and the undergrowth, and as we hit the first tree trunk, the spotlight went out.

'Jesus Christ!' shouted Hugo again. 'Stay close. Stay close. Don't lose her!' Without the mobility of the spotlight we had to keep her within the arc of the car's headlights, or she would disappear into the darkness and the trees and bushes would swallow her. I accelerated again, trying to close the gap while manoeuvring the Cruiser through the forest at speed, avoiding the bigger trunks and flattening anything else that stood in our way. I heard and saw the thin trees crashing all around us, heard the metallic sound of bushes and thorns scratching the sides of the car.

'Keep going, keep going,' Hugo was shouting unnecessarily from the back seat. The night was even darker in here; the forest seemed to close in on us, and its density, its smells, appeared to engulf us. I felt a sudden sense of disorientation and struggled to keep my eyes on the only fixed point in this maze, the ghost-like shape of the lioness weaving through the trees in front of us.

We finally emerged into open ground once more, on to the deeply crevassed cotton soil. The lion was still running in our headlights. The radio crackled, we heard Arthur's voice.

'Where the hell are you?'

'Arthur, we managed to follow her through the *Lonchocarpus* grove. If you circle around the north edge of the forest, you'll see us. We're still with her, just on the edge of Chembwe lagoon.'

'Roger, see you there. Standing by.'

The lioness had slowed down and stopped. She stood, swaying uncertainly, and suddenly it seemed that all her charged-up power left her at once, as if someone had pulled a plug, and she collapsed like a rag doll. I switched off the engine five metres from her and all of a sudden the night was still, like the silence at the end of the movie before the house lights come on and the audience starts shuffling to their feet.

We climbed out of the car and looked at each other. An owl called from the trees and the croaking of frogs sounded from the nearby lagoon. A small cloud of fine powdery dust rose where she had fallen. It eddied and swirled and drifted through the twin columns of our headlight beams and slowly settled on her motionless body and the great head lying on its side on the ground. Her eyes were open and staring into nowhere.

Tyres crunched on the clay behind us; Robin and Arthur drew alongside, stopped and climbed out of the HiLux. It was time to go to work.

Arthur pulled her tail and stretched and measured her from her muzzle to the black tuft at the end of her tail. He stood up straight and looked down at the immobile form for a long moment, then he straddled her and lowered himself on to her chest. Crouching astride her, supported by his knees on either side of her body, he reached for the wire-cutters sticking out of his hip pocket.

Katinka knelt beside him with a bottle of disinfectant and the contents of her medical kit laid out next to her but although the radio collar had bitten deep into the folds of the animal's neck, it had not broken the skin and there was no

evidence of infection. Katinka held up her thermometer and made notations on her clipboard. Arthur shifted forward and, still astride the lioness, opened her jaws with both his hands, pulling back the flaps of skin with his thumbs and exposing the teeth. 'Do you want to measure her canines?'

I shuddered involuntarily. Katinka nodded.

'Yes, good idea.'

There was something almost affectionate in the way he bared her teeth, an intimacy that would, of course, not have been possible if the lion were conscious and that was therefore all the more intense. I would not have been surprised if Arthur had bent down and quickly kissed her.

They worked quickly and efficiently like a team of well-trained surgeons (perhaps mechanics was a better word?). Arthur had one hand inside the lion's mouth. With the other he fished in his shirt pocket for his cigarettes. Hugo held out his lighter and flicked it. Arthur inhaled deeply, dropped the pack back in his pocket and briefly knuckled his eyes. He passed his hand over the rough surface of the lion's tongue, grabbed the thick muscle firmly and pulled it. He blew out a plume of smoke and muttered softly, 'There you go, we don't want you to choke now, do we.'

The owl called again. The leaves above us swayed in a slight breeze. I looked at the quarter moon drifting on its back in the clouds like a small boat on a vast sea.

Arthur grabbed one of the massive paws, lifted it and pressed hard on the pads to extend the claws. He stared at the sharp points as if in meditation, then gently dropped the paw on to the ground. His gaze shifted to her face, her unblinking eyes, and lingered there intently, almost lovingly, in what seemed to me an attempt at non-verbal cross-species communication.

Robin and I looked at each other.

'Most unusual way to pass the evening, this . . .' Robin grinned.

Later that same year, in September when the weather had turned hot and the mopane trees had lost their leaves and their branches stood out bare and brittle against the white-blue sky, some of the drivers encountered a male lion with a snare around his neck. He was often seen in the company of another male of similar age, possibly a sibling. They were three or four years old, neither of them with a particularly impressive mane but both of them healthy lions about to reach their prime.

The wire snare had cut deep into his neck, exposing flesh and sinew festering with infection.

Hugo Jachman was in the Valley flying aerial transects for his annual elephant survey and he decided to try and dart the

lion and remove the snare. But it was easier said than done.

Although game viewers saw him often, and although Hugo and Arthur followed every lead, the lion eluded them. They had numerous reports of sightings in broad daylight but when they went after him with the dart gun, he was gone. They finally decided that the only way to get close enough for a shot was to bait him. After liaising with the Parks Department and obtaining permission, they went out and shot a zebra in the GMA on the other side of the river, not far from where the lion had last been seen. Lions regularly cross the river, and the idea was to lure him to the other side and dart him while he was feeding on the zebra. But things went wrong. After covering the dead zebra with branches to keep off the vultures, they started walking back to their car. But where was it? They had parked it under a tree when they first spotted the zebra herd and followed them on foot, and now they suddenly weren't sure. The country was featureless and monotonous; small plains among the hills, and endless yellow elephant grass dotted with occasional thorn trees.

They kept walking, trying to look over the tall grass and scan the country in all directions. Perhaps they walked past the Cruiser, just twenty metres away, and missed it in the yellow grass. In any event, they spent the entire day walking among the maze of plains below the Nchindene hills. They had no compass and no water and with the temperature over forty degrees and the heat reflecting off the stark hills, their mood slowly turned sour.

But there was no option other than to carry on and the sun was almost down and the eastern slopes of the hills lay in shadow when finally, exhausted and dehydrated and bad-tempered, they found their abandoned vehicle and made it back to Kapani by nightfall, only to be told that the lions had been seen that afternoon at Luangwa Wafwa lagoon, twenty kilometres to the north.

Although dog-tired, they decided that they could not afford to miss this opportunity. They radioed Jake at Flatdogs to join them and also got Nick Aslin, the new Kapani manager, to bring one of Kapani's rifles. After a quick supper, they found themselves out in the bush again, once more looking for lions.

They spotted the two males off the north road on the west side of Luangwa Wafwa lagoon and Hugo darted the snared lion who ran sixty or seventy paces and went down in the sand by the edge of the lagoon while his companion took off into the moonlit night. They worked on the immobilised lion by the light of a torch and the moon and a million stars that reflected off the quiet water. Arthur used wire cutters to remove the deeply embedded snare. Once again there was a familiarity in his movements, an attitude of casual intimacy, as if he and the lion knew each other well and had been friends a long time. There was something in his gestures that was reminiscent of the camaraderie of two soldiers, an unspoken agreement, like helping a drunk buddy off the bar stool and into a taxi.

They cut out the dead flesh and

doused the wound in iodine and antibiotic powder. They injected penicillin and, because it is unsettling to touch and push and pull an adult lion who is asleep but breathing and may just wake up any minute, Hugo administered a second dose of the immobilising agent, Zoletol 100. When they had finished their work, it was an hour before midnight, and they retreated to their Land Cruiser, which they had parked up on the ridge fifteen metres behind them, to sit and watch.

Now came the long wait. Every ten minutes they shone their spotlight on the unconscious lion and on the surrounding bush and over the water where the crocs were waiting. Nick had the Lodge's .375 Parker-Hale and Jake held his Winchester 12-bore pump-action in case a hyena should venture too close. They were dressed in nothing but shorts and T-shirts, which were all they needed during the hot day but which proved totally inadequate as the night grew colder. One of them had had the foresight to bring a bottle of whisky to keep them warm which, as Jake later recounted, may have had something to do with the events that followed.

By 2 am the lion had still not moved. They sat in the open vehicle shivering, bored, impatient, Arthur and Hugo more tired than they'd ever been. At one point Hugo got out and walked over to the lion shouting, 'Wake up, you!' and gave him a gentle kick in the ribs. The lion didn't move. The second dose of Zoletol had ensured a long and sound sleep.

Finally, at about three in the morning when the night was at its darkest and coldest, and the four men were weary from fighting sleep, the lion slowly got to his feet. He looked around uncertainly, and the four, instantly alert again, started the car, checked spotlight and weapons, and got ready to follow. But instead of moving off into the bush, the lion, obviously still drowsy and confused, headed in the opposite direction and ran straight into the shallow water of the lagoon.

They have the spotlight beam on him and see him standing there in three feet of water with his head just above the surface. Jake pumps a round into the chamber of the shotgun and Hugo grabs the .375 and flicks the safety catch; they can see the green eyes of crocodiles moving in.

Suddenly, without a word, Arthur drops the spotlight he is holding and rushes into the water after the lion. Jake sees the crocs sliding closer. He hesitates only a few seconds, then he follows, splashing into the lagoon with the 12-bore held high. The other two watch incredulously as Arthur catches up with the lion who has now reached deeper water and is beginning to sink. Three times he has gone down and three times he has come up again.

Jake's eyes widen in disbelief as Arthur puts his arm around the lion's neck, straining to keep the big head above the water. But the lion has already swallowed a lung-full. Arthur looks wildly around him, at the flat water, the distant trees. Then he takes a deep breath and puts his open mouth to the lion's nose and starts blowing, a desperate attempt at the kiss of life. Jake can't believe what he is seeing and hears himself shout, 'Arthur, if this works, what are you going to do next?'

For second after second nothing happens. The cold moonlight seems to have frozen the moment – a strange tableau – in a paralysis of arrested time, to be for ever etched on the participants' memories. Jake in the water and the other two behind him, up on the bank. But in the end there is nothing left for them to do but stand by impotently with their guns and watch as the lion finally slips out of Arthur's grasp and drowns.

Most people who hear this story flatly refuse to believe it. But it is true, it happened.

Others say, Oh what a shame, the lion died.

They miss the point, don't they?

16 Snakes

A two-metre long, black-necked spitting cobra, one of the scariest of all snakes, once came into the Kapani bar. No one saw it slither across the cool dry cement floor but when Chitumbe opened the bar that evening and moved some crates and boxes that were stacked against the wall behind the counter, he noticed something black moving behind them. He called 'Njoka!' in a voice both cool and matter of fact and took some hasty steps backwards. In the doorway he collided with Arthur, who had come off his barstool like a cat off a windowsill.

'Where? Oh, I see it.' Then, his voice assuming its military tone, Arthur commanded, 'Stand back everyone.' Everyone did. Everyone except Patrick who never could watch his older brother steal all the limelight, and who could sniff out a potential accident with the nose of a bloodhound, often not only to be the first at the scene, but to be its first victim.

'You too, Patrick,' said Arthur but Patrick had already squeezed through the open doorway and, elbowing his brother out of the way, he faced the snake. Its head was half a metre off the ground now and weaving from side to side, its hood spread like an evil black shield behind its neck. Its intended menace was unmistakable. It is said that cobras mesmerise potential victims with the slow weaving dance of their heads and their unblinking eyes; if this is true, then Patrick was a willing subject. With hypnotic deliberation, he lowered himself into a cowboy crouch and stared back at the snake.

There is something atavistic about facing a cobra with its hood spread – a threat and a sort of arrogance completely out of proportion with what is actually taking place. A shield of skin and muscle extending behind a snake's head is not dangerous in itself; and, after all, the snake is a good deal smaller than you, and poses no threat as long as you keep your distance. But the sight of it nevertheless produces an immediate rush of adrenalin and quickening of the heartbeat, along with a feeling I can only describe as insulting: how dare that thing scare me so?

'Don't move, anybody,' said Patrick. As if we would. Even Arthur, more competent and experienced in handling snakes than his brother, stood still. Marvelling at Patrick's stupidity, it seemed.

'Someone find me a stick. Or a broom handle. Quick!' Arthur hissed. But it was too late. The snake spat. The venom left its dark mouth in a fine mist that seemed to hang in the air, clearly visible under the bar lights, and struck Patrick's eyes. Patrick jumped, stood ramrod-straight for a second or two, and then collapsed on the floor, both hands clamped to his eyes.

The cobra recoiled. Chitumbe said, 'Ah-ah-ah.'

Arthur uttered a short string of clipped vowels like a parade-ground order and hurled himself at the snake, a short bamboo stick clamped in his hand like a baton. There was a flurry of movement – arms, stick and black snake – and in a matter of seconds he had the head pinned to the floor, the long body writhing among the reflections from the overhead lights that danced on the polished cement. Kneeling beside the cobra, he clamped his right hand around its neck just behind the angular jawbones, thumb and fingers squeezing like pliers, and released the downward pressure of the stick. Then he wiped his forehead with the sleeve of his left arm and looked up at me. 'What do we do now?'

I stared down at the sinister-looking head. 'Croc Farm?' I suggested. The Croc Farm had recently added some snake pits and reptile display cases to its exhibit area, and the boys were always on the lookout for new residents.

'Good idea,' nodded Arthur, slowly raising the snake off the floor. His left hand was now fastened firmly about its body, roughly midway, the right still clutching the neck. 'How do we get it there? Can anybody find a sack of some kind? Chitumbe . . . a sack!'

'Sack,' nodded Chitumbe and hurried across the courtyard behind the bar. We heard the screen door of the kitchen slam behind him. A crowd of tourists had gathered around Arthur, all staring at the snake straining to free itself.

'You gonna drive me?' said Arthur. I looked at the fighting snake. The power of its contracting muscles made Arthur's

arms move sinuously as if they were fellow reptiles. It reminded me of the mating dance of some giant lizards that I had once seen on National Geographic.

'Ah . . . sure.'

We heard Patrick moaning and thrashing about on the grass of the little courtyard, and Pam's voice, soothing but firm: 'Hold still, man. Christ, how can I

wash out your eyes if you keep moving?'

'But it hurts!'

'Of course it hurts. Now shut up!'

Arthur said, 'Serves him right.' Then, with an impatient look at the kitchen door where Chitumbe had disappeared, 'Oh, let's just go.'

When we reached my Cruiser, Arthur climbed on to the passenger seat. I saw the key wasn't in the ignition and patted my pockets.

'Jesus,' muttered Arthur.

'Hang on. They've gotta be here somewhere. Oh, here we go.'

I could see Arthur's arms were getting tired. The veins on his forearms were bulging, and there were beads of sweat on his face. It was a ten-minute drive to the Croc Farm. With the thought of a two-metre cobra loose in the cab, we did it in about five.

Early the next morning we stood around the fire watching the red charcoal hissing under the tea kettle. The dawn was still grey and uncertain, still trying to make up its mind what sort of a day to present to us. Patrick's eyes were hidden behind his dark glasses and his face looked puffy.

'So you made it to the Croc Farm?' he asked.

'Only just.' I grinned at Arthur. 'How are your arms?'

'Can't be as bad as my eyes,' said

Patrick.

    'Oh, did that hurt?'

    'Jesus.'

    'You asked for it. Bloody hell, you invited him to spit at you.'

    'Jesus, you guys. No sympathy, hey?'

    Arthur shook his head, 'No.'

My own last encounter with a dangerous snake was more straightforward. I shot it. A visiting friend was staying in one of our grass huts, and one afternoon the soporific silence of siesta-time was shattered by a piercing scream for help. When I entered the dim interior of the hut, I saw Noreen lying rigid on her back on top of the bed, her eyes fixed on the ceiling where a light-green snake was moving about in the thatch. It was a boomslang. A big one.

    Boomslang carry a deadly venom, but being back-fanged and timid, they seldom pose any real danger to humans. If they do manage to bite and inject a full dose into you, you're done for. Unless you receive immediate medical attention, your chances of survival are almost zero. I didn't want that to happen to Noreen. But I suppose I also wanted to impress her, to show her what a cool customer I was and how calmly I dealt with hazardous situations like impending snake attacks. So I told her to stay put and fetched the shotgun. When I returned, the snake was still in the thatch above her head. It hadn't fallen on her and savaged her, but I raised the gun anyway and pulled the trigger.

    The shell, at such close range, cut the snake in two. It fell out of the roof in two separate parts that twitched and thrashed on the floor next to the bed. I stared down at the floor, the acrid tang of gunpowder in my nostrils, and watched, mesmerised, as the head raised itself on its bloody torso, opened its mouth wide and came for me. The forked tongue flicked at me, the jaws were hinged open in a ninety-degree angle, and the dying half-snake slithered towards me, its eyes filled with undiluted aggression.

    It is hard to say what I felt. Revulsion, panic, awe, horror. But that wasn't really it. Human language must have evolved long after we had to deal with situations like these on a regular basis, for there are absolutely no accurate words for it. Perhaps an inarticulate grunt, a wordless gulp for air is the only appropriate response.

    Before the half-snake could reach me, it died. Somewhere at the back of my mind, I felt a quick stab of guilt. Sorrow at having destroyed a living thing, yes, but it cut deeper. What had just happened touched on the mystical, the snake as archetype – as symbol of evil, of temptation.

    And it also revealed the desperate struggle of a living organism to cling to life and, by extension, the preciousness of all life, even a snake's.

Later that day, Norman waved a knobbly finger at me and asked, 'Was that a shot I heard earlier on?'

    I told him I had shot a boomslang. 'That was brave of you,' he said. His expression was neutral, but did I detect a note of disapproval in his voice?

    Maybe I blushed, maybe not. But I was

not particularly proud of myself, and that night I had strange dreams of two-headed reptiles and fire-spewing dragons.

I still had a few things to learn, it seemed. I remembered how Norman once handled a similar situation.

We are standing on the beach of Lake Malawi. Far out on the lake, a solitary cormorant is bobbing in the waves, drifting slowly in our direction. Norman points with his arm.

'That's Monkey Bay over there, to the right of that range of hills. You see that cormorant? In line with that palm trunk sticking out of the water. About three hundred yards behind it.'

But as it comes closer, it doesn't really look like a cormorant any more. Its black head is weaving from side to side, and even from this distance there is something sinuous about its movements, something very unbirdlike. Norman frowns and raises the binoculars hanging round his neck.

'You know, I think it's a snake. Looks like it has swum all the way across the bay. Let's see what kind it is.' We walk towards the spot where the thing has chosen to come ashore, and sure enough, a long black snake slithers out of the water on to the warm sand. Norman drops on one knee and quickly, with a blur of his right hand, grips the snake behind its head. He slowly straightens, grimacing at a twinge in his back, and holds up the snake for us to see. 'It's a mamba,' he says and looks around for some bushes where he can release the snake. Although obviously exhausted after its long swim, the snake still has enough fight to struggle in Norman's grip.

Some barefoot village children have come along the beach and are staring at us.

Norman looks at them and shakes his head.

'I can't let a mamba loose among these kids,' he says. 'It's a pity but I'll have to kill it.'

He holds the snake behind its head – strong muscles contracting – with one hand while with the other he fishes in his shorts pocket for his Swiss army knife. He opens the main blade one-handed, and in a gesture of extreme nonchalance reminiscent of Indiana Jones, he cuts off the struggling snake's head and throws it in the bushes behind us.

'Sorry about that,' he murmurs as he folds his knife. I stare at him in secret amazement. I have never seen anything quite so cool.

Later, Norman and I are standing at the bar of a nearby lake hotel.

He says, 'I think I spot my favourite whisky up there,' eyeing the shelf behind the barman. 'I'm sure you'll join me in a dram of Scotland's finest?'

I think of the Swiss army knife in his trouser pocket and I picture a group of solemn-faced Swiss factory technicians supervising the honing of the blades. Do they know, I wonder, to what use some of the owners put their knives?

Norman says, 'I once shot a cobra from the hip. I was showing off, I suppose. The snake reared up at us and I had my old army service revolver and shot it in the head. Pure luck, of course, but I pretended there was nothing to it. When you do something like that, you must make sure you don't shoot again that day, because you'll definitely miss. Of course I was much younger then.' He sipped his whisky and smiled ruefully at such foolishness.

Mambas are the most feared snakes on the African continent. Their venom is neurotoxic and strikes at the respiratory system of the victim, causing rapid deterioration and paralysis of the heart and lungs. A full mamba bite is invariably fatal unless immediate action is taken. The antisera of the past were largely ineffective, and to-day's treatment demands the availability – within minutes if possible – of an artificial respirator and a well-equipped hospital.

A mamba advertises its deadliness by its appearance alone – long and slim with a thin elongated head whose oblique-angled jawbones give it the rhomboid appearance of a small coffin. Unlike most snakes, which are shy and avoid confrontations unless they're hunting, the mamba's arrogant willingness to strike raises goose-flesh at the mere thought of it.

But the most frightening aspect is its sheer size – they can reach more than three metres in length – and the ability to stand on its tail: mambas are able to support themselves for short periods on one third of their body length, with the front two thirds rising up in the air.

I was driving along the dusty Chipata road with Tamara one day, and as we climbed out of the Valley into the foothills, we both suddenly saw a movement on the left shoulder of the road. A large snake was in the process of crossing the road and had stopped, picking up the noise and vibration of our approaching car. We were travelling in our open Land Cruiser, and as we sped by the snake reared up. Its long body stood vertical like a slim tree trunk, and its head suddenly swayed above us. One minute, the snake lay on the ground, as snakes do, the next we were passing underneath it. Despite our speed, the moment seemed to pass in slow motion and we both pulled our necks into our shoulders as we stared at the coffin-like head with its chilling round eyes inches above us.

We looked at each other in silence for a moment, hearts in our throats, our skin crawling. Then Tamara shook her head, the wind in her hair. I know we both like snakes and are usually not afraid of them but this was a moment of pure primeval terror.

'That was evil,' said Tam. 'No snake should be allowed to do that.'

17   Baboons

A baboon lands with a thump on our roof and wakes me. Through the mosquito-gauzed window, I see that the sky is streaked with colour. The sun has not yet shown its face on the horizon but the growing light above the treeline is pink and orange and glows with the promise of another hot day. The night birds have fallen silent, and the leopard has stopped coughing in the mopane forest behind camp. It is time for the daytime sounds to start.

Monkeys rustle the leaves and baboons grunt in the trees as they wake up and start coming down from their sleeping places in the high branches.

The early birds not only catch the worms, they also begin the frantic business of defending territories and warning off potential rivals. The harsh sounds of aggression and the sweet calls of attracting mates are everywhere. The *meeee-ooop*, the croaking and squawking, the shrill cries and soft warblings, the *Poor-Fathers* and *Piet-My-Vrous*, the distant boom of the ground hornbill and, high above the river, the effortless call of the fish eagle, smooth as a violin.

And it's not only the vocal vocabulary we hear: some birds beat their wings together in movements too rapid for our eyes to detect, producing a sound like a stick being pulled across an iron grate. Some clack-clack their beaks, some rattle their tail feathers. I am reminded of our own frenzied showing-off in clubs and at parties, of our posturing and swaggering.

I lie in bed, still tired after a late night, rub my gritty eyes as another baboon hits the roof, pull up the sheet and think, why do they have to do it *now*? At this time of the morning?

No one else is awake as I walk into the *chitenje,* but there's a baboon sitting at the breakfast table. A big male with a thoughtful-looking face. He must have hurdled the low wall of the dining room and he's sitting on a chair, apparently waiting for breakfast. It must be the same animal that has been hanging around for the last couple of weeks, getting bolder every day.

He watches me walk towards him and reluctantly slides off the chair. He vaults back over the wall like a hairy gymnast and squats under the tamarind tree, leaning back against the trunk.

Iwomba arrives with the tea tray, and the baboon watches as I pour tea into a mug. His eyes never leave me as I add milk and sugar and raise the mug to my lips.

When we first moved here – when Norman first staked his claim to this piece of mopane forest – a resident troop of baboons lived on the island across the *dambo*. There was nothing of interest to them on our side, apart from a few tamarind and *mchenja* trees which they probably raided during fruiting season. Then they saw our cooking fires, leftover maize porridge from the labourers' lunch, food scraps in the dustbin behind the kitchen, and came to investigate. As the signs of our comings and goings grew, they started visiting more frequently and they stayed longer. They must have discovered something else, too. The constant presence of humans keeps the leopards away from this piece of forest, and no doubt they feel more secure spending their nights in our trees than in the wilderness across the *dambo*.

At first they were good company. It was fun to watch their antics and they were still shy enough to keep their distance. They seemed curious about our activities, and when the building of the lodge began in earnest and there were bricklayers and carpenters at work and trucks arriving with loads of sand and poles and stones, they seemed drawn to the noise and bustle and watched the proceedings with interest. Of course the more people who came to work, the more food was cooked, and the more leftovers there were for the baboons to steal. It seemed a perfect arrangement, and with each week that passed, the baboons grew bolder.

An electric saw suddenly shrieks from the carpentry workshop and shatters the morning's quiet. The baboon takes no notice, and at breakfast time he is back on the wall, squatting just beyond arm's reach of the table.

Norman stares hard at him and says, '*Ee-we*! Hey, you.' He points his finger at him, and the baboon stares back. He shifts his buttocks and watches Pam drop two pieces of bread into the toaster and slides a few inches closer along the wall to be ready when the toast pops, just in case the opportunity for a quick snatch should present itself. It doesn't. Pam is faster, but his eyes follow the knife dipping into the butter with the fixed stare of an airline passenger watching the approaching food trolley.

Norman says, with a look at Patrick, 'Can't say I approve of this. But at least this chap has better table manners than some of my safari guides.'

I nod. 'He only grabs the food when no one's looking. But it's a hard life out there, digging in the dirt for roots and shoots all day. Sitting at the table with us must feel a lot more civilised to him.'

Miranda says, 'Ja. And maybe he's sick of the other baboons, maybe they had a fight.' She chews her toast. 'Maybe he prefers human company.'

'Naw,' says Pam. 'He just likes bread.'

The baboon follows our conversation, turning his eyes from one to the other, as if watching a tennis match.

Norman gets up from the table, scraping the chair on the irregular stone floor. 'Thanks for breakfast,' he grins.

'Thanks for gracing us with your presence,' Pam grins back. 'Now that your lodge is finished, we don't see you at mealtimes.'

'The clients expect the company of the great Bwana ...'

'So do we,' says Tamara, 'and who is more important, clients or grandchildren?'

'Oh, grandchildren any day, especially when they're home for the holidays,' Norman replies. 'But now,' he swings his walking stick, 'the great Bwana must get back to work.' Over his shoulder, he adds, 'Unlike artists who can sit on their arses all day.'

Now that the lodge is finished and there are tourists coming and going, the baboons have become full-time residents. They move between our camp and the lodge, checking out the kitchens and the dustbins. They pass their time at the edge of the big garbage tip like old men on park benches, and at night they roost in the leafy *mchenja* trees between the two camps. There are many more of them now; it seems that over the last couple of years the troop has doubled in size.

They shit everywhere. On the lawn, on the paths, on tables and chairs, and occasionally on people. Now that the weather is hot and the first hint of humidity is in the air, the clients eat their lunch out in the open, on a wooden deck overlooking the lagoon. More than once, a foul-smelling baboon turd has landed with a liquid splat on the white linen amongst the lunch plates.

The lodge manager chases them across to our side, clapping his hands, shouting, throwing things. They come and sit in the trees behind our kitchen and dining room waiting for opportunities. Iwomba guards his supplies with the vigilance of a private detective but his eyes can't be everywhere. When they have again outwitted or out-waited him and made off with a newly baked bread loaf or a prize watermelon, he throws things at them, and when the stealing from our kitchen becomes intolerable, and when the baboon shit lies deep on the ground at the Ruins, we chase them back to the lodge.

At lunchtime a baboon pees on the table, narrowly missing somebody's dessert bowl. Enough! When the guests go out on their afternoon drive, Craig gets the .375 out of the gun safe and takes up position in the bushes flanking the deck. He doesn't have long to wait. When he spots a baboon face peering at him from amongst the leaves, he raises the rifle and fires.

Nothing happens. There is no panic in the tree, no startled screeching. The face simply disappears. Craig shrugs, shoulders the gun and walks back to the office. Maybe it taught them a lesson. Maybe not.

Three days later, the decomposing carcass falls. Craig, at lunch with the guests, happens to glance up into the tree just as it begins to dislodge itself from its resting place, wedged in a fork between branches perhaps. Maybe he has heard a soft noise, a slipping of fur on bark, a rustle of leaves. He can't believe his eyes as he watches a formless black shape fall towards him, growing in his field of vision. It lands on the white linen with a dull thud, sprawled in grotesque imitation of sleep: stretched out on its back, arms flung wide, one back leg dangling an inch above the bread basket.

There is a sudden bad smell, and a hush around the table, six pairs of eyes staring in shocked disbelief. Then a quiet voice says, 'Oh my God', as if in silent prayer. It belongs to a woman in a silk khaki blouse, a silk scarf at her throat. All through lunch, her eyes have been covered by a pair of Ray-Bans. There is a scraping of chairs on wooden floor planks and one or two suppressed retching sounds.

'Oh my God,' the woman says again, but through the hand clamped over her mouth it sounds more like 'Uh-bikard.'

'Holy shit,' Craig hears himself mutter, hoping that no one has heard him. 'Don't worry, everyone,' he adds, trying not to catch Patrick's eye. 'We'll get this cleaned up immediately.' Sure enough, two of the waiters are already moving in and grab the dead animal by the legs, one of them trying to look serious, the other grinning broadly.

'But why, I mean what . . .'

'Must be snakebite,' says Craig. 'Only thing I can think of.'

Mark and Ginny Evans are the new managers. Ginny is an efficient manageress. She handles the demands of housekeeping, catering, bookings and entertaining with equal ability, while her husband Mark organises the safaris. The rooms are always spotless, the staff always friendly, the meals on a par with top restaurants.

To Norman, this is a problem.

'Ginny is spending far too much money on food,' he tells us. 'People don't come on safari to eat.'

'But having nice meals helps them to enjoy their holiday.' I say. He gives me an irritated look.

'I'm not suggesting we starve them. But Ginny goes over the top,' he answers sharply.

'Norman, you're running an upmarket safari lodge. I think people expect four-course dinners, and it's in keeping with the high standard of the lodge, the game-viewing . . .'

'You're playing devil's advocate again,' Norman says and storms off, swinging his bamboo stick.

'Remember how your clients hated the meals at Mfuwe?' I call after him.

Norman himself takes no pleasure in eating. Food is fuel to him, a necessary bodily activity. A piece of bread is exactly the same as a meal in an expensive restaurant. On the few occasions when he finds himself in such a place, he scrutinises the menu almost suspiciously, skipping the pretentious foreign-sounding dishes for something familiar, like an omelette.

Pam remembers how she once accompanied him on a trip to London, and they found the most humble, *unthreatening* restaurant in the neighbourhood of their hotel and ate there every day, Norman ordering the same meal for every lunch and dinner: omelettes. I doubt he even varied the filling: *yes, tomato is fine, thank you very much.*

He is so much a naturalist that he regards humanity as just another animal species. He often refers to the act of his own eating as feeding. He will stand next to the breakfast table, reach for a piece of toast and spoon a lump of jam on it and chew while looking out at the *dambo*.

'Dad, don't you want to sit down?' Pam says.

'No, I'm feeding on the hoof,' he'll reply, scanning the distance for signs of wildlife.

Ginny won the food battle in the end, through sheer stubbornness equal only to Norman's own. When Norman argued with her, she stood her ground. When he cancelled a food order, she reordered. Finally she showed him the Visitors Book with its glowingly complimentary entries about the high standard of the cuisine, equal to the gushing game-viewing comments.

Norman read them and shook his head.

'People don't come here to feed,' he said again, but it is Ginny's legacy that her example of culinary excellence set the standard for all the other lodges in the Valley.

Our own lunches have improved, too. We have electricity now, and two fridges and a deep freeze. At this time of year we need them. It is October and the sun is burning in the white sky like a nuclear fire. We barely make it through the morning, our energy levels flagging in direct proportion to the rising thermometer. By mid-morning, the mercury is already nudging the forty-degree mark, and there is not a cloud to be seen in the dead-white sky.

None of us really feel like the pork chops and baked potatoes Iwomba has

cooked for lunch. It is a day for cool salads, not hot pork. It has been a *month* for cool salads.

'Iwomba, there is a lot of garlic in this *nyama*.' Patrick chews rhythmically. 'You like using garlic, hey?'

Iwomba nods, his long front teeth showing in a rare grin. 'You don't like?'

'No, it's fine. Just … you know, not so much.' He looks across the table at me, soliciting support. 'Hey Vic?' I start to nod, but I catch Pam's stern look that says, Not now! Not in front of the staff! Patrick looks at her and mutters, 'Jesus, I can start a bushfire with my breath.'

Iwomba is smiling, but there is no way of telling whether he feels confused or complimented.

After lunch, everyone collapses on their beds. But it is too hot to sleep. The heat whispers to me; it taunts me in a slow sullen monotone. 'What are you going to do about me?' it murmurs. 'You are weak, you are powerless to stop me, there is no escape, no respite.'

Outside, I hear baboons calling from the direction of the river. If I listen hard, I feel that I can *hear* the heat. It ticks in the brittle grass. It sings in the crowns of the trees along with the cicadas. When a breeze rises and enters our gauzed windows, it feels like someone has opened an oven door.

I lie on the damp bed, sweat pooling in my hair and around the base of my neck. A moth with RAF wing markings is tapping against the gauze. I look at my watch, the leather strap slick with sweat.

The clients will be climbing into the game-viewing vehicles now, setting off for their afternoon and night drives. Rather them than me, I think hotly, but perhaps it's different when you're on holiday. Although it surely couldn't feel any cooler? Driving in the open Land Cruisers on the road to the bridge, I know the wind sweeps across the hot tarmac like a blowtorch. It will suck the breath out of them.

I think of the big freezer room at the Croc Farm. Perhaps I can ask Charl to rent it to me and move in.

The swimming pool will be vacant now that the clients are out, but the pool is three hundred metres from our house, a long weary walk in the heat. The ground is hot like a beach but I hate the feel of shoes on my swollen feet. The pool water is tepid, like a cooling bath. Standing waist-deep in the water, I can't decide if there is a difference in temperature between the upper and lower parts of my body. Sandy and Janelle are here with the children. The children splash and shout and I envy them their energy.

On the walk back the ground has not cooled. The thicket that forms the boundary between the lodge and the Ruins has lost its previous denseness, the branches and twigs are brittle and bare. Back at the house, the sun has moved around to the back. The light is still intense and falls on the veranda at a low angle, gleaming on the polished cement floor. Outside, dense clouds of small insects vibrate in the still air.

Pam says, 'Are you going back to work now?'

'I must.'

'You never stop, do you? What happened to the carefree old days? We never have time for each other any more.'

I look at her and nod slowly. It's become a familiar subject.

'I know, I know,' she breathes. 'School fees are due, pressure is on.'

Making a living from painting is a great job, I know we both agree about that. But it's not easy and it's not reliable: no one pays our salaries at the end of the month. And the responsibility of two daughters at an expensive private school weighs more heavily on me than I like to admit.

'Come on, I'm an artist. I have to paint.' The heat is making both of us argumentative. I know these moods will blow away with the first rainstorm.

'I'd rather spend more time with you than buy a new Land Cruiser.' She sighs. 'Oh well, off you go.'

The temperature is still above forty, but if I wait much longer, the insects will start swarming into my studio and make concentration impossible. And I do want to finish the section I started this morning. I trudge across the bare earth of the camp towards my studio. Jesus, this heat.

The sun is down. The falling light has drained the colour from the trees and I sit on our porch and count twenty-four baboons still feeding on the *dambo*, fifty metres from me. Every few minutes, some of them raise their heads in my direction, and I know they intend to climb the trees above our camp for the night. That means another too-early wake-up call tomorrow morning, and a fresh layer of baboon shit on our struggling lawn and on the paths between the huts.

Today, a big male baboon broke into Adrian's house, flew around the kitchen in a three-minute frenzy, and left by way of a big front window, shredding the mosquito gauze as he went.

'I'd love to shoot one of these bastards,' he hissed. 'In fact, I wouldn't mind a little massacre.' I grinned at his frustration. I knew that Sandy, his beautiful girlfriend, would never forgive him.

'Maybe *you* could shoot a few,' he said hopefully. 'It probably wouldn't help much, but it might buy us a few days' peace.'

I'm thinking of that now, watching the troop in the twilight, and I'm thinking of another disturbed night of baboons jumping on my roof and grunting in my sleep. The slim-barrelled two-two feels good in my hands, the stock smooth against my cheek. Through the scope, the grey figures hunched out on the short-cropped *dambo* grass are tantalisingly close. The four-power lens brings their fate into my hands, and I feel my finger taking up the slack of the trigger as one hairy torso fills the round eyepiece.

Squeeze and ... I think of Sandy, and move the barrel fractionally down as the sharp crack of the rifle breaks the evening's stillness. I see a clump of earth erupt a few feet in front of the baboon. Several animals look in my direction but continue feeding. I line up another one and pull the trigger again; again a puff of dusty earth. But not the hoped-for shrieks and hasty retreats. They feed on, leisurely.

I step out into open and walk towards them, the rifle barrel pointing at them. I've got their attention now. They know the thing in my hands, they know what it can do. But still there is no panic. I know they are merely biding their time.

I fire another round into the ground but now the light is almost gone and with it my visibility. It is too late for a good shot even if I wanted one. The baboons seem to know this. They suddenly stop tearing at the roots in the ground and start towards me, all twenty-four of them, sauntering into camp with the rolling gait of an arrogant soccer team.

At night I crawl out from under the limp mosquito net. I leave the sodden sheets, the veins of sweat that have gathered in the folds of the damp-crumpled pillow. My hair is wet, beads of moisture stand on my forehead, my shoulders; the hollow of my neck. I stand under the shower with barely enough strength to keep upright and feel the tepid water run over my body and slowly bring its temperature down to a tolerable degree. Wearily, with bones like stone, I collapse back on the damp bed and lie there, a wet towel covering my chest, too exhausted to sleep.

I listen to the baboons in the trees. Now and then a breeze blows through the mosquito gauze. It smells of distant rain.

18 Gwat

I have known Alistair Gallatly aka 'Gwat' about as long as I have lived in Zambia and have always been impressed by his imperturbable stoicism. The man is unflappable; in the most dire circumstances, Alistair remains calm. This is a good thing, because Alistair seems to attract adverse circumstances like a dog attracts fleas.

Early on in our friendship, his father died of a botched routine operation. I had met the old man – who wasn't that old, or that sick either – a few weeks before and saw how close the bond was between father and son. Yet when he heard the news, Alistair showed no outward sign of grief. He busied himself with chores at the Zambia Safari headquarters in Lusaka where we were staying and took every new day as it came. It was the start of the hunting season, all the professional hunters were in town having their vehicles serviced, buying camp supplies, telling stories of near misses and close shaves, and competing for the few available women in town.

Alistair listened to the stories and sat and drank with them. What he felt inside, I don't know because he never showed me. When I asked him, 'Aren't you sad', he simply nodded and carried on with the task at hand. He may have muttered something like, 'Nothing I can do about it', and he may have asked me to bring a round of beer, seeing that I was going to the kitchen.

At the beginning of another season some years later, Alistair had become a hunter himself. He did not yet have his own concession, and moving from camp to camp to be someone's second hunter was not going to be a lucrative business. He decided to supplement his income by running a load of camp supplies and other essential goods down to the Valley. All the hunters were building camp at this time and needed all kinds of things, usually more stuff than they could fit in their own Land Cruisers. Alistair reckoned he could make a little money on the side.

He borrowed a truck from a friend, a big Mercedes Benz, and loaded it with boxes of canned food, bags of maize meal and *kapenta*, gas cylinders and generator spares, plumbing pipes and fittings, six hundred-metre rolls of plastic water hose, bags of cement, baling wire, a grader blade and four big grader tyres; he searched Lusaka for French wine and managed to buy some Scotch instead. He spent the last of his money on ten gallons of engine oil and eight drums of fuel. He gave directions to the driver and early one morning they left Lusaka, Alistair in his Land Cruiser, the big Mercedes truck following behind.

'Take it slowly, drive carefully,' Alistair instructed the driver. 'I'll get there a couple of hours before you, and when you reach Luangwa Croc Farm this evening, you'll find me there.'

We stood around in a loose circle under some trees by the riverbank. The sun was sliding down into the trees on the opposite bank, birds standing in the shallows on long legs looking for fish were casting long shadows on the still water. Charl Beukes, owner of Luangwa Crocodile Farm, was a hunter, and the Croc Farm had become a kind of a staging post, an informal headquarters for the professional hunters and guides who worked for his outfit. Others had come to visit or were passing through. Once the first clients arrived and the season got under way, there wouldn't be much time for socialising, but now there were seven or eight of us, telling jokes and hunting stories, everyone holding beer bottles or whisky glasses. Charl was showing us his new hunting rifle, and someone asked, 'Has anyone got any spare .375 rounds?' Alistair kept looking at his watch.

People came and went, leaving the circle and rejoining a few minutes later, drifting between the bar tent, the store-rooms and their parked Land Cruisers, while the sun sank lower and Egyptian geese chattered in the river.

'Vic, your daughters won't speak to me.' Alistair was looking at me over the rim of his glasses.

'Neither of them?'

'Ja, specially Miranda.'

'Why, because you shot that dove last season?'

'Ja. You can't win, can you?' He smiled ruefully. 'I mean your wife asks me to shoot a dove for her so she can catch a falcon, and now your daughters hate me. Tammy sort of understands, being a bit older, but Miranda says I'm a murderer.' He shook his head.

A Land Cruiser came down the dirt track and pulled up on the dusty hardpan where a random collection of other bush vehicles were parked. Robin Pope climbed out.

'Hi Robin, howzit, man?'

'Yes, good to be back, good to see you all.'

A few handshakes, a few smiles of welcome.

'How's the road? Long drive?'

'You know, the usual potholes, road-blocks. No problems though.'

Alistair said, 'Did you pass a green Mercedes truck on the road?'

'Don't remember. I passed quite a few trucks between Lusaka and Chipata, but none since Chipata that I can remember.'

'You sure?'

'Ja, pretty sure. You know how difficult it is to overtake a truck on that dirt road.

All the dust they throw up. Why?'

'Just wondering,' Alistair shrugged.

'What I *did* see was a burnt-out truck blocking the road. Had to drive right off the road to get past.'

'Shit. Where?' asked Charl.

'Outside Chipata, coming down here. Just by Kalichero, the market there. People and hordes of kids standing around, all excited, all shouting. I suppose it must have happened not too long before I passed.'

Alistair had gone quiet.

'Did you see anyone else around?' he asked, pushing his glasses up on his nose with a finger. 'Someone who could have been the driver?'

'They said the driver gapped it. As the truck drove by, there was a loud noise and the next second the whole truck was in flames. It stopped in the middle of the road, flames everywhere, and the driver baled out of the cab, ran into the bushes and just kept going. Nobody saw him after that.'

Robin looked at Alistair. 'Probably still running,' he added. 'Probably on the way to Malawi ...' he stopped. 'Why, are you expecting a ...'

Everyone was looking at Alistair.

'Ja. That's my truck.'

'Oh Jesus. Are you sure?' said Robin.

'Ja. Of course. Must be.'

'Hang on,' said Charl. 'Was this a Merc?' Frowning at Robin.

'Couldn't really tell,' Robin shrugged. 'The thing was so charred. All the paint burnt off, the doors and the roof of the cab buckled from the heat, you know.

Must have been some fire. But yes, I guess it could have been. One of those snub-nosed jobs.'

'Holy shit,' someone said.

We were all staring at Alistair.

'Anyone know how it happened?' said Basil. 'I know you had fuel drums on the back, maybe something got too hot? Someone in the back, smoking?'

'One of the drums could have started leaking,' someone said. 'That road ... the corrugations.'

'Well,' said Charl, 'let's go and make sure. It's only a hundred k's, we can be there in an hour and a half. We'll take my Cruiser.' He nodded at Alistair. 'Let's go, Gwat!'

'I'll come,' said Basil. 'Maybe we can save something.'

But Alistair wasn't moving.

'Why don't we go in two cars,' said Willie Cloete, 'maybe there's stuff to ...'

Robin looked doubtful.

Alistair shook his head.

'No point,' he said. 'I'll go tomorrow some time. Whose round is it?'

❊

Every safari season seemed to follow a pattern. It started with the optimism and high spirits of renewal. Like birds in spring

we built camps, repaired fallen roofs, mended fences, fixed cars, scrubbed and painted. Before we knew it, it was August and the first chinks appeared in our armour of enthusiasm. Catering to tourists was tiring. Everyone expected to see a leopard and a lion kill and seemed to blame their guide if they didn't. The endless repetitive night drives, the same questions.

It was even harder for the hunters. Up at four, leaving camp before dawn to check baits and be in the right spot when the sun came up. Following tracks all morning, scanning the bush for those big horns. While the clients rested after lunch there were all those logistical problems to be dealt with that take place behind the scenes of a successful camp. Out again in the afternoon, return for dinner, and then the suppressed yawns at the campfire every night, listening to the client's boring stories. And the stresses of the hunt; avoiding dangerous situations, keeping the client out of trouble, and the constant pressure – the *tyranny* – of the trophy. Not every animal they shot could be the biggest in the area, but that was of course what most clients desired.

In October the weather became so hot that every footstep under the burning sun required an effort, but by now it was more than the heat that felt oppressive. We watched the first rain clouds build up on the horizon and watched them drift away again.

When the first rainstorms lashed the country in late October, they signalled a rebirth for the plants and the animals but for most of us they meant the end; the exhaustion after another season that felt much longer than it really was. The relief of going home. By November most of us couldn't wait to leave. People were breaking camp and packing up. The real rains were looming, swarms of insects came in dense clouds at dusk, beetles and moths and tiny gnats.

All the plans we had made in May – *let's build a raft and float down the river, let's explore the hill country, let's do all that stuff that we never have time for* – were suddenly forgotten. Even the parties and get-togethers which held such promise and optimism before the season, felt compromised by regret and an indefinable melancholy. We were still jolly on the surface of things, and there were stories to be told – *did you hear about Arthur and the wounded buffalo, have you seen so-and-so's Cruiser since it hit that hippo* – but we knew another season had come and gone, somehow far too quickly. It would be six months before we would see each other again; some of us might not come back, and somehow even the new green grass and the sight of the first newborn impala fawns could not lift our spirits.

The constant rain had already driven the last tourists from the Valley, the season was already being classified, labelled for future reference (... wasn't it '96 when the Japanese lady fell into the river?); it was turning into history before it was properly over. But still there was always one more story to tell, one more claim to the most dangerous encounter, the client with the most beautiful daughter, the biggest snake; and it wasn't until the morning after the last of the end-of-season parties that you felt it was really time to go.

Alistair Gallatly was sitting on a bar stool, the same one on which he'd been slumped all evening. The wooden bar counter was littered with empty glasses and bottles, crushed cigarette packets. The tape recorder had come to the end of a cassette and no one had bothered to put in a new one. The earth floor between the bar stools under Alistair's feet was strewn with dead cigarette butts and beer bottle tops. Alistair had taken off his glasses and laid them on the counter next to him, taking a little time over this, his hand like a circling vulture looking for a dry place to land between the drying pools of spilt beer and other sticky liquids.

He stared across at the shelves of

bottles and at the life-size inflatable doll that someone had placed there earlier, when the party started, a needless reminder that although women were scarce in the safari camps, the season was over and the towns were full of available girls waiting to be swept off their feet by these love-starved sunburnt adventurers from the bush.

She sat there on the shelf facing Alistair, squeezed between the bottles of whisky and gin, her bright plastic lips and dead eyes a grimace, a grotesque parody of a come-hither look. A wood owl called nearby and her mate answered, the booming sound echoing along the dark river like a foghorn.

Nearly everyone had gone to sleep, collapsing on the stripped beds in the empty cabins. I thought I heard an elephant tearing the branches off the winter thorn behind reception but it was too dark to see. Alistair slowly put his head down on his folded arms.

The night was too short. Suddenly, it seemed, the small birds were chirping and twittering, rustling in the bushes. A pair of fish eagles were exchanging greetings over the river, and I heard voices and the clattering of a tea kettle outside. I rose and stepped into the thousand-watt glare of a November morning, rubbing my eyes. A fire was crackling on the ground between the huts and two blackened enamel pots stood next to it. I ignored the tea and went looking for water. The kitchen was at the far end of camp, so I made for the bar instead, where Alistair

was still asleep on the bar stool with his head on his arms. He appeared not to have moved at all since I left him there four hours earlier, and he still didn't move as I searched behind the counter and in the fridge for drinking water. Facing Alistair, the sexy doll was still sitting on the shelf. She had lost a little air during the night and was slouched forward, her head dropping down on to the twin rubber cones of her breasts, as if she too had had a hard night. Neither Alistair nor the doll looked likely to wake up and move any time soon, so I went and sat on the riverbank to watch the hippos basking in the early morning sunshine.

❊

A few years later, Alistair went fishing on the Zambezi with his friend Arthur Taylor, Taylor's wife and parents-in-law. Taylor was a rough-and-ready, born and bred white Zambian like Alistair himself, but his wife Fay and her parents were English. The father, Clive, had once worked in Chipata, teaching at the secondary school, and had filled the school holidays working as a guide on Norman Carr's safaris. His wife Brenda was a short woman with a round face, and their daughter Fay was so small and delicate that to see her stand next to the stocky bulk of Taylor was like seeing a dainty deer fawn next to a bull.

Taylor, who prides himself on being barely human, untainted by the superfluous ballast of higher education and fancy manners, was an unlikely candidate for Fay's affections. But when the shy and

sweet seventeen-year-old had finished school and was sent out from England to help at Chibembe camp for a season, something in this rough-hewn stone, a glint of mica in this block of granite, must have touched her, and it amazed us all to see them always together. At the end of that same year, when Fay found that she was pregnant, a proud Taylor, very much in love, phoned her parents in England to tell them the happy news.

'So,' said Clive after the shock had worn off, 'when are you going to get married?' There was a silence on the telephone line, and then Taylor said, 'Oh, when I find the right girl.' Fay, standing next to him, could see his grin, but Clive could not.

It was a calm April day. The weather had not yet turned cold, and they were drifting on the Zambezi under a cloudless sky. Small waves lapped at the fibreglass hull of their boat and their soporific sound and the gentle rocking of the boat on the wide flat water soothed them, and the effect of the beer that the three men had drunk during the morning's fishing added to their overall feeling of sleepy relaxation. Their lines trailed lazily in the water. There was more cold beer in the ice box and the warm afternoon stretched before them. They were totally unprepared for the hippo that appeared out of nowhere and hit the side of their boat.

Alistair, Brenda and Clive went overboard immediately. The hippo turned and attacked again but instead of zeroing in on the thrashing bodies it hit the boat a second time, perhaps seeing it as a rival hippo, and capsized it. Everything sank immediately: their cameras, binoculars, all their fishing tackle, cooler boxes, and – worst of all – the boat. They were left splashing around in the deep river, treading water, gasping for air, expecting worse to come. The hippo bellowed like some demented hellhound, but instead of going for them with open jaws and gleaming tusks, it submerged in a whirl-pool of white water and disappeared from sight. They were lucky to be alive, but the nightmare had only just begun. Fay, Clive and Brenda were not strong swimmers and struggled to keep themselves afloat. The river was too wide to think about heading for the shore, none of the three would make it, and it was even further to the Zimbabwe side behind them.

Alistair had seen a small island, nothing more than a sandbar, in the middle of the river, and they slowly made their way towards it, breathing hard, swallowing water, helping Clive and Brenda to stay afloat. When they reached the sandbar they realised that the bul-rushes and reeds they had seen from a distance had given them false hope – the island was submerged in two feet of water and only the tallest of the vegetation showed above the surface. Still, it was good to find solid ground beneath their feet, infinitely better than the deep dark water all around them, and with waves lapping at their knees and thighs, they

tried to settle their nerves and analyse their situation. It didn't look good. There were more hippos in the water around them, and crocodiles everywhere. Some they could see, and some they could not. They looked again at the Zambian shore, but knew that Clive and Brenda would never make it. They looked towards the Zimbabwe side, a similar distance away, where the sun was beginning to make its way slowly down the western sky towards the distant trees.

After cursing themselves for not having arranged emergency back-up of some kind – radio, rescue instructions to a driver if they failed to return, the simple precautions that should be part of any expedition – Alistair decided he would swim to the shore and try to find help while Taylor would stay with his family and try to protect them if he could.

They waited for hours, rooted to the spot, unable to move. They had no weapon of any kind, no food, and they shivered as the afternoon turned cooler and the sun grew larger and eventually sank beneath the surface of the river, just like their boat had done.

There was no sign of Alistair.

Just before dark, Taylor spotted a paddle, apparently lost from a canoe, drift-ing towards them and he swam towards it, grabbed it and stuck it into the ground where they were standing. Later, when all other landmarks had disappeared in the night, they would use it as a beacon to orientate themselves in the darkness of the river.

Intermittently, they called out to

where they thought Alistair might have reached the shore, but there was no reply. Maybe he had drifted too far downstream to hear them, maybe he had already started walking to find help and was out of earshot. But they also had to face the possibility that he might have drowned.

If they stayed there, it was likely that one or more of them would not survive the night. The thought of spending the next twelve hours standing knee-deep in the swirling water as the night grew colder and darker all around them, and the hippos grunted and the crocodiles moved silently, sent shivers down their spines. But they had no choice, and as the hours passed and the last light faded from the river, they prepared themselves for the longest night of their lives.

Alistair had swum in long strokes towards the Zambian side. He had almost reached the shore and was eyeing the steep bank, looking for a place to climb out, when he felt a crocodile grab his left arm. Within seconds, he was more than three metres below the surface of the water, out of breath and fighting for his life.

'The thing had me by the arm and was trying to spin me,' he told me afterwards. 'I couldn't breathe but I thought if I could spin with him, at least he wouldn't pull my arm out, you know.'

He rolled up the sleeve on his left arm showing where a red line of jagged scars ran all the way from his hand to his shoulder.

'At the same time I was hitting him and trying to get my thumbs into his eyes. I kept jabbing, you know, but it wasn't easy under water, and at the same time I was trying to drag us both up to the top so I could catch a breath.'

Fortunately for Alistair, the crocodile was not particularly big by Zambezi standards, otherwise he would not be alive today. He kept jabbing at the eyes and when the croc finally relinquished its grip, Alistair managed to push his arm all the way down its throat and force his fist into that narrow space to open the valve that seals the back of its gullet. Swallowing water, the crocodile let him go.

But Alistair's troubles were not over. Exhausted and bleeding, his body weak and shivering, he dragged himself up the steep bank and lay on the ground, trying to catch his breath. Blood from his arm was seeping into the sand. A hyena started whooping close by, and he suddenly heard voices calling him from the open water. He managed to draw a deep breath into his lungs and called back, not sure whether his voice was strong enough for them to hear. 'Ja, I'm here. I'm okay!'

But he knew he wasn't. It was dark now, and he was too weak to walk. There was nothing he could do to help his friends, certainly not until morning.

He dragged himself under a thorn bush and lay there as the dark gathered around him and the first stars began to appear in the sky.

'I must have passed out for a bit,' he said later. 'And then I began to hear lions. They seemed to be coming closer. I thought, oh no, man, *now* what.'

Everything went blank for a while but

the pain in his arm kept waking him up. He kept thinking of the blood dripping from his arm, the *smell* of it, as he heard the lions calling again, closer now.

And then a strange thing happened. What had taken place so far that day was a hair-raising sequence of events, part negligence and part bad luck. But it was not unique; it could all be explained. What was to follow, could not be explained. That is, neither Alistair nor anyone who has heard this story can offer any explanation.

Alistair heard a new noise, something heavy moving in the dark scrub, and saw the black shape of a buffalo lumbering towards him in the pale moonlight.

'I couldn't believe it. At first I thought, okay, now I really am done for. After all

that had happened this would be the final straw. This buffalo had come from hell with the specific aim of delivering the *coup de grâce*. I watched him and thought, okay you can have me. Go on, finish me off.

'He stood there, not three metres from me, and stared at me, his head low as if in thought. In the moonlight I saw the red eyes in his wrinkled mud-caked face. He turned and raised his head in the direction of the lions once or twice, then lowered it again. And then – I couldn't believe my eyes – the buffalo lay down, and he lay there all night until the sun came up. I have never heard of anything like it. He was a big bull, and the lions must have been wary of him. Or of his scent mingled with mine. Whatever – they stayed away,

174

and as the sun rose behind the trees, the bull got to his feet and shuffled away.'

'And then what happened?' I asked. 'How did you finally find help?'

'Well, I shouted across to the others – they were still in the river – to hang on while I tried to find some people.'

'And did you?'

'Ja, there was a little village a couple of k's away, with some fishermen.' He paused. 'Took me three hours to get there. I mean, I crawled all the way.'

*

Alistair is not in good health these days. A hunting accident two years later with a different buffalo, one of a less benevolent disposition, left him badly mauled and without a spleen. It was as if one buffalo saved his life, and when he didn't repay the debt and stop hunting them, another came to admonish him. His doctors advised him to stay away from the bush. Another bout of malaria might kill him. Lacking the resource of a functioning spleen, his body might not have the resistance to fight it.

I saw him down in the Valley shortly after he had recovered. 'So Vic, how's it going?'

'Okay, Al, and you?'

'Ja, fine.'

'I'm surprised to see you here. I thought you had to stop hunting, stay out of the bush.'

'Ja, well. But ...' he shrugged and snorted. 'What else is there for me to do? Hunting is what I do, so ...' He trailed off, then added with a lopsided grin, 'Anyway, I like it here. You know?'

The following January he arrived at the Safari Club Convention in Las Vegas looking wasted and yellow from malaria. He had come to book clients for another season and was not about to let the minor obstacle of bad health interfere.

A month later I ran into him in Lusaka, standing outside the Holiday Inn.

'Do you want to buy my Land Cruiser?' he asked me. 'I need to sell mine. You've heard that they've banned hunting in Zambia, haven't you ...'

I nodded. 'Your luck's finally run out. What you gonna do?'

He shrugged. 'Something will turn up.'

'Like that buffalo on the Zambezi.'

He grinned at me. 'Vic, that buffalo didn't come to protect me.'

'No?'

'Come on, man, a buffalo doesn't do that.'

'I know, but why else was he there? Have you ever heard of anything like it before?'

'No, I haven't. And I haven't got the answer to that.'

I said nothing. Out on Church road, the Lusaka traffic clanged and hummed, and the exhaust fumes shimmered above the hot tarmac in a silvery-blue haze.

'Anyway, it makes a good story,' he said.

19   Rain

November. I have been away for two weeks and when I return, the whole country, not only Kapani, has changed. When I left at the end of October, the mopane forest was bare. Like the trees of the northern hemisphere at the end of winter, the branches stood out stark and empty against the sky. Not a single leaf shielded the ground from the intense heat of the sun. Walking between the trees had felt like being caught in an overexposed photograph where everything was glaringly black and white and in high contrast.

Now there is a sudden softness. The flush of new leaves is all around us, and the whole camp has a bright emerald green ceiling. Quick shoots of new green grass, delicate yet already robust, are growing in clumps where the rainwater from the first storm is still standing; it is sprouting at the edges of puddles and dotting the plains in lush islands of deep-pile carpets.

Everything has its own green. The emerald of the mopane, the pale green skin of the new fruit of the sausage tree, the Christmas tree canopies of the winter thorns, and new grass shoots, each species in a different shade of green.

Golden orb spiders have stretched their webs, tough as nylon string, across the paths where I walk. The track between the kitchen and my studio is overgrown and slippery under my feet, and every morning I walk the obstacle course, trying not to lose my balance, trying to stay relatively dry under the dripping leaves, and dodging the glittering gold-green webs strung between the trees like a ship's rigging. Some of them are two metres wide, the thumb-sized spider vibrating hopefully in the centre. If I don't pay attention, my face gets caught in the sticky mesh like an unwary insect. And what size insect are they hoping to catch in these webs that are as strong as small fishing nets?

Some of the individuals in the newly materialised swarms are admittedly large and fearsome: rhino beetles with armour-plated bodies and inch-long horns, cicadas tough as acorns, dung beetles. Praying mantis the size of cigars.

Every evening we are surprised by new swarms. Some consist of millions of tiny black flying organisms that get into our eyes and noses. We walk through clouds of insects. Sometimes we can't help breathing insects. Others crash into our faces and buzz against the mosquito gauze like tiny helicopters.

Some of them are familiar from last year, others we have never seen before and perhaps will never see again.

Tens of thousands of flying termites erupt from termite mounds in the evenings, flitting around light bulbs with glittering translucent wings. Iwomba, Alefer, and the gardener place water-filled pots and pans under the kitchen lights to catch them. They take bundles back to their villages for the frying pans, but there are still thousands that complete the nuptial cycle. Shedding their silk-sticky wings, they find a partner among the hundreds. (How? What criteria make one termite more suitable than another? Or is the pairing-off completely random?) Every surface in the kitchen, as well as the ground outside, is covered with these new couples; they move about slowly, earthbound now, two by two, as if glued together head to tail. And everywhere the discarded wings shine like patches of old silk rugs.

The big *mukwa* easel in my studio has a row of holes in each leg for the adjustable pegs of the canvas support. Each of these holes is sealed now with the hardened clay of a mud-wasp nest, and every time I want to move the canvas up or down, I have to take a sharp nail or knife point and unblock the holes. The wasps buzz around me irritably while I paint, looking for new openings to lay their eggs.

And, bloating their throats, thousands of frogs that have been silent for six months, announce themselves. Their sound is not uniform. Not all frogs croak. Some sound like distant wind chimes, glass tinkling softly on crystal. Others are like a hundred small hammers beating on a hundred small anvils. Still others remind me of the tinkling of piano keys in the middle distance, low on the ground (small pianos hidden in the reeds).

Some sound delicate, like silver bells, others bounce along the wet ground with the ping-pong sound of breaking billiard balls. Then, as if obeying some unseen command, they all stop at once and there is a sudden silence. And slowly, timidly at first but quickly gathering volume, a new sound rises from the river, the grating of a slow rasp on hardwood.

And new life everywhere. Wherever we look, the countryside is alive with the mewing, bleating, croaking and singing of the newborn. The big and the small are now breeding and everywhere there is evidence of renewal: baby monkeys dangling big-eyed from branches like animated Christmas decorations, loose-limbed antelope fawns nudging their mothers' bellies; nests in secret places.

A dormouse has bitten a hole in my canvas. A dormouse is a cuddly little rodent with a big bushy tail, and if you can manage to tame one, it makes a nice pet. This one isn't a pet, in fact as of this morning it's on the 'most wanted' list.

The painting has been hanging on the big white back wall of the studio, and because it's a big one, I've been working on it intermittently, when I feel in the mood for it. I know it is going to take me the better part of the year to complete it, and that is fine by me. Some canvases need that much time to develop and change, and to grow. I've been busy with other work and haven't looked closely at this painting for some weeks, but this morning I discovered the hole. About the size of a jam jar lid, in the bottom left corner.

'How do you know it was a dormouse?' asks Patrick. 'It could have been anything.'

A small beetle is making its way across the breakfast table. It is mostly black, with a bright orange abdomen and two short stubby wings. It somehow reminds me of a small military aircraft, perhaps of Italian design. I shake my head. 'I *know*. And furthermore, I know that it is the same mouse that has been eating my Cobalt Blue.'

'No way. You can't be sure of that.'

'Patrick, why're you being so argumentative? It's just a mouse.'

'Yeah, but you may be accusing this mouse wrongly.'

'I have proof,' I smile.

'How? You got the mouse?'

I shake my head.

'Then you're just guessing.'

I smile again. Miranda says: 'Promise you didn't kill the dormouse?'

'Promise.' I nod and walk back to my studio. I take the big painting off the wall and, sure enough, there is a small nest snuggled into the bottom corner behind the canvas, just next to the hole. It has been made from pieces of string and cotton wool, matted bits of toilet paper that I use for cleaning brushes, dried grass and shreds of chewed canvas. I also find some short pieces of black wire that have been missing from my Walkman earphones for some time. The whole thing is wedged comfortably between the canvas and the wall, resting on the stretcher frame, with the hole as its entrance.

In my paint box, I find the tube of Cobalt Blue with the tooth marks in its metal skin.

At lunchtime, I approach the table with an exaggerated frown.

'I know I'm facing a group of people who are set on defending a criminal just because he's cute and has a bushy tail. But I'm here to show you beyond all reasonable doubt that the rodent is guilty. Guilty as sin.' I bang the table with a soup spoon.

Patrick shakes his head. 'Rubbish. You got no case against our client.' He winks at Tam and Miranda.

'Innocent until proved guilty,' says Tam, her face stern.

I stare at her. 'You may be making a serious mistake, counsellor. You may be protecting a dangerous felon.'

Miranda raises her hand: 'Our client is an upstanding member of the animal community, a respected mother and –'

' – and a known fugitive,' I interrupt her.

Patrick puts his fingers to his chin. 'Okay, granted. Our client may have bitten a hole through your painting and made a nest behind it. I say *may have*, but as a zoologist and observer of mice, I submit that dormice are known to do this.' He takes a breath and raises his voice. 'But you have no proof that the mouse who did this also ate your paint!'

I eye the defence team, each one in turn. Miranda is grinning, Tam wears a slight frown; Patrick lights a cigarette.

I slowly lay the tube of Cobalt Blue on the table. It has a collar of irregular holes around its circumference, clearly the work of sharp teeth. Inside, the bright blue paint is visible. Next, I pull the carefully preserved mouse's nest out of my shirt pocket and place it next to the paint tube.

Three faces eye me expectantly. I prise the nest open. Inside is a small cluster of seven or eight mini sausages of dried mouse droppings. They are thin and hard and bright blue, a perfect match with the colour inside the paint tube.

'I rest my case. What's for lunch?'

'One of Iwomba's stews.' Miranda laughs. 'That was brilliant. You should have been a lawyer.'

'Would make more money, anyway,' says Patrick with a sidelong glance at me. 'Pass the salt please, Tam. Where's Pam today?'

'Gone with Norman to look for a Red-Necked Falcon nest.'

'Why didn't they tell me? I'd have liked to go with them.'

Tam said, 'Jeez, Patrick, you use a lot of salt. Doesn't it make you thirsty?'

'It does.'

'So?'

'That's why I eat it.'

I sit on the veranda and watch the rainstorm race across the *dambo* towards me. A minute ago, the trees on the far riverbank were still and in plain view. Now they are swaying like dancers and are almost obscured, swallowed by the bluegrey wall of rain. The river itself slowly disappears in the mist and I don't need binoculars to see that the rain has reached our side. I can hear it drumming as it flattens the tall grass in its path, hear the wind in the bushes, and feel the advancing rush of cold air blow into my face, raising the hairs on my forearms and shivering down my back.

And the unmistakable damp-dusty rain smell. Just as the bouquet of a fine wine can't be described in one word, so the African first-rain smell defies easy description. It is a complex mix of scents: wet clay, ripe mushrooms, with overtones of warm summer breeze.

The trees on the *dambo* vanish from sight just as the first drops hit the house, then my skin as the wind pushes them under the roof and on to the veranda. And then it is upon us. Horizontal rain hits the front of the house like a hail of bullets. Our camp suddenly seems small and defenceless, houses of cards against the savage power of the storm. I roll down the bamboo blinds and slam the shutters down over the windows. Through the wet haze I see Iwomba run from the kitchen, the wind slamming the door behind him, Iwomba slipping on the wet ground, the clay already saturated and slick. He reaches the *chitenje*, races around it unhooking the blinds, covering books and moving cushions.

Pam comes running from her studio, sliding and splashing, the water already an inch deep on the ground. We shout at each other through the noise of the rain: *check the car covers, have you done the bathroom windows . . .*

I see Norman outside his house, hastily throwing a tarpaulin over the open cab of his Land Cruiser.

When we get back to our house we are drenched and shivering from the sudden cold. None of the blinds are completely rainproof, not against this onslaught, and water enters the house through gaps and

rumbles in the distance but the sky no longer pours water. There is a great muffled silence disturbed only by the sound of dripping trees, frogs splashing in the puddles, and the sucking and rushing of the small channels that have cut into the soil connecting one puddle to the next.

Clear blue spaces open up between the clouds and their sides are lit as if by a spotlight, and suddenly, incongruously, like a prisoner upon his release, a bird starts singing. The air feels like it's been washed and hung out to dry. Flapping softly in the slow breeze. Steam rises from the damp grass and evaporates quickly in the clean sunlight.

Sounds suddenly travel farther than before, and we hear elephants trumpeting far in the distance.

Now it is time to inspect the damage. The blinds around the *chitenje* haven't held and the inside is like the deck of a sinking ship. The floor is covered in an inch of green water and all the grass mats are soaked. The wind has blown cups and mugs off the sideboard; they lie half submerged in a mosaic of shards on the stone floor. Someone left the lid off the big tin of instant coffee on the table; it is now a brown sludge. Someone also forgot to put away a loaf of bread (where were the baboons?). It sits on the table like a wet sponge, weeping a thick white-yellow pus on to the sodden white tablecloth. The shelf on which the books and magazines stand has taken a direct hit. The magazines are solid bricks of pulp. Someone will no doubt

hangs in the room in a fine mist. The sheets and blankets are suddenly damp, the mosquito net hangs limp, and the walls are slick with a film of moisture. Outside, the puddles are filling quickly, lightning flashes between the huts and thunder rolls through the mopane trees.

The roof is alive with white noise, echoing the whiteness of the landscape outside. It drowns out every sound beneath it. We mouth words at each other but cannot hear, like people under water, which of course we are.

And suddenly it stops. Thunder still

have the patience, today, tomorrow, or next week, to sit and separate the more interesting pages (those with the fashion models in skimpy underwear).

Roberts Birds of South Africa will be dried out in the sun, its lumpy pages still useful. The book 'Where there is no Doctor' is indispensable, we can't afford to lose this one, so it, too, will receive first aid.

The wind has entered through the slatted windows of my studio and blown a half-finished canvas off the easel. It is lying face down in a puddle on the floor, leaving smears of ultramarine and yellow ochre when I lift it.

Tomorrow, everything will be back to normal, just in time for the next storm.

Caught up in the exuberance of all this renewal in the air, Pam and I ride our bikes in the game reserve. This is not allowed, but the tourists have all gone and, with weary good humour at the end of a long season, the guard at the gate merely grins and salutes.

The puku in Nsefu-sector look freshly showered, their orange-brown fur gleaming with the morning sun on them. We scatter a small flock of crowned cranes, sending them into the sky, their lazy-shrill *owani owani* competing with our engine sounds. The sky is clear after months of haze, and there is the freshness of spring all around us. It seems to have infiltrated my brain too. For no reason I can think of other than perhaps what is commonly known as spring fever, I shut my throttle and slow down. I see Pam racing ahead,

splashing through puddles, and I think I hear a '*Yee-haa*' over the sound of her motor. I put the bike on its stand, take off my shoes, shorts, boxer shorts and T-shirt, roll them into a ball and look around for a tree or bush that I will remember later.

When I catch up and overtake Pam, I'm naked. Looking back over my shoulder, I see her bike wobble uncertainly. I shout and whoop and ride through puddles, splashing mud and spraying greenish water over myself. Zebras and impala raise their heads at us. We are breaking almost every rule in the Park, but we know there is no one here to catch us. Or is there? This would not be a good time to run into the warden. I have a quick thought for my stashed bundle of clothes, wondering if I will recognise the tree again, but the thought passes.

The next morning is again damp and humid. I'm in my studio and examine the canvas I've been working on, scrutinising last night's final brush strokes. Am I happy with them? Not sure. I look out the window. A giraffe bull stands motionless among the trees by the lagoon, the reticulated brown patterns on his neck in perfect harmony with the swaying branches. The baboons are out feeding on the *dambo*, the young ones playing. Half of the *dambo* is now covered in water and the lagoon at its far end has risen and expanded towards us.

A red-chested cuckoo is moving about in the branches above my studio, nearly driving me crazy with his monotonous, endlessly repeated three-syllable call. '*Piet-*

my-vrou' is how they describe it in South Africa. '*Piet-my-vrou. PIET-MY-VROU*'. He has been calling incessantly since early morning and if I weren't a conservationist, I would now get out the shotgun and blow him away.

I look back at the canvas. How to continue? What will the next move be? To delay the day's first decision and buy myself time, I pick up a rag in order to wipe the work table. The instant my hand touches it, a searing pain shoots up my right arm. It feels like a hammer blow to the vein in my wrist; a minute hammer, but the impact is just the same. Within seconds my hands goes numb and the pain has travelled up to my shoulder and into my chest like a subcutaneous electric current. I can feel it approaching my heart and for a second I stand immobile, as if paralysed. I take a few deep breaths. I shake out the rag and stare at the small yellow scorpion sitting on the oiled wood of the table, tail curved with its sting touching its back.

My response is instant and instinctive.

Then I run outside for cold water and when it touches my skin, my hand jerks back in involuntary shock, as if the flow of water were a stream of boiling lava. I think of how a tree trunk must feel at the touch of a chainsaw.

'Okay, I tell myself. It's only a scorpion sting. Look at the thing, now lying squashed on the floor, see how small it is. I'm not going to let such a tiny thing upset my working day. I kick the dead scorpion into the corner and pick up a paintbrush. But the pain pierces my concentration, the

pain has its own ideas about my working day. It throbs in my wrist, obliterates thought. Hopping from one foot to the other, I laugh out loud. I shout, 'No! I will not let this thing mess up my day! I am tougher than that.' But I'm not really. At the end of the working day, I realise that it's been a waste of time and effort and the painting was better before I touched it this morning.

Twelve hours later, almost to the minute, the heat in my arm starts retreating and the pins and needles start. The pain slowly ebbs, as if going home after a long day at the office, leaving a tenderness, a tingling, a sensitivity to touch. That too soon disappears, and I laugh at my own weakness, at how once again there was no defence, no matter how determined I was.

But pain has its own memory, and for days afterwards, I look at each washcloth, each harmless towel, with suspicion. I kick at last night's discarded T-shirt before gingerly picking it off the floor, I shake out my shoes thoroughly every morning.

December. The rain has set in now; it hasn't stopped for weeks. It rains every day, sometimes in cloudbursts that send even the hippos scurrying for the safety of the river, sometimes in a steady drizzle that soaks the ground on which we walk, the air that surrounds us, and gets between our toes even when we wear boots. Our clothes are damp all the time and feel clammy on our skin. They smell musty, they never quite dry after washing; minutes after they leave the ironing table, they are damp again.

Still, they have to be ironed thoroughly to kill the small eggs of putzi flies that cluster in unironed clothing. Putzis attach their eggs to items of washing drying on the line; when they come into contact with our bodies, the eggs can get under our skin and grow there. Most of the time, we will be unaware of this until we suddenly – several times a day – feel an unexpected sharp pain as if the maggot growing under the skin has decided to take a bite.

A few more months of this, and we will be bored with the rain. End-of-tether, last-straw bored. Just as the heat of October threatened to overwhelm us, so the constant mud, the clammy clothes and the sheer wetness of it all saps our energy and good humour. Malaria is alive and thriving in our shrunken community, and our conversations are preoccupied with who is sick, who has just recovered and who's had a relapse.

Small sores don't heal. Every scratch seems to get infected and if we don't keep it meticulously clean, it will fester and swell into an ugly red welt, promising eruptions of yellow-green pus full of unspeakable bacterial life. One of the guides has knocked his shin just below the knee and opened a small gash in the skin. In a matter of days it has grown into a small erupting volcano. Every morning and evening, Paul Murphy drains his wound; milks it of cupfuls of foul fluid. We crouch around him passing him balls of crumpled toilet paper and cotton wool, and marvel at the sheer volume of each eruption. But it won't stop producing more; like a bountiful tropical harvest, it bubbles and ferments below the skin and in the marrow of his shinbone, and Paul Murphy hobbles through camp with a mixture of pain and pride.

Our food supplies are usually at their lowest during this time. A shopping trip to Chipata will be put off again and again. It will take half a day to get there over a road surface that has become rutted, gouged by deep erosion channels, and sometimes disappears altogether under a foot of water as far as the eye can see.

But Iwomba insists on serving us dessert with every meal. He has discovered a carton of custard powder in the pantry, and the one other thing we seem to have plenty of is jam (home-made by Iwomba from wild marula fruit in July). At lunchtime Iwomba carries his tray into the *chitenje* and places the bowls on the sideboard (where we can watch them from the table in case of a baboon invasion). Often these days the bowls contain rice and beans or *nshima* and beans, or rice and stew, or just beans. Sometimes we have a fresh salad, but not often. The tomatoes rot quicker than we can eat them and the lettuce lies wilting on the pantry shelves. But always, every day, we get Iwomba's new dessert invention, a glue-like mixture of lumpy custard and globs of marula jam.

'What is this, Iwomba?' we ask him.

'Is trifle,' he replies with his sad smile.

Iwomba may call it 'trifle', we call it 'Murphy's knee'.

When the rain stops for a day, we can hear elephants trumpeting miles away across the river and, if it is the beginning of the month, Dolly Parton's 'Queen of the Silver Dollar' drifts across the lagoon from the game department offices. Dolly is out of place somehow and I would rather listen to the elephants, but I know the batteries will soon run out and the tape player will fall silent till next payday.

The wind blows hot and wet and thick with mosquitoes at night.

20 Noah

Noah was the name someone gave to a baby elephant that got washed up on the riverbank late one afternoon without his mother. It was the rainy season and the river was high and flowing fast. Elephants are strong swimmers, and cows are extremely protective of their young, especially at a vulnerable time such as a river crossing when the calves bob in the water, almost totally submerged like miniature submarines, with only their trunks showing above the water.

Nevertheless, this baby somehow lost his mother and was found by a game scout trying to clamber up the steep bank. The bank was muddy and slippery from a recent rainstorm, and at least five times the calf's height. The scout called for some helpers, and together they managed to pull the exhausted elephant on to solid ground while lightning flashed in the indigo sky on the far side of the river.

No one quite knew what to do with him. He was tiny, less than a year old, and needed his mother. Or at least a mother of some kind.

As was their daily routine, several groups of elephants had crossed the river to the east bank and were moving off to the distant trees where they would feed during the night, returning to the safety of the Park in the early morning hours. The scouts could see them in the gloomy distance: lumbering shapes made indistinct by the low rain clouds and the falling darkness. They walked the calf up to the closest group, approaching as near as they could while still keeping a safe distance, but the cows made no attempt to accept him into their midst – they wouldn't even let him come near. Either they were traumatised by the event of losing one of their calves, spooked by the rumbling thunder and the lightning flickering through the trees, or – most likely – it was the wrong herd.

The scouts were at a loss. They knew they couldn't abandon the calf. If none of the wild elephants would adopt him, he would die. With much pushing and cajoling, they managed to walk him to their offices half a mile away and reported the matter to their ranger.

The ranger knew the difficulties involved in trying to raise a wild elephant calf. He also knew it wasn't strictly legal. But he had to act quickly, and perhaps the necessary permits could be dealt with later. There were only a few likely candidates to assume the role of surrogate mother, only a few people with the resources, the willingness, the understanding and passion – the foolishness – to accept such a challenge. One of them was Adrian Carr, and the ranger decided to contact him first.

The scouts loaded the calf into the back of their Land Cruiser and dropped it off at Kapani, and someone named it Noah. As in the flood.

It is a mammoth task – no pun intended – to raise an elephant. Adrian had loved elephants all his life and felt that he understood them better than most; he had lived among them since childhood, had observed their habits and their different characters. He had read all he could about them, was awed by them, their intelligence and their almost human traits. He had hunted them, he sometimes dreamt about them – but he had never nursed one.

The first thing to do was to get some advice. How much milk, how often, what kind, what dilution? How to avoid stomach infections, how to keep him calm and create a stress-free environment for him. What to do if he got sick? In the following days, Adrian phoned a wildlife veterinarian he knew in Lusaka, he perused the Wilderness Guardian handbook, he talked to John Coppinger from Tafika camp, who had successfully raised elephants himself. He asked friends in Lusaka to shop around for the right milk formula – Nestlé's S 22 – and if necessary to import some from South Africa.

But in the mean time, night had fallen, and the small elephant calf in his yard was obviously scared and disorientated. And hungry. It took short running steps from one person to the next but could not find reassurance from any of us. We are told not to anthropomorphise, not to read human emotions into an animal's behaviour, but there was no mistaking the fear in his small black eyes.

'Someone go and find Miranda,' said Adrian. 'Tell her there's a baby elephant in my garden.'

Pam was in bed with malaria and couldn't help, but Miranda was home from university for the Christmas holidays. Deb from Kaingo Camp happened to be visiting, and while Adrian worried about the bigger picture and wondered how much it was all going to cost (several tins of S 22 a day for … how many years?), the two girls took charge of the calf's immediate future. They walked him in slow circles around the yard, scratching behind his ears and the soft underside of his trunk, talking to him in low voices. Slowly they felt the tension draining from him, and each step – each soft word – seemed to calm his shaky nerves.

'My God, he's cute,' said Miranda.

'Tiny,' said Deb.

'And scared. Hope he'll be okay.'

Deb nodded.

'Don't worry, little fellow,' said Miranda, 'it'll be fine. Look at his long eyelashes, Deb.'

Someone had found some powdered milk somewhere, probably in the lodge storeroom. What about a bottle? Would a coke bottle do? Those low rumbling sounds that Deb produced deep in her throat, were they close enough to the real thing, the sounds that elephants made? It seemed to settle the calf so she kept on purring. But where was he going to sleep? Who would stay with him? There was nothing in camp that could serve as a stable, except perhaps Tamara's small pottery shed. But it was too far from our houses, and it was full of pottery wheel, tools, and shelves of pots and clay objects.

Adrian was in the process of building a small house for his cook at the edge of his garden. The building was less than half finished: unplastered man-high walls, but no doors, no roof. Still, the rain had stopped, and it would have to do. We hastily barricaded the gaping doorway with some building planks and a fuel drum, cut fresh grass at the edge of the *dambo* to cover the rough cement floor, and the two girls enticed the calf inside with the help of his milk bottle.

The night passed slowly. The calf's intermittent squeals kept all of us at the edge of sleep. Everyone within earshot slept fitfully that night, and we could all hear the baby moving restlessly about within his enclosure, knocking against the makeshift door, rattling the fuel drum, scraping the walls, whimpering.

The girls didn't sleep at all. They soon realised that they couldn't lie down for fear of being trampled or squashed. And they couldn't leave. Once or twice, thinking the elephant was asleep because he

was leaning against the rough brick wall with his eyes closed, they tried to climb over the planks for a break. But as soon as one of them moved, he was alert again.

Somehow, between the last owl and the first call of the fish eagle, the night passed, but it was a long night, and in the light of the new day, some practical aspects had to be decided on.

Feeding him was no problem; he seemed permanently hungry and, once he got used to the milk bottle, willingly followed anyone who held it. Miranda assumed the role of elephant mother as comprehensively as she knew how. Making the low rumbling sounds of elephants in the back of her throat, she walked about the patchy lawn between the huts of our camp with the unhurried dignity of a real elephant, pausing every few paces to let Noah nuzzle up, his trunk searching for the bottle. They would both stand for a while, the calf making soft sucking sounds while Miranda scratched behind his ears, stroked the soft skin at the base of his trunk, and searched his skin for ticks. Another few steps, another few inches of milk from the bottle, and all the while Miranda's soft voice telling the elephant in reassuring words that all would be well, telling him stories.

After each feeding session, the milk had to go back in the fridge, and before the next session it had to be warmed again on the stove.

That afternoon it started to rain again, and we still had not found a better shelter for Noah. We needed a permanent place, a stable of some kind, an elephant house.

'I know what we can do,' said Miranda. 'I'll move out of my room, he can sleep there. Tammy is not coming for the holidays, so I'll just move into her place. I know she won't mind.'

Our daughters' rooms were two thatched rondavels connected by a communal veranda. Miranda emptied her room of all movable objects. She shifted the chairs, the desk, the bed, her personal things, her clothes. She piled the furniture and tin trunks in the corner of the porch, and when the room was completely bare save for a built-in cupboard, she put some grass on the floor.

'There,' she said. 'A perfectly nice elephant house. I'll be sleeping in Tam's

room, right next door and I'll hear him if he has a problem.'

He did have a problem. He refused to sleep. All night, again. The round wall of the room only served as an enticement to keep running – it had no end. He ran and ran and never reached the end of the wall. When Miranda was in the room with him, he seemed calmer. His steps slowed down, and he even stood still for long moments. But as soon as she left the room, Noah would squeal and fret and start running again. He was obviously accustomed to the comfort of the herd, of other warm bodies surrounding him. Of the herd always on the move. It was clear that he simply could not be left alone, not even for a minute.

Miranda sent a message up to the lodge to say that as soon as her boyfriend Huw returned from his night drive he should come and join her. And bring a couple of beers because it was going to be a long night.

It *was* a long night. Miranda and Huw sat in the darkness on the hard cement floor, back to back in the centre of the room, trying to stay awake. They talked in low voices, which seemed to please the elephant, and they touched him every now and then to reassure him. It was hot under the thatched roof, with the warm body of the elephant inside and the humid and still night air pressing through the open window. They could see the leaves of the trees motionless against the rising moon in the pale square of the window. They began to sweat and decided to strip down to their underwear. But they were still hot.

They did not dare fall asleep and kept each other awake with stories, and with the thought of a restless body weighing well over half a ton in the room with them.

When Miranda closed her eyes to try to snatch a few minutes' sleep, she felt the soft padding of his feet going round and round inside her head, and against her closed eyelids she seemed to see only *his* eyes, black and impenetrable as the night outside.

At some point in the middle of the night, Huw opened the door to let in some night air. The calf, who had appeared to be sleeping, was instantly awake and out through the door. Before Huw or Miranda could react, he had disappeared into the damp night.

The rain had stopped but the air still felt moist, as if a sea mist was hanging between the trees. Where had he gone? They saw flat round depressions in the muddy ground that looked like his footprints, and decided to follow them. Out past Norman's house on to the open *dambo*, out towards the distant trees. The moon had drifted behind a cloud, and Huw's small torch was useless against the darkness that surrounded them. Soon they lost the spoor among the puddles, the clumps of mud and the tufts of soggy grass.

The sound of hippos rumbled along the river.

They looked at each other, then up at the dark sky. After long minutes, the moon broke through the clouds again and they saw a shape moving rapidly across the *dambo* in the direction of the river. Moonlight on its back, ears flapping.

They started to run, and when they caught up with him they were completely out of breath and, Miranda realised, completely naked.

It could not go on like this. We needed help. It was obvious that we had to find a full-time elephant minder, a kind of African mahout. We asked Alefer and Iwomba to enquire around their villages and see if they could find someone who wanted the job.

The person who showed up at dusk did not look like the sort of man who would inspire confidence. He was a low-browed individual with hooded eyes that shifted constantly as if caught in a spotlight while doing something immoral, or something private and depraved. Pam, who had recently suffered a series of minor burglaries, immediately locked up her laptop computer and other valuable possessions.

'Hmm. Not sure about this guy.'

'Shall we give him a try? We're not exactly overrun with applicants.'

'Let's see how he copes. If he lasts the night.' Pam shivered, the malaria still in her bones.

But perhaps we did the man an injustice. First impressions can be misleading, and he seemed to settle down to his task with unexpected sensitivity. We showed him how to use the bottle, and he sat on the dry grass on the floor and kept the elephant quiet and amused by talking to him and touching him. Whenever one of us peered in through the window, the calf seemed content. The man sang to him in a low monotone, stroking him and scratching behind his ear.

When we came back from dinner (soup and bread on Norman's porch), they were both still quiet, and we nodded at the minder through the window. Exhausted from two consecutive sleepless nights, we all went to bed.

An hour later the elephant started screaming. Miranda got out of bed quickly and ran across the veranda. She shone her torch through the window and saw Isaac (I seem to remember that was the man's name) crouching on top of the built-in cupboard, wedged under the thatched roof, arms around his knees, rocking back and forth in the small space. Below him, the elephant was running in hysterical circles.

'What's wrong? What happened?'

The terrified man on top of the wardrobe shook his head.

'Madam, I am frightened.'

'Of what?'

'I don't know. Of the night.'

Miranda opened the door and tried to soothe the spooked calf, and at the same time reassure the man on the cupboard that there was no need to be afraid of the noises outside, he was perfectly safe inside the hut.

The next night at about eleven, a herd of elephant circled the edge of camp, caught the scent of the youngster and started demonstrating. The night was black, and a steady rain was falling again. Several elephants trumpeted at once, no doubt a scary sound to the man inside guarding the baby. Unable to see them, he heard them coming closer, trumpeting again.

The baby answered with a plaintive squeal. Then a cow outside – a big cow by the sound of it – bellowed with a volume that seemed to shake the trees. The thought of a herd of elephants advancing through the falling rain to snatch the baby from his care – and probably kill him in the process – was too much for the man. His nerve broke. Who knows what thoughts ran through his mind? Did he think perhaps that he had been employed for this specific task? To defend the youngster against all odds, and if necessary pay with his life? Die in the line of duty?

Whatever his thoughts, they were not happy ones, and he too began to scream. 'Help! Heeeeeelp. Help me, please help me! Do something!'

Pam, who still had not shaken off her fever, had been lying in bed listening to the commotion outside. Never one to ignore cries for help, she jumped out of bed, hastily wrapped herself in a blanket, and sprinted the twenty metres through the rainy night to where the terrified man was crouched inside the hut, on top of the wardrobe again, to reassure and comfort him. But the man, sensing a possible escape from certain death, bolted from the doorway when he saw Pam approaching, and disappeared into the night. With the diligence of a new employee on only his second night on the job he remembered to shut the door and to snap the padlock.

Pam stood shivering on the threshold, her back to the driving rain, and listened to Noah's panicked screams inside the hut.

The watchman was whimpering somewhere behind her in the darkness, and elephants still trumpeted among the trees. Where was the key? She turned in the direction of the moaning watchman and spoke across the empty space, trying to placate the terrified man. Trying to calm him and tell him it was okay, elephants often came through at night, they hadn't come specifically for him, it was all going to be fine, now please come back with the key.

The man went home in the morning and never came back, but at the end of that week, the elephant had settled down. Looking after him was still a job for three or four people, but with Alefer's, Iwomba's, and the gardener's help, Miranda managed. The gardener replaced the night watchman and became Noah's official minder, on the premise that we needed a cook and a handyman more than a gardener. The lawn was looking good and the vegetable garden could survive on its own for a while since it didn't need watering, and our new fence and diamond mesh cover seemed to be keeping the baboons out. Besides, the gardener had the right temperament for the job; after all, he had the patience to watch plants grow.

After a month, the baby elephant had become an established member of the household, and it was a common sight to see him wandering around the paths between the huts, the kitchen, and the winding track up to the lodge. Often a small noise outside my studio would make me look up from my work and I would see him pushing through the tall new grass shooting up on the bank. Or I would see him standing on the lawn, Miranda sprinkling his back with the garden hose. He used his trunk to explore, and let it wander up Miranda's legs, arms and face, touching her gently like a lover.

But it had also become clear to everyone, especially Adrian, that we would not be able to keep him in the long run. Miranda had to go back to university eventually, Pam and I had our own work keeping us busy, and Adrian his.

Adrian knew a game rancher in South Africa who had a small herd of young elephants on his ranch, and who was keen to add Noah to his tribe. It took time to arrange the necessary permits in both countries but after a week of faxes and phone calls, all initial problems had been ironed out, and a date was set for Noah's departure. The South African would send his plane, accompanied by a wildlife veterinarian and a couple of handlers, and fly him south to his new home.

'I'm going to miss you, little Noah,' said Miranda. 'Not so little, hey? But I'm happy for you. You'll be with your own people. There'll be other ellies there, you'll see.'

Noah stood in the puddle while water from the hosepipe rained on his forehead. He shook his head and swung his trunk, stepped on his trunk and almost lost his balance in the slippery mud. Miranda thought she saw embarrassment in his expression, as if he was aware of his clumsiness.

'You'll be the new kid in town, and maybe the others will play jokes on you, as elephants will.' She looked into the dark eyes with their long lashes. 'Because

you guys can be real clowns, can't you? Bunch of stand-up comics.' Her voice grew serious. 'And what's more you seem to know it.' She scratched behind his ear. 'But they say animals don't have consciousness.'

It was a solution that pleased everyone, and it seemed that the story was going to have a happy ending. The stage was set.

What we hadn't counted on was the obstructive nature of the Zambian bureaucracy. Or, to be more precise, of one bureaucrat who took it into his head to stick to the rules, regardless.

A high-ranking official in the headquarters of the National Parks Department in the distant town of Chilanga, returned to his office from a trip out of town, was briefed on the elephant situation by a member of his staff, and said *No*. He sent instructions to the ranger at Mfuwe to have the elephant released in the National Park. The ranger telephoned Kapani Lodge on our radio-telephone and relayed the message. The elephant was to be taken into the Park and released.

Adrian phoned the official and tried to explain that the calf had been given into his care by the official's own department in the first place, that he had gone to a great deal of trouble and expense in order to keep it alive, and that he had now made arrangements to have it relocated at no expense to the department. The official still said no.

Adrian pointed out that if the elephant were abandoned in the park, he would die. No wild herd would adopt a semi-domesticated orphan; he would wander around the bush on his own, unable to feed himself and would slowly starve. Lions and hyenas would do the rest. The director told Adrian that he was aware of these facts, and should the outcome be what Adrian predicted, then so be it. 'Nature,' he added, 'is cruel. You may not understand, but it's tough out there.'

Adrian was about to point out that in this case it was man, not nature, who was cruel, and that an alternative solution was at hand, but he thought better of it. He thought of reminding the official of the tame baboon that had been the subject of a similar 'release' exercise. The baboon hadn't wanted to go and, frightened of being abandoned, had tried to follow the vehicle until the scouts had finally given up, tied the baboon to a tree and driven off. But what would be the point?

Logic, reason, and common sense don't seem to carry the same weight in Africa as they do elsewhere. The trouble with Africa is that things are seldom as they seem, that there are hidden motives that we can only guess at, forces hiding under the surface of things – like crocodiles – of which we are only dimly aware.

Maybe the wildlife official had his own reasons; perhaps they were personal or perhaps they were reasons of principle. He had the authority, and perhaps that was the only reason he needed.

It was one of those bright rainy season days when the storm clouds have drifted away and the sun is back in a high blue sky – cerulean and white – and the trees' outlines have lost their fuzzy edges and were hard and clear again, and the hills on the escarpment appeared closer than they really were. Hippos had left the river and looked black and deep purple against the bright light reflecting off the water. They stood at the edge of the river or lay in tight clumps in the white sand, their heavy heads resting on each other's backs.

Noah was standing on the high grassy bank with his minder. Below them the wide sandy beach sloped gently down to a strip of black mud at the water's edge. Egyptian geese chattered and plovers flew in low circles above the sand.

Noah shuffled a few steps towards the edge of the high bank and turned his head into the breeze that blew off the river. Tilting it this way and that, he caught the wind behind his ears and they made a loud slapping sound. He lifted his head and held it still for a moment. The wind off the water raised the sparse black hairs on his wrinkled back. His dark brown eyes with their impossibly long lashes reflected the river, the trees on the other side, and all of the wide sky, it seemed. He lowered his trunk and let it wander between the tufts of grass and explore the smells of the earth.

The minder looked up and saw dark rain clouds gathering behind the treeline on the other bank. He touched the calf's side and spoke quietly to him in his native Chinyanja.

'Okay, you! Look at those clouds. Rain is coming, let's go back to camp.'

Miranda was standing near the kitchen, talking to Jake who had just arrived and was standing next to his vehicle. His dog Milo was running among the puddles with his head high and ears forward, scouting the tree tops for monkeys. The wind in the mopane trees had died down and it had started raining again, a light drizzle that shrouded the forest in a silver veil and muffled the sound of the approaching vehicle.

A white Land Cruiser splashed through the sodden and rutted road and braked hard to stop abruptly at the end of the driveway. Two uniformed game scouts were sitting in the cab and four more crouched in the truck's open back.

'Where is that animal, that elephant?' one of them asked Jake.

'We have come to take him!' grinned another, jumping from the back of the Land Cruiser.

Jake looked at the man, shrugged and whistled for Milo.

'Come on dog, let's go.'

The scout turned away from him and shouted in the direction of the kitchen where he saw Iwomba standing in the doorway.

'*Ayeee* . . .' he yelled, '*njovu ali kuti?*'

Iwomba pointed towards Adrian's house, his outstretched arm like a silent indictment. Then he turned wordlessly into the kitchen. The six scouts marched through our camp like a military commando on the brink of victory, shouting and laughing.

Miranda followed them at a distance until they passed her hut. There she stopped and turned into her doorway to step inside but she turned again and stood there, her eyes following them through the trees.

They found Noah on the lawn in front of Adrian's house where the gardener was splashing him with a hosepipe. They circled around him. Noah turned away from them, his eyes rolling back in his head.

'We have come to take this animal. You can tell Mr Carr. Mr Adrian,' said the man in command, addressing the minder. Miranda saw him look towards the house and she saw Adrian standing at the kitchen window, his face like marble. The scout stared back: immobile, his back straight, the olive-green beret at a slight angle on his head. Then he turned to the men.

'Let's go. *Tien*. We are wasting time standing around here like . . . you know like we are sleeping. You!' He pushed at the elephant, 'Move.'

They crowded around Noah and began pushing. Miranda heard a thin squeal like steam escaping from a high-pressure boiler. She saw one scout reach for the elephant's tail, laughing, and as the elephant turned, another quickly grabbed his trunk and began to pull. A third one took hold of the left ear, and with the others pushing from behind and shouting encouragement, they shoved and dragged him through the wet grass towards their vehicle. The elephant struggled and slipped and screamed – a shrill sound like a frightened piglet – but there was no escape from the laughing men. They pushed and pulled him past Miranda's house where Miranda leaned in her doorway, arms crossed; past Tamara's pottery shed and past the empty kitchen until they reached the circle at the end of the driveway where their vehicle was parked.

One of the men reached into the cab for a coil of rope. They tied the struggling elephant's front legs together, then his hind legs. Noah was weakening but still fighting. One of the scouts slipped and fell into a puddle, causing one of the others to dance a loose-limbed jig in imitation of a man slipping on a banana skin.

'OK, *tien! Tien.* Lift! Push! Altogether . . . One, two threee. Sakala, don't be lazy. You should be pushing like a, you know . . . like a tractor.'

One scout stood in the bed of the cruiser and pulled the elephant's trunk, the others lifted and pushed, bumping and scraping until they finally had him lying on his side on the steel floor of the truck's loading bed. Their shouts and guffaws almost drowned out the elephant's screams.

The driver climbed into the cab. A puff of black diesel smoke burst from the exhaust pipe and drifted away on the rising wind. The driver gunned the engine. One of the scouts stood erect in the back of the moving vehicle and sang in a clear, high-pitched voice, 'Oh Lord, won't you buy me a Mercedes Benz . . .' The others laughed, their laughter dying in the falling rain as the car pulled out of the drive and disappeared slowly among the sodden mopane trees.

The Kapani game drive saw a white Land Cruiser offload a baby elephant late that afternoon in an open space near Mbangula lagoon. A group of elephants was busy feeding in a nearby grove of winter thorns, and after a while the calf appeared to take a few uncertain steps towards them. But the group moved off before it could get close. They were all bulls.

The following day, another drive came across a small elephant calf standing alone among tall acacias not far from the edge of the lagoon.

After that, he was not seen again.

21   The Ebony Grove

I've been away again, in the USA for an exhibition. This time I stayed longer. The time had come for me to take a long break from Africa.

Sooner or later, it seems, every white person in Africa will reach the end of the line. When the apathy of the local people and their sometimes flexible relationship with the truth has begun to get you down. When you have been touched one too many times by hijackings, armed robberies, death from disease and wild animals. When the lack of honour and honourable behaviour, the all-pervading lethargy and selfishness has ground you down. When enough has finally become enough!

Africa is chaos. It's upside down, back to front,

lawless chaos, with no bottom to its dysfunctional despair. We cannot lean on our familiar Western structures or systems because they do not exist here. We know we will never truly belong. Even the second or third generation whites, like Lester and Rolf Shenton, who were born and raised in Zambia will always be outsiders.

'Where are you from? I mean *originally*, where are you from?'

'I was born here.'

'Yes, but still. You must be from somewhere, your parents … I mean you're white!'

Those of us who have the option, who can pack up and leave, will sooner or later reach the point where we do just that.

Then we go and live in some First World suburb and work in a First World office. We are surrounded by people who have not shared our experiences, have never been drenched by the intense light of an African sunrise, have never seen the smile of friendship – of brotherhood – on the face of a crippled African beggar on a dusty street corner.

And we are bored. Deep-down-disinterested bored by the conversations, the aspirations and preoccupations that sound childish and unimportant to our Third World ears. Bored by the comfort zone, the obsession with material success. We have, after all, proved to ourselves that we can manage fine without them, that our lives are in fact fuller, more complete, the less they are encumbered by the trappings of capitalism.

We jeer at the grey throngs of subway commuters, the peacock-costumed bicycle riders. We are miserable; all we can think of is going back. We are lost in no-man's-land. We are the lost white African tribe, displaced and discontent. We know we are doomed to be forever unhappy with Africa's contradictions, and we know we can never be happy anywhere else.

I lived for several months in Colorado, and spent the deepest part of the winter in a cabin on the Wyoming state line.

The Americans I met were decent, honest, law-abiding, hard-working. They have to be. Their society expects nothing less and tolerates no misfits. The abundance of laws and regulations has made them into the people they are. From my outside vantage point, the people appear programmed, all chasing the same goal, a homogenous army of commuters congesting the highways in an orderly fashion twice every day.

From an African viewpoint, the efficiency of the system is staggering, the absence of litter and debris the first thing you notice: the towns and highways look freshly scrubbed. Often, they are.

From across the ocean, this is a society at the summit of civilisation.

Is it already teetering on the brink of inevitable collapse like the Egyptians and Greeks and the Romans before them? Or will global warming and unchecked population growth end life on our planet before that can happen? Or is America indeed the Brave New World that will set the example to the rest of the world and show the way to an enlightened future?

The land of the free. Freedom of the state and freedom of its people. But are the people of America really free, or are rules and laws and regulations choking the very concept of personal freedom?

Of course, every civilised society has

detail. Noise reduction and littering laws. Marriage, divorce, and custody laws. Bar opening, liquor licensing and anti-smoking laws. How we may treat our pets. How we recycle our garbage. Where we may walk our dogs.

to have rules and laws. The opposite is chaos, like Africa is chaos. Laws that guarantee fundamental human rights are as necessary as the air we breathe, and the basic tenets of the American constitution (and the British, German, French, Italian …) should indeed be carved in stone, like the Ten Commandments.

But now there are laws pertaining to every single aspect of our lives in minute

Speed limits that sometimes change every few miles or less – in Boulder, Colorado, on a stretch of Broadway, you must drive 25, then 35, then 25 again, then 30, 35, then 25 and 15. The speed limit has changed ten times on a five-mile stretch, and you ask yourself, is this really necessary? Am I really this stupid, this irresponsible, that I cannot think for myself? Is it not common sense to slow down in front of a school, can I not be trusted with so simple a decision?

Out in the woods, there are rules, too. Where we are allowed to camp, where we may hike.

We are intrigued, even exhilarated, by the noise and colour, the street-parties, the laissez-faire 'vibe' on a Caribbean Island. Yet we go to great pains to make sure that nothing remotely resembling that atmosphere will grow in our own suburban streets. We regard our neighbours with suspicion, and when Halloween comes around once a year, most American kids may only go trick-or-treating under adult supervision.

People drink expensive bottled water and ride their bicycles in multicoloured spandex outfits with matching boots and water bottles and odd-shaped plastic helmets. My friend Bobo says, 'God, you'd think they're on their way to invade Afghanistan when all they're doing is ride their bike around the block.'

We try and protect ourselves from every possible eventuality. We pay insurance premiums that cripple our budgets – and that may pay out for a coffin and a gravestone when someone dies but can never alleviate the grief we feel at their funeral.

And when something does go wrong – as it always must because it is inherent to the core of our existence – we can sue. The obsession with law and order has created a comfort zone around each individual, but seems to have bred a citizenry who do not know how to take responsibility for their own actions. Who

are quick to blame someone else for any mishap, and are encouraged to do so by the busy machinery of the legal system. People have sued McDonald's for not warning them that they might get fat if they eat too many Big Macs. To an African, even a white African, this is incomprehensible.

The Yellow Pages – again in Boulder, Colorado, a town of less than one hundred thousand people – has 719 listings for attorneys.

A dog-owner was reported to the police by a neighbour for allegedly hitting his dog. The owner claimed that he had not touched the dog but had hit the ground next to it with a rolled-up newspaper; he was attempting to house-train the dog – his own dog. In the absence of eye-witnesses, the judge was apparently unsure how to rule, but finally sentenced the man to ten hours' community service and prescribed several sessions of (state-funded) therapy for him to learn to manage his anger.

There are day-care centres for dogs, with personal trainers and stress-relieving massages as options. In Africa, most dogs never have enough to eat; many *people* can't find enough to eat.

When I face an African dawn on an empty plain, these laws seem superfluous, even ridiculous: I am capable of making up my own mind whether smoking is good for me or not, and I will certainly consider the rights of others if I do smoke. (But I'm not standing in a crowded subway, so it's easy to say.) If I drive too fast in my car and

cause an accident – or a death – I will have to live with my conscience afterwards, as I would in Germany or America – and no threat of fines or imprisonment would change that.

The arrogance of all governments is their inability to credit their citizens with the intelligence to make their own choices. Wasn't it Plato who said, act responsibly so that every one of your actions could become law. The law makers of our Western systems have diverged a long way from that simple maxim.

A bumper sticker in Colorado read: YOU ARE ALL SHEEP.

It's the same in Europe. My brother in Germany buys a new car every two years and a new suit every few months. His wife redecorates their home once a year. They are insured against every possible misadventure; except of course the big

ones – those real disasters and tragedies that lie in wait during the course of a life and which no insurance can cover. Their medical policies will take care of all hospital bills, and their pension is secured until the end of their lives. For this, my brother works a fourteen-hour day, with two weeks' leave a year.

I ran away from his world a long time ago, and it has become as alien to me as mine must be to him. My Land Cruiser is eight years old and going strong. I'm happy to keep it a while longer – the older it gets the less likely it is that someone will steal it (there is nothing like driving a brand new car in Africa for raising blood pressure). I have another fifteen-year-old Cruiser that I'm keeping because they don't make them that tough any more.

I'm back in Africa now. I am sitting in a patch of late afternoon sun on the rough, leaf-strewn ground, my back against the dark trunk of a

tall African Ebony tree that rises twenty-five metres into the sky. Above my head is a tapestry of leathery grey-green leaves, near-black branches and a slowly darkening blue sky.

A troop of baboons is still busy on the ground despite the deepening afternoon. Their shadows are long as they dig with bony human-like hands below the carpet of matted leaves. They find fresh shoots and edible roots and seedlings and pull them from the ground.

Sometimes they sniff them briefly or inspect them by holding them in front of their eyes before pushing them into their mouths. The older animals are always watchful: their heads are constantly turning from side to side, up into the trees, and down to the ground. Some of the animals have begun eyeing the trees more purposefully: with the approaching dusk, it is almost time to climb into the high branches and settle for the night

A short distance behind me is Norman's grave. The straight boughs of five tall ebonies form a semicircle with a cathedral-like roof of interlocking branches and deep green leaves. In the centre of this space rests the stone, an oblong monolith of solid granite that was brought here from the hills above Chichele. A brass plaque is set in the weathered surface of the stone, the straight lines of its shiny square the only evidence of man in this quiet natural space.

> *Norman Carr*
> *Conservationist*
> *May he rest in peace here in the quiet of the park*
> *Which will forever be his monument*

Most early evenings, when the sun has cooled and the last daylight is fading from the sky, elephants gather in this grove in calm preparation for their river crossing, and I have often seen them moving quietly among the dark trees, grey on grey, solemnly filing past the stone as if in silent tribute.

But the Africa that Norman knew no longer exists. The days of exploring new territory on foot where no white man had ever set foot before belong to the past, and Norman was one of the last of the generation who knew that world. The era of the elephant control officer is over. The world has moved on, and Africa has moved on with it, albeit reluctantly. Albeit at a slower pace.

The game is now confined to relatively small pockets of land set aside for its protection. But already the cry is for more land for agriculture, for the spreading towns – for the people.

The truth is that Africa can't afford wildlife. The trouble with Africa is that its rapidly increasing population is spreading fast and unplanned in all directions, and the natural resouces can't keep up. Around the big Zambian towns wild game has all but disappeared. Where bush pigs and antelope, baboons and leopards were plentiful only thirty years ago, there are now spreading villages, ugly compounds, or empty silent bush. Even birds are under constant threat from slingshots and snares and traps.

Lusaka was once surrounded by *miombo* forests. Today, the trees are mostly gone, and every day rusting trucks limp up the dirt tracks from the surrounding hillsides and valleys huffing under their heavy loads of felled trees or sacks of charcoal. Every day the trucks have to go further, and these days there are fires burning in the forest reserves, too. The charcoal burners have to make a living.

The *mzungus* who live on the outskirts of town and see the endless procession of charcoal trucks are outraged.

'They're cutting down every single tree for miles,' they say. 'And no one ever seems to plant a new one!' All this is true, of course. Ideally, this wholesale harvest of trees should be controlled and managed. But the concept of a managed infrastructure is still quite new to this part of Africa. Civil or social awareness is a luxury; responsibility an alien concept.

Meanwhile, the population of Lusaka has grown to more than a million people. The vast majority of them live in hopeless shacks in 'informal settlements' – the politically correct term for the abysmally squalid shanty towns that surround the inner city and its few affluent suburbs like strangler vines. The people who live here have left the suffocating poverty of village life to find a better future in town. But life in the towns is, if anything, harder, sadder, more desperate.

A few scrawny chickens scratch in the lifeless dust, sewage runs between the small houses in open drains, a fertile conduit for dysentery, hepatitis, or worse. And there is the all-pervading, stifling haze from the charcoal fires that burn in front of every shack. The people have to eat; they have to cook. And the trees are still cut down by the thousand, without a thought to replanting.

The Aids epidemic is adding fuel to the fire of poverty, unemployment and misery. The sexually active run the highest risk: the able-bodied are dying young, leaving behind dependant orphans and the elderly.

But we want wildlife.

Excuse me? Come again?

Most urbanised Africans have never seen a zebra or an elephant. The carvers of tourist curios are ignorant of the true identities of their models. There is a large settlement along the Kafue road outside Lusaka where forests of wooden giraffes stand tall by the roadside. If you stop and ask the carvers if they've ever seen a live giraffe, they will grin and shake their heads. To the millions of poor in Africa, wild animals are meat. They are not good for anything else.

It's the same word: *nyama,* wild animal; *nyama*, meat.

But we – we Europeans and Americans – think Africa should preserve its wildlife.

And we'll help. From the comfort of our suburban armchairs, that's easily said. We lecture, we cajole, we 'educate'. We send our 'experts' from Denmark or Norway to establish systems and projects. The experts have finally understood the fundamental truth that if wildlife in Africa is to survive, it has to pay for itself. (Norman Carr knew this simple fact fifty years ago.) Tourist dollars have to be channelled back into local communities who live on the boundaries of game reserves to help them understand the value of their wild heritage. But the concept of tourism as a policy of national interest is still struggling. To many Africans, the notion of a foreigner hunting – or even simply enjoying – their game is fraught with mixed emotions. Jealousies and xenophobia are still massive stumbling blocks to the proper development of tourism.

Meantime, the poaching continues.

In the Luangwa Valley, you can walk along any river or lagoon within a strip of a kilometre or two, and if you're observant and know where to look, you will find snares. Dozens of wire snares in a single day. You will see elephant calves with half their trunks missing, lions with festering and obviously agonising wounds around their necks. A baboon might chew off the useless foot and survive on three legs, but the leopard cannot reach the noose around his neck, and the more he tries to pull it, the more it will strangle and suffocate him.

Black rhino have completely disappeared from the Valley, and the elephant population has shrunk from close to a hundred thousand forty years ago, to eight, or ten, or perhaps twelve thousand, depending on whose statistics you want to believe.

There is a noise somewhere behind me, and between the dark tree trunks I see that two bull elephants have entered the grove. For a moment they are silhouetted in the gaps between the trees; then their shapes lose their distinct outlines and blur into the soft-edged landscape. I see them ambling slowly towards the river in the gathering twilight. I know that later this evening, just before the light is completely gone, they will cross the river to the other side.

They seem in no hurry. Elephants have almost the same lifespan that we do, but their lives must seem longer to them. Everything they do is leisurely; time for them must move at a slower pace, and it is not often that you see an elephant hurry or lose his dignity in pursuit of a material goal or under pressure of time.

When Norman became ill, there was no doctor in Zambia who could help him. He arrived in Johannesburg on a night flight, pale and fragile. His eyes were deep and hollow. The medical prognosis was straightforward: with the right care and under the correct supervision in the appropriate facilities, he could recover. But he would have to stay in the city and could not return to Luangwa. Ever. The other alternative was a potentially dangerous operation that might restore the functioning of his kidneys and allow him a modicum of free, if limited, movement. He might even be able to return home; and with self-administered procedures and medication, he might persevere. But it was risky.

Norman's decision was equally straightforward. Operate.

It didn't work.

His memorial service in the ebony grove was attended by more than five hundred people. His staff were there, and everyone from the local camps and lodges. Friends flew in from Lusaka and Johannesburg and distant parts of Zambia. The Kapani choir sang and the BBC was there to record it. Miranda recited a poem from the seventh century BC.

> Oh girls of honey-sweet voices, my
>   limbs are weak
> They will not bear me. I wish, ah, I
>   wish I were
> a carefree kingfisher flying over
>   flowering foam
> with the halcyons – sea-blue holy birds
>   of spring.

Kenneth Kaunda, Zambia's first president, came and paid his last respects to a friend, a man he admired. That evening at Kapani Lodge, I spoke to him.

'I was thinking the other day about my first years in Zambia, and about your concept of humanism. I was trying to write about it, and I asked myself how to describe it, what exactly was meant by it? Well, I'm standing face to face with the man who invented it.' I smiled at him, 'So who better to ask.'

Kaunda looked at me a long time. Then he said, 'You are an artist. I think you know.' I smiled and nodded slowly.

'It's not a doctrine,' he added. 'It's a way of life.'

Miranda has finished university and is back in the Valley, a permanent resident and one of the most popular and respected members of the community. (A senior resident, ex-ambassador and close Kaunda friend suggested that if she ran for parliament as the local representative, she would be elected hands-down). But her ambitions are not political. At twenty-five, she is an artist like her parents, if in a different field. Her theatre group, Malambo Drama Group, educates villagers and delights tourists with plays about poachers, conservationists, and the dangers of sexual carelessness. Audiences sit enchanted on wooden benches or dirt floors as the actors bounce around the dusty stage in hilarious and convincing imitation of warthogs, rhinos, chickens, rickety Land Rovers, and – three up – feeding giraffes.

Tamara pursues her own career in a similar field in Cape Town and misses the bush. But she needs the stimulation of the city and the proximity of like-minded artists and writers and theatre people. The Grahamstown Arts Festival, the Johannesburg and Cape Town theatres are a long way from the Zambian bush.

'I need to be here for the time being,' she says. 'But who knows . . .'

Patrick Ansell never finished his house amongst the *mchenja* trees. He lives in his stone cottage in Cornwall and dreams of Africa, not the first to do so. The abandoned walls of his African dream home have collapsed and the bricks lie among tufts of grass, covered by dust and dried baboon droppings. He swears he will never return. The Africa he knew is gone, he says, and he has no interest in seeing the new one. His brother Arthur, being the less romantic of the two, still flies out every year for his four-month season. He is a shareholder in Jake da Motta's new Flatdogs camp and has earned the right to sit on his bar stool in the evening, tell stories and check out the girls from the overland trucks with their wild hair, brown legs, and their skimpy shorts.

Jake finally married Gillie, who came to the Valley over fifteen years ago, a pretty blonde twenty-year old London girl. All the boys gave chase but Jake was her first boyfriend. Somehow they drifted apart a few years later and Gillie teamed up with a professional hunter for nine years. But in the roundabout way these things take, they found each other again, and now they are the newest married couple in the Valley.

Craig and Janelle have moved to Tanzania.

Robin and Jo Pope run Robin Pope Safaris, one of the biggest Safari companies in Zambia.

Chibembe camp has fallen into the river.

The big *chitenje* near the edge was the first to go but, apparently not satisfied, each season the river bit deeper into the bank until only three of the twenty-four chalets were left and the swimming pool behind the chalets where Cliff Bishop taught my kids to swim hangs over the edge.

I have seen Cliff once or twice over the years. One time several years ago was a chance meeting in Lusaka when he was hobbling awkwardly on homemade

crutches that he had welded from strips of angle-iron. They were painted black, dotted with red rust spots. He had told me then that a rare infection of the bone marrow had caused new problems for his bad leg. No money, no steady job, and of course no health insurance had taken proper medical care out of his reach. He'd had another operation, but now the old plastic leg no longer fitted. They made some very nice ones in Switzerland, he told me, with articulated heels and toes. But they were expensive, and the only kind he could afford was the kind they were handing out at the University hospital. Of course they were black. His friends thought that was funny, but Cliff didn't seem to care.

I ran into him again not long ago in a Lusaka hardware store. His jeans were oil-stained and hung loosely from his angular hip bones, and when he shuffled across the linoleum floor to the cashier's desk I noticed that his limp was worse and that walking seemed hard work.

'Hey, Cliff.'

He turned. 'Hey man, what you doing?'

I saw that the lines around his smile were deeper now, but the smile was the same.

'You keeping okay these days?' I asked him.

'Sure, man. I'm living on a small farm out of town, working for my keep, sort of. Come out some time, we'll have a few frosties, talk about the old days.'

'Yeah, why not. I've been thinking a lot about those days. Trying to work on my book again.'

'Oh yeah? I bet there're some stories there …' he grinned. We exchanged telephone numbers, and as he walked out of the store's big double doors into the dusty Lusaka sunshine, he turned back and said over his shoulder: 'And, hey boy, don't you write anything bad about me now.'

I wouldn't, Cliff. I wouldn't.

The road between Lusaka and Chipata has been resurfaced, in parts even completely rebuilt, and driving on it feels almost like driving on an American highway. And on my last trip to the Valley I encountered only a single roadblock.

But the first cracks in the new tarmac have already opened up, and no doubt in time the policemen will reappear along with the potholes, as surely as the grass fires will blacken the hillsides come the next dry season. The one thing you can always rely on in Africa is that nothing is ever permanent, and that every change is short-lived and will open the door to new change.

Like the Luangwa River that keeps altering its course, never content with the way things are, so Africa teaches us this simple truth: that life itself is never constant, and never predictable. You can wear a plastic bicycle helmet with matching shirt and spandex pants, but it does not protect you from other misfortunes, like the unannounced cancer that is already taking root in the dark pulses of your vital organs. Life itself is uncertain, ever-changing. Every one of us has it in his or her grasp to fashion the life we want to lead. We may not be able to dictate our financial prospects, our health or ultimate fate. But we can ensure that we have built good foundations, and we can rise and greet each day and embrace it and say, by God, I will make the best of this life.

The beggar in his rags wearing a plastic bag on his head and a crazy smile; the hunter standing squarely in the path of a charging buffalo; the politician who must decide whether to put his hand in the till or use his head and his heart to improve the prospects of his people; we all have a choice to make.

Cross the Zambezi, and you will see for yourself.

Karen Blixen saw it in the Ngong Hills. Denys Finch-Hatton must have felt it in his plane, in the windy updrafts over Voi before he lost control and crashed. David Livingstone experienced it as he made his way up the Zambezi River for the first time, and it never let him go until he died, years later, in a remote corner of the Bangweulu swamps. Ernest Hemingway wrote about it. And Norman Carr lived his life according to its unspoken rule.

Africa makes us believe – or at least suspect – that there is more than one layer to our existence on this planet. That there is a dimension from which we have been excluded through our upbringing, our education, our environment – through being conditioned to focus on our corporate destiny, to function in our role as consumers. Does this sound like Big Brother? Those of us who have been in Africa long enough think we can look across the oceans at Europe and North America and see him there, Big Brother, with eyes like blank computer screens, trying his utmost to keep that dimension secret from us.

Listen: the elephant raiding a village garden is real. The results – a destroyed maize crop – is as real as a stock market crash is to you and me. The villager is poor, he has no economic power, no political voice of any significance. In the great scheme of things he doesn't count; on a practical level, our reality is light years removed from his.

But has our journey towards civilisation really been such a long one? Has it really taken us so far away from the time when we huddled together around the crackling fire and listened in fear to the noises in the night? From the time when wolves were stealing our sheep?

There was a time when wild animals occupied a more prominent place in our lives than they do now, when their destinies were interwoven with ours. They still visit us in our dreams; and sometimes in dreams they tell us of their plight and their problems and force us to take a look at our own.

They share with us the same bone structure, eyes and ears; the same hearts and lungs and blood. They breathe the same air while they are alive, and when they die, they decay back into the same earth.

We have domesticated many of them, much like our governments have domesticated us, and will continue to do so if we let them. Farm animals are not free. Wild beasts feel the wind in their manes and see the stars at night; they live by the maxim that it is better to die by the hunter's gun than live in the prison of the automated feeding stall where their only prospect is the certainty of the abattoir. The wild animal may die younger and it may die violently. But it lives by its own rules. Norman Carr understood this better than anyone I've ever known.

In the last of the twilight, minutes before the evening fades to black, I listen to the elephants cross the river to the other side. I hear them now, tearing at branches among the distant trees. The hoarse alarm call of a baboon echoes along the river.

And so I came back. Because the simple fact is that I'm in Africa's spell. Africa, of course, doesn't care. Like a beautiful but dangerous woman who turns a cold shoulder to my attentions, her indifference is an added incentive, goading me. Her aloofness only adds to my eagerness to follow her to the edge of the whirlpool.

I know that any day I may be stomped by a marauding elephant, wiped out by an unlicensed car in Lusaka's chaotic traffic or hit by a bullet from a robber's gun. I may incur the displeasure of a zealous bureaucrat who can change the course of my future with the stroke of his pen.

I have had malaria more times than I can remember. I have seen friends die from it. I've seen others die from recklessness, from getting too close to an elephant, or from that senseless random violence that seems part of the African landscape.

I have also experienced more joy here than the human heart has any right to expect. The joy of being awake and alive and out on a vast open plain when the sun's first light floods over the horizon. The joy of hearing the cry of the soaring fish eagle, its voice like liquid honey. The beauty of the blood-red sunsets that seem to hint at some great truth just beyond our grasp. Of watching a herd of elephants crossing the Luangwa River at dusk and shuffling slowly up the bank to mingle with the dark trees, speechless at how something so big can be so ghostlike, so ethereal and so delicate.

I have been awestruck by the raw fury of an African thunderstorm.

And by the African people who, with their stoical acceptance of life's hardships, can teach us all some basic truths about life.

The trouble with Africa is that once it is in your blood, like malaria, it is almost impossible to get rid of, and I know that I can never leave. I feel like a prisoner. A prisoner of freedom.

Epilogue

For the past week I have been coming to this waterhole, this small lagoon slowly drying up in the late September heat. Every day the sun seems to suck up more of the tepid water, exposing the mud at its edge. The mud is soft at first and pockmarked by the hoof prints of a hundred animals that have come here to drink; then it dries quickly to a hard surface, grey and solid as rock.

It is a quiet place, a good spot to be alone, to observe and sketch. There are tall trees on all sides, and I sit in their shade and hear the vervet monkeys feeding high in the branches. In the late afternoon the air is still and feels heavy, golden highlights flicker on the water. Five Spoonbills stand in the shallows today, cutting the surface with endless circular motions of their heads, beaks half submerged, fishing. A pair of Egyptian geese chatter somewhere.

I become aware of a different, heavier sound and look up to see an old buffalo bull, a *kakuli*, materialising among the trees opposite, fifty metres away, and lumbering slowly towards the water. He approaches cautiously, pausing repeatedly to test the wind.

An emerald-spotted wood dove calls mournfully from somewhere behind me. Above my head there is a masked weaver's nest. An erratic September breeze has been blustering, carrying the hot air off the dusty plain, and the nest sways precariously at the end of a thin branch overhanging the water. All afternoon the male weaver has been at work; flying to and fro, alighting on the branch with blades of grass in his beak, and threading them into the intricate quilt of his nest.

I feel myself getting drowsy and wonder idly how many hours, how many days, this bird has spent working on his nest. He doesn't know why he is doing it. He doesn't have the consciousness to understand the cause and effect of nest building, of attracting a female, mating, procreating. His small brain cannot fathom the fabric of life: the unending cycle of birth, fruition, death, and rebirth. He

simply follows his instinct and does what he must do: he weaves.

The old buffalo bull has reached the edge of the water. He stands there silently, his forelegs sinking up to his knee joints in the purplish grey mud. He briefly flicks his massive head, propelling two ox-peckers into the air, then lowers it to the water to drink.

The wind has been gusting sporadically all afternoon in short but violent bursts of hot dry air that stir the branches and raise the dust and rustle the stands of *kasense* grass at the edge of the lagoon.

Suddenly I hear an agitated chirping above me. I don't recognise the sound; is it an alarm call of some kind? But no, I look up to see the weaver flying back and forth excitedly, beating its wings and chattering. His nest is gone. Blown off its

216

fragile moorings at the end of the branch. I see it floating on the water, useless.

✳

Another drowsy afternoon. Two collectors stand in front of my art display at Safari Club International, Las Vegas, Nevada. They are discussing my work, a painting of a buffalo at a waterhole. One of them is wearing a blue suit and is sweating slightly despite the air conditioning. The bright spotlights reflect off the glass of bourbon in his bejewelled fist. The other one, clearly a hunter, is wearing a tanned leather waistcoat covered liberally with pockets and cartridge loops. The waistcoat is open in front so that I can see a huge solid gold belt buckle in the shape of a buffalo head. All around me there is the soporific hum of droning voices discussing muzzle velocities, bullet weights, trophy measurements, the art investment market, taxidermists.

I close my eyes and let the voices wash over me: 'Shot him with my .458 Weatherby. Killed him with a heart shot. Fifty-two inches. Number three in the book. Gotta use soft-nose for those guys . . .'

This is a far cry from the kind of hunting I know. I don't see any evidence in this hall that there is more to hunting than the kill. I miss the sense of communion that I feel when I walk in the African bush. I don't see any respect for the animals.

I'm suddenly sick of all this and find myself thinking of New York and my short visit there on the way over; the galleries, museums, the vibrancy of the city. One gallery is showing one of the rising stars on the American contemporary art scene. Huge canvases with flat mechanical-looking surfaces (airbrushed to deny the artist's touch) and commonplace, banal subject matter. A plastic knife and fork, a tray of airline food. The hubcap of a Cadillac with another Cadillac reflected in its polished surface. Realistic graffiti on peeling *trompe-l'oeil* subway walls. Some have real pieces of subway stuck to them: number plates, direction signs. The work has elegance. Urban and urbane.

Down the street is another exhibition, a series of assemblages: TV sets stacked one on top of the other, more than four metres high, their screens endlessly repeating the same electronic image, ad nauseam, for ever.

I find myself excited by this. I don't see this kind of exhibition often enough, not where I live. A cocktail waitress passes with a tray of drinks; the sculptures stand menacingly in the room among us, towering over the gallery crowd, the waitress and me.

A few blocks away is Wall Street, the financial capital of the world where decisions with global repercussions are made every minute. I feel the dynamic excitement of being in this place, at the centre, the hub of this great wheel. And all around me art is being made, art that accurately reflects the state of the society that spawns it. Fast food. Fast cars. Deals and wheels. Big bucks and small consciences. Fake tans and genuine liposuction. Consumerism running away and moral rectitude struggling to keep up.

But New York is real, it vibrates with its own pulse, and you can see the arteries of its influence reaching out into the rest of the world.

The flight to Las Vegas seemed like a descent into the underworld. It couldn't possibly be more different from the world I know. A place that owes its very existence to an illusion: the myth of eternal bliss through quick riches, where nothing seems real, least of all the croupiers' smiles and the gamblers' optimism.

Each building pretends to be something it isn't; the big casinos imitate exotic places and past times. There is an Egyptian pyramid, there's King Arthur's castle; a volcano that erupts on cue every two hours. There is the battle of two galleons, with 'real' sailors diving out of the crow's nest into the water on the street corner.

Up the Strip is the new PARIS hotel, where signs direct you to toilets and restaurants in French and the waiters speak in fake French accents. The whole interior has been designed to look like a Parisian *quartier*, complete with its own small Eiffel tower.

Why?

Where is the American spirit that opened up the West, this place right here on the streets of which I'm walking? Those must have been tough people. Has all original thought been banished from this town? Where is the American vision that built the Brooklyn Bridge, the Empire State Building? In Las Vegas in the new millennium even New York is a fake, a replica of itself. This morning, with the desert wind blowing hot-dog wrappers and empty Coke cans around her feet, the statue of liberty on the pavement outside looks sad somehow.

Is this our Brave New World where Big Brother is not the Orwellian omnipresent police state but – more chilling even – the all-powerful cold eye of state-of-the-art capitalism?

In Las Vegas, one doesn't need much imagination to see us all as a race of worker ants. Europe and North America are our termite mounds. Our soldier ants stage raids on distant, unseen enemies. In our shopping malls we reap our harvest, corporate scandals are our diversions. And Las Vegas is our reward.

The interior of my hotel has a Venetian theme. Among the forest of glittering slot machines, Renaissance-looking statues hold up the canopy above the bar. There are canals upstairs, on the second floor, complete with gondolas. A Rialto bridge spans the canal and marries the shopping piazzas on either side of the water. When you finish shopping, you can take a ride in a gondola and pretend that you're in Italy. But I am not floating on a gondola in Venice; I am adrift (becalmed and bewildered) in the Nevada desert.

The displays at the hunting convention do nothing to allay my sense of dislocation. When I walk through the aisles, the glassy eyes of a hundred dead and stuffed animals are on me. Their heartbeats have been silenced, their blood long soaked up by hot African earth many thousands of miles away. But the weight of their bewildered innocence presses down on me here in this cavernous hall. They seem to vibrate under the heat of the spotlights with the same sense of dazed disorientation that I feel. Some of them are so lifelike that I tremble involuntarily as I walk past them.

In the aisle behind me, someone has set up a video projector in his booth, and a big circular screen mounted in the roof girders high above. All day long, video images of shot and dying animals chase each other across the screen in an endlessly repeating loop. They are visible from halfway down the hall. A soundtrack of gunshots and electronic keyboard music accompanies the video carnage.

The big-racked buck has just died for what must be the fiftieth time today when I notice that someone is standing in front of my booth. A man wearing a khaki shooting jacket stretched tight over his belly. A lion claw set in gold is dangling from a gold chain between the wings of his collar. He stands with his feet planted wide, a hand on his hip. He points at my lion painting and turns to the woman next to him.

'That's about the size mane mine had,' he says, his voice strident above the hum of background noise.

'The one you shot last year?' she asks.

'Yeah. In Tanzania.' He nods. 'Except mine had a long white scar on his nose. This one doesn't.' He stares at the painting for another full minute, paying no attention to me.

'Good lion,' he says, nodding his head, then turns across the aisle where my friend, a painter from South Africa, is asleep in his booth.

Artists are not known for their social skills, and most of us find it difficult, if not downright embarrassing, to sell and promote our own work. My friend has overcome this problem by drinking Bloody Marys since breakfast, and he is slouched in his chair, his head resting on his folded arms on the table in front of him.

The man in the shooting jacket is examining the paintings on the wall of the booth.

'Say, that elephant painting. How much is that?'

There is no reply, and he has to say it a second time before the artist raises his head. I can see his tired red eyes, and I see his mouth is set, like a tight pencil line hidden in his beard. He stares at the man, at the gold-encased lion claw.

'Fuck you,' he finally says, and lets his head drop back on to his folded arms.

I know how he feels.

＊

The wind has come up again. It prickles my skin and wakes me from my reverie.

The buffalo has gone back to the safety of the treeline. I can still see his great grey head among the thorns, his black horns glinting in the late sun. The water is quiet again. A flight of skimmers approaches low from the west, difficult to see against the sinking sun. Flying in a straight line, single file, inches above the water, the four white birds dip their beaks and gently ripple the surface, then they are gone.

On my way home, I come around a bend in the road and my foot automatically touches the brake. A bull elephant is stretched to his full height, his weight on his hindlegs, trunk reaching up into the high branches of a winter thorn. It is dark and dust hangs in the air. I have Mozart on the tape player, a violin concerto. The music is loud in the quiet night, drowning out any bush sounds. The elephant stands in the middle of the track, eyeing me now, his dark eye glinting small in my headlights with the remoteness of a black amethyst.

He has torn off a long branch and is chewing on it slowly, methodically, his eyes on me. I turn up the Mozart, the violin soaring into the night sky just as the bull stretches his trunk again high into the top branches. I remember Norman telling me once that he had measured a bull elephant's reach at almost eight metres.

It is usually like this. The bull is calm and there is nothing aggressive in his body language. I know sooner or later he will make way for me. But he is not in a hurry, and it seems that he wants to show me so. I turn the concerto down to a murmur and listen to him chew. He advances a few steps towards me, and I let out the clutch slowly, gear in reverse. He stops. I stop. He resumes chewing. I put the Cruiser into first and let the car roll towards him, a few feet at a time.

It is a game. I know it. I wonder if he knows it. It seems to me that he does, and it is clear that he is playing with me, not I with him.

I turn the Mozart up again, and with a final glance in my direction he lumbers slowly off the road and disappears in the darkness between the trees.

Early next morning I'm back at the water-hole. The quick-rising sun has cleared the trees and the gap between the red-white ball and the treetops is widening as I watch. The whole pan is lit as if by a slow fire in the sky and the outlines of the trees are blurred and gold-embroidered. A group of first-year impala rams is standing at the edge of the water, their tan-black-white rumps glossy in the dense sunlight. They jostle each other, briefly knock budding horns, and jump stiffly on the spot, not going anywhere.

I look up into the tree above and find the weaver and see that he has started work on a new nest; gathering material, placing the right straw in the right place, intertwining each strand; weaving, weaving.